DEFYING THE
WINDS OF CHANGE

Defying the Winds of Change
zimbabwe's 2008 elections

edited by
ELDRED V. MASUNUNGURE

Konrad
Adenauer
Stiftung

WEAVER
PRESS

Published by
Weaver Press, Box A1922,
Avondale, Harare
and the
Konrad Adenauer Foundation,
Box 4325, Harare

© Konrad Adenauer Foundation, Harare, 2009
This collection and each individual chapter,
with the exception of Chapter 3.

© Andrew Moyse and the
Media Monitoring Project, Harare, 2009
Chapter 3: 'The Media Environment Leading up
to Zimbabwe's 2008 Elections'.

Typeset by forzalibro designs
Cover painting: 'Stitched' by Walter Mapondera
From the exhibition 'Post-Election Selection'
at the Gallery Delta, Harare, 2008
Printed by Sable Press, Harare

The Konrad Adenauer Foundation also notes that any
opinions and views expressed in this publication are
the responsibility of the individual authors and that
the Konrad Adenauer Foundation does not
necessarily subscribe to these opinions
and views of the contributors.

ISBN: 978-1-77922-086-8

Contents

CONTENTS

Introduction

To the ancient question, 'Who will guard the guardians?' there is only one answer: those who choose the guardians.

On 29 March and 27 June 2008, Zimbabwe held two historic elections. Both were 'critical' in the sense of defining or redefining the strategic direction of the country and ensuring that it would never be the same again. Though they were different in every fundamental way, both had a profound effect on the tenor of national politics and firmly put the country on what appears to be an irreversible though bumpy journey towards democratic transition and away from resilient authoritarianism.

The 29 March elections were the first ever 'harmonized' elections, for the presidency, the Senate, the House of Assembly, and local government councils; they were held on one day, and results were posted at the polling stations for all to see. The 27 June election was the first presidential run-off in the country's history and, as some of the contributions in this book will demonstrate, was also the most controversial and violent election since Independence in 1980.

Elections and democracy

A country's people are the ultimate source of political legitimacy, and this is most often expressed through free elections. In the contemporary world, elections are and remain the best known and most effective device for connecting citizens to policy makers. They are a formal expression of democratic sovereignty.

Paul Clarke and Joe Foweraker make a distinction between 'thin' and 'fat' conceptions of democracy and argue that the former centres on electoral democracy.[1] Most such conceptions borrow from Joseph Schumpeter's now

1 See Paul A.B. Clarke and Joe Foweraker (2001) *Encyclopedia of Democratic Thought*, Taylor and Francis, Portland.

1

classic definition of democracy as 'an institutional arrangement for arriving at political decisions in which individuals acquire the power to decide by a competitive struggle for the people's vote'.[2] Adam Przeworski and colleagues adopt and extend this notion by insisting that elections encompass: (1) *ex ante* uncertainty; (2) *ex post* irreversibility; and (3) repeatability.[3] For these writers, if a system regularly holds elections to choose its chief executive officer and the seats in its effective legislative body; if there is some chance that one or more ruling parties can lose office in a particular election; if any winner of a free and fair election can assume office; and if the winner of one election cannot prevent the same competitive uncertainty from prevailing in the next election, then the system is a democracy.[4]

It is immediately apparent from this 'thin' conception of democracy that elections are not only central but are an indispensable part of democracy. Few would fault this approach, but many would dispute establishing equivalence between elections and democracy. It is truer to posit that while elections are held even in non-democracies, no modern democracy exists without elections. In other words, elections are a necessary though not sufficient condition for democracy.

While the 'thin' or minimalist conception is limited to one necessary institutional characteristic of democracy – namely electoral competition and its uncertainty – the 'fat' or 'maximalist' notion requires other extra-electoral imperatives for democracy to fully flourish. Thus Clarke and Foweraker write that: 'Fat, or more fully articulated, conceptions identify a wide range of other types of institutions, processes and conditions that must also be present for a regime to be called a democracy.'[5]

Further, the minimalist conceptions are accused of committing what Terry Karl calls the 'fallacy of electoralism'. Larry Diamond explains that this fallacy:

… consists of privileging electoral contestation over other dimensions of democracy and ignoring the degree to which multiparty elections, even if genuinely competitive, may effectively deny significant sections of the population the opportunity to contest for power or advance and defend their interests, or may leave significant arenas of decision-making power beyond the reach or control of elected officials.[6]

In short, the fallacy is committed when one assumes that elections are a sufficient measure of democracy and ignores other essential attributes. The bottom line though is that elections are a required condition for democracy. As Michael Bratton and his colleagues argue, '… elections are the

---

2 Joseph Schumpeter (1976) *Capitalism, Socialism, and Democracy*, Allen and Unwin, London. p. 260.
3 In Clarke and Foweraker (2001) p. 149.
4 Ibid.
5 Ibid.
6 Larry Diamond (1996) 'Is the Third Wave Over?' *Journal of Democracy*, vol. 7, no. 3. p. 22.

most fundamental democratic institution';[7] they are also the most visible form of mass political participation.

Defying the Winds of Change does not seek to join the debate about the 'thinness' or 'fatness' of democracy in Zimbabwe. It has no theoretical ambitions beyond engaging in descriptive analysis of the landmark 2008 elections. Nonetheless, and as the various contributions demonstrate, Zimbabwe is struggling to fulfil the requirements of democracy even in its 'thin' sense. It falls short of being what Diamond prefers to call 'electoral democracy'.[8] Instead, Zimbabwe seems to falls squarely into that category of regimes that he calls 'pseudodemocracies', that is, regimes that 'have legal opposition parties and perhaps many other constitutional features of electoral democracy, but fail to meet one of its crucial requirements: a sufficiently fair arena of contestation to allow the ruling party to be turned out of power'.[9]

Elections in Zimbabwe

Zimbabwe has a chequered electoral history. The first comprehensive study of Zimbabwe's post-independence experiment with elections was by Jonathan Moyo in 1990. At the design stage of his study, Moyo reveals that many wondered why he was wasting his time and resources 'setting out to study the obvious', in that it was almost preordained that ZANU(PF) would win.[10]

Ten years later, no analyst would have dared categorically to predict a ZANU(PF) win, not after the February 2000 referendum defeat of the Government-sponsored draft constitution and the near-defeat of the long-ruling party in parliamentary elections four months later. In fact, what made the post-2000 elections interesting (and dangerous too) was their cliff-hanger quality. Elections in post-2000 Zimbabwe no longer produced 'obvious' results, notwithstanding concerted efforts and huge investments allegedly made by the incumbent regime to transform them into a contest that produced predetermined outcomes.

In fact, the contestation for power and the attendant bitter and often violent conflict between the major political gladiators – notably Robert Mugabe and ZANU(PF) on one hand and Morgan Tsvangirai and his Movement for Democratic Change (MDC) on the other – was at root about whether the outcome of elections would be certain – even predetermined – or uncertain. Democratic elections are inherently uncertain and it is this uncertainty that

---

7   Michael Bratton, Robert Mattes and E. Gyimah-Boadi (2005) *Public Opinion, Democracy, and Market Reform in Africa*, Cambridge University Press, Cambridge. p. 144.
8   See Diamond (1996) 'Is the Third Wave Over?'.
9   Ibid.
10 Jonathan N. Moyo (1992) *Voting for Democracy: A Study of Electoral Politics in Zimbabwe*, UZ Publications, Harare. p. 6.

Table 1: Importance of Elections in Choosing Political Leaders, 2004-2009

Method	2004	2005	2009
A: Choosing leaders through regular, open and honest elections	75	74	80
B: Use other methods for choosing leaders	21	26	18
Agree with neither	1	0	1
Don't know	2	0	2

Question: Which of these statements is closest to your own opinion? Choose statement A or Statement B.
Statement A: 'We should choose our leaders in this country through regular, open and honest elections'.
Statement B: 'Since elections sometimes produce bad results we should adopt other methods for choosing country's leaders'.

makes the study of elections interesting, salient, and even imperative.

Richard Joseph, a seasoned analyst of African politics, recently observed that African citizens face two 'daunting challenges: securing the right to elect those who will govern them in fair and honest elections, and ensuring that elected officials do not continue to treat state treasuries as their personal bank accounts'.[11] Zimbabwe has been confronted with both 'daunting challenges', but this book is about the first. The county has had extreme difficulties conducting even remotely free and fair elections since 2000. The road to democratic development was incrementally narrowed via questionable and highly contestable elections organized by the incumbent regime. The narrowest road was one leading to the June presidential run-off election. And the public agrees with this assessment.

Public perceptions of Zimbabwe's elections and democratic status

Empirical data on the attitudes of Zimbabweans on a wide range of issues has been collected under the auspices of the Afrobarometer, a comparative series of national mass attitude surveys on democracy, markets, and civil society. Four rounds of surveys have been conducted in Zimbabwe and several other African countries. For our purposes, we focus on Zimbabweans' perceptions of elections and democracy in the country. Questions on these matters have consistently been asked from Round 2 in 2004 to Round 4 in May 2009.

11 Richard Joseph (2008) 'Progress and Retreat in Africa' *Journal of Democracy*, vol. 19 no. 2. p. 104.

Table 2: Reactions to Abolition of Elections and One-Person Rule

	1999	2004	2005	2009
Strongly disapprove	64	55	66	51
Disapprove	13	24	24	26
Neither approve nor disapprove	6	5	5	2
Approve	5	6	3	6
Strongly approve	6	4	1	3
Don't know	5	5	2	4

Question: There are many ways to govern a country. Would you disapprove or approve the following alternative: 'Elections and the Parliament are abolished so that the president can decide everything.'

Table 3: Freeness and Fairness of Elections, 1999-2009

	1999	2004	2005	2009 March	2009 June
Completely free and fair	16		19	30	6
Free and fair, with minor problems	15		16	15	7
Free and fair, with major problems	21	14	13	9	

Table 1 demonstrates beyond reasonable doubt that Zimbabweans invariably prefer elections as a mechanism for choosing their leaders. Three-quarters said they preferred this method in 2004 and 2005, increasing to eight out of ten in 2009. The importance of elections has therefore increased since 2004 and the attractiveness of alternatives has diminished in the same period from 21% to 18%.

Answers to another question reinforce Zimbabweans' deep predilection towards elections. From 1999, Afrobarometer has been asking respondents whether they would approve or disapprove if: 'Elections and the Parliament are abolished so that the president can decide everything' and the results are shown in Table 2. Again, not less than three-quarters disapprove of one-person rule attendant on the abolition of elections and parliament. The proportion that disapproves has in fact risen by 9% in ten years, meaning the inclination towards elections is increasing rather than diminishing.

Despite the strong desire for open and honest elections, adult Zimbab-

Table 4: Perceived Supply of Democracy in Zimbabwe, 2004-2009

	2004	2005	2009
Not a democracy	15	35	29
A democracy, with major problems	22	21	29
A democracy, with minor problems	27	10	22
A full democracy	9	4	6
Don't understand the question	21	22	5

Question: 'In your opinion, how much of a democracy is Zimbabwe today?'

weans are unhappy with the manner in which elections are conducted in the country, a fact demonstrably confirmed in Table 3.

If the first two responses are combined, we find that about a third assessed the previous elections as free and fair in the 1999 and 2005 surveys. Nearly half (47%) in 1999 and more than half (58%) in 2005 judged the previous elections as either not free or fair or just marginally free and fair. And voters can recognize traits of fairness when they see them. As the various chapters in this book illustrate, the March 2008 harmonized elections were the 'fairest' for a long time, and survey evidence in Table 3 confirms this. But still a full half lambasted the elections. As for what Masunungure calls a 'militarized election' i.e. the June 2008 presidential run-off, adult Zimbabweans are unambiguous: 81% condemn the election as 'not free and fair', and only 13% regard the violence-drenched elections as free and fair.

It is probably because of the perceived dirty elections that the citizens of Zimbabwe dismiss their polity as 'not a democracy'. There is a clear disequilibrium between demand for and the supply of democracy. To the question, 'In your opinion, how much of a democracy is Zimbabwe today?', 36% said the country was a democracy (see Table 4). This proportion declined to only 14% in 2005 before recovering to 25% in 2009. The recovery was probably due to the euphoria accompanying the formation of the transitional government in February 2009, three months before the survey. Even then, the proportion of Zimbabweans who said the country is not a democracy was at its highest at 58% in the latest survey.

We can conclude with a high degree of confidence that Zimbabweans want free, fair and honest elections but so far have not got them. Further, the evidence supports the proposition that Zimbabweans do not even regard their political system as an electoral democracy, i.e. as fulfilling even the 'thin' sense of the words.

Zimbabwe's pseudo-democratic status is in contrast its almost 'perfect' juridical framework, particularly the Electoral Act itself (see Chapter 6). This Act, as amended in February 2008, explicitly states the general principles undergirding democratic elections in the country. Section 3 of the Act states:

> Subject to the Constitution and this Act, every election shall be conducted in way that is consistent with the following principles:
>
> (a) the authority to govern derives from the will of the people demonstrated through elections that are conducted efficiently, freely, fairly, transparently and properly on the basis of universal and equal suffrage exercised through a secret ballot; and
>
> (b) every citizen has the right:
>
> > (i) to participate in government directly or through freely chosen representatives, and is entitled, without distinction on the ground of race, ethnicity, gender, language, political or religious belief, education, physical appearance or disability or economic or social condition, to stand for office and cast a vote freely;
> >
> > (ii) to join or participate in the activities of and to recruit members of a political party of his or her choice;
> >
> > (iii) to participate in peaceful political activity intended to influence the composition and policies of Government;
> >
> > (iv) to participate, through civic organizations, in peaceful activities to influence and challenge the policies of Government;
>
> (c) every political party has the right:
>
> > (i) to operate freely within the law;
> >
> > (ii) to put up or sponsor one or more candidates in every election;
> >
> > (iii) to campaign freely within the law;
> >
> > (iv) to have reasonable access to the media.[12]

When these provisions are read in conjunction with the fundamental civil and political freedoms, rights and liberties guaranteed in the Declaration of Rights (Chapter 3 of the Constitution of Zimbabwe) – freedom of assembly, freedom of expression, freedom of movement, protection from torture, inhuman or degrading treatment, the protection of the law, freedom of conscience, etc. – it is clear that the juridical framework supports the general principles of democratic elections. However, it is at the empirical level where serious deficits arise.

The manner in which elections are conducted in Zimbabwe has been to vitiate even the 'thin' conception of democracy. This is in part what prompted this study. This book is about those who choose the guardians, and how that choice was partly fulfilled in the March 2008 harmonized elections but frustrated in the presidential run-off that followed.

12　The term 'reasonable access' though not defined in the Electoral Act, is presumably defined in the ZEC Act, Part 1VA, especially Section 16C (1) which covers access to public broadcasting media which states that 'Public broadcasters shall afford all political parties and independent candidates contesting an election such free access to their broadcasting services as may be prescribed in regulations, made by the Commission, with the approval of the Minister ...'

Overview of the book

Each chapter covers a different aspect of the elections and each adopts a descriptive, analytical approach rather than a theoretical one.

Eustinah Tarisayi's chapter sets out the socio-economic contexts which, she argues, 'define the electoral playing field and determine the process and outcome of an election'. She describes the extent to which Zimbabwe stood on the edge of a precipice that threw many voters into a state of despair in an economy characterized by the highest inflation in the world, shortages of virtually every basic commodity, high levels of skills drain, and over 80 per cent unemployment and poverty levels. It was in this context that voters effectively passed a 'vote of no confidence' in the ruling ZANU(PF) party.

In Chapter 2, Anyway Chingwete Ndapwadza and Ethel Muchena focus on public opinion and the challenges of conducting political research in a fragile state like Zimbabwe, and trace the shift in political support and public mood. They demonstrate how public opinion studies were used to predict the outcome of the March elections, and conclude that 'in predicting political developments, people can sincerely rely on public opinion'. Unfortunately, public opinion surveys are a new phenomenon in Zimbabwe, and Bratton and his colleagues note that they are 'an unfamiliar tool in Africa, rarely encountered in everyday life'.[13]

In Chapter 3, journalist Andrew Moyse examines the media environment in which the elections took place, but dates the poisoned environment back to the referendum defeat in February 2000s: 'Apart from the country's pending total economic collapse that crippled the operations of most domestic media institutions and the capacity of the public to access them, a host of blatantly unconstitutional and repressive laws were enacted that effectively emasculated the independent media and deprived the nation of its rights to freedom of expression, including the right to be informed.' Given such an unpropitious environment, Moyse is emphatic that 'there could not have been free and fair elections of any sort in March 2008.'

Eldred Masunungure covers the 29 March and 27 June 2008 elections in Chapters 4 and 5 respectively. He describes them as 'critical but sharply contrasting', in that while the March elections 'were the most peaceful (and even enjoyable) since the genesis of Zimbabwe's mega-crisis in 2000', the June run-off 'will go down in history as the bloodiest since independence.' Chapter 4 looks at the political party and presidential contestants, dissects their platforms and examines the pre-poll arena for the harmonized elections, especially the use of state-financed patronage, poor voter education, the decrepit state of the voters' roll and the pronouncements by members of the military-security sector, all of which skewed the playing

13   Bratton et. al. (2005) p. 57.

field in favour of the incumbent regime. Nonetheless, he concludes that: 'On balance, it is fair to say the pre-election environment was relatively peaceful and sufficiently conducive to the free expression of the people's will in the ballot box.'

Chapter 5 describes and analyses 'a militarized election', one with an unprecedented role for the military/security complex – and the attendant systemic violence and intimidation – which made the presidential run-off an election without a choice. It argues that this election lost its political quality and took on a military character and as such, 'the resultant ballot was more a barometer of people's fears than of people's choices',

In Chapter 6, constitutional lawyer Greg Linington largely confines himself to the presidential elections in March and June. He exposes the wide divergence between what the law (domestic law and the SADC Principles and Guidelines Governing Democratic Elections) says and what happened in practice in respect of the conduct of the elections. He interrogates the actions and inaction of various electoral institutions, notably the Zimbabwe Electoral Commission and the Electoral Court, reviews the complex legal issues surrounding the run-off, and concludes that 'the 27 June election was invalid' and that 'Morgan Tsvangirai ought to have been declared President after the 'first' election'.

John Makumbe, in Chapter 7, looks at one of the key electoral institutions, the Zimbabwe Electoral Commission (ZEC), from the perspective of a political scientist rather than a lawyer. He outlines its characteristics and functions, examines its role in the harmonized elections and finds fault with the manner in which it conducted itself, particularly regarding its partisanship. Makumbe concludes that 'ZEC is not an effective and autonomous electoral body' but an instrument 'defying the winds of change in Zimbabwe.'

The role of civil society in the elections is covered by Derek Matyszak in Chapter 8. He traces the birth of an activist civil society in the late 1990s that focused on the civil and human rights of Zimbabweans and describes the brutal response of the party-state with the military and police taking leading roles. He argues that the state's *modus operandi* explains 'why an "orange" or "popular" revolution has not taken place in Zimbabwe', and highlights the role of civil society organizations, notably the Zimbabwe Human Rights NGO Forum, the Zimbabwe Election Support Network and the Zimbabwe Peace Project, in monitoring, documenting and exposing human rights violations and providing assistance to victims. Matyszak concludes that the March elections 'conformed more closely with democratic requirements for free and fair elections than any other in Zimbabwe's history', while the June presidential run-off was a 'bloody electoral farce'.

In Chapter 9, Simon Badza considers the regional and international responses to the elections. He traces the evolution of worsening relations with the West and argues that 'regional and international reaction has been marked by continuities rather than discontinuities of the policies governing the world's diplomatic interactions with the government of Zimbabwe', and faults the manner in which SADC brokered the 15 September 2008 pact between the three parties, regarding it as an inadequate solution to Zimbabwe's post-election crisis. He concludes that 'the only lasting solution to any election crisis can be one that affords primacy to the freely expressed democratic will of the people'.

Defying the Winds of Change demonstrates that the 2008 elections, like previous elections before them, failed as a mechanism for ushering in political change. It is in that sense that the winds of change were systematically defied.

1

Voting in Despair
The Economic & Social Context

Eustinah Tarisayi

Introduction

Social, political and economic contexts define the electoral playing field and determine the process and outcome of an election. The March and June elections in Zimbabwe were held in an atmosphere of uncertainty, confusion and a deepening sense of crisis. The polarized political situation and a highly unstable macroeconomic environment emphasized the danger of social and economic meltdown. In addition, the elections came at a time when governmental relations between Zimbabwe and the West were at their lowest.

Economic context

The declining economy, a collapse of the democratic process, failure of the rule of law, land seizures and the way inflation was manipulated to make the very rich even richer shaped the manner in which the people of Zimbabwe voted, particularly in the March polls, which were effectively a 'vote of no confidence' in the ruling party.[1]

Until the end of the 1990s, Zimbabwe had been regarded as the breadbasket of southern Africa by the International Monetary Fund and the World Bank. It had also established and maintained one of the best educational systems in Africa, along with a vibrant political system, a free press, an independent judiciary and a rapidly growing economy. However, after 28 years of ZANU(PF) misrule, Zimbabweans are one-third poorer than they were at independence; according to the IMF, Zimbabwe is the world's

1   ZESN Election Report, Harare. October 2008.

11

fastest-shrinking economy – at a time when the average annual growth rate in sub-Saharan Africa was 6 per cent. The 2008 elections were held within an economy in which over 80 per cent of the population was living below the poverty datum line (PDL, the minimum income required in order to survive on an ongoing basis in reasonable health) and 80 per cent of the population was below the food datum line (the income necessary just to buy sufficient of the right food to avoid malnutrition). According to the International Crisis Group's May 2008 update, over 4 million people were in desperate need of food. Although Zimbabwe's economic problems can be traced as far back as 1997, 2008 saw the economy taking 'giant steps' backwards.

State of the economy

Characteristics of economic crisis included:

1. Hyperinflation. According to Steve Hanke, 'Zimbabwe is in the late stages of a classic hyperinflation'.[2] Zimbabwe can now lay claim to second place in the world hyperinflation record books. Table 1 illustrates the world's highest hyperinflationary countries.

    Zimbabwe is the first country in the 21st century to hyperinflate. Hanke asserts that in February 2007, Zimbabwe's inflation rate topped 50 per cent per month, the minimum rate required for a country to qualify as a hyperinflationary.[3] The Central Statistical Office (CSO) failed to release official inflation figures for February, March, April, and May, only to release the July figure that stood at 231 million per cent. However, unofficial figures by independent economists are as follows: February 165,000 per cent; March 355,000 per cent; April 732,604 per cent; May 1,694,000 per cent; in June it was over 2,000,000 per cent, the highest outside a war zone.[4]

2. Chronic shortages of foreign currency, fuel, electricity, water and basic commodities.

3. A dearth in human capital due to brain and skills drain (an estimated three million Zimbabweans are in the diaspora).

4. High levels of corruption.

5. Unemployment and poverty levels in excess of 80 per cent.

6. Informalisation of the economy.

7. Poor socio-economic policies.

2   Steve H. Hanke is professor of Applied Economics at Johns Hopkins University and a fellow at the Cato Institute. He developed a hyperinflation index for Zimbabwe beginning 5 January 2007, a month before Zimbabwe entered the hyperinflation zone.

3   www.cato.org/zimbabwe

4   The *Financial Gazette*, 20 June 2008.

Table 1. Highest monthly inflation rates in history

Country	Month with highest inflation rate	Highest monthly inflation rate	Equivalent daily inflation rate	Time required for prices to double
Hungary	July 1946	$1.30 \times 10^{16}\%$	195%	15.6 hours
Zimbabwe	Mid-November 2008 (latest measurable)	79,600,000,000%	98.0%	24.7 hours
Yugoslavia	January 1994	313,000,000%	64.6%	1.4 days
Germany	October 1923	29,500%	20.9%	3.7 days
Greece	November 1944	11,300%	17.1%	4.5 days
China	May 1949	4,210%	13.4%	5.6 days

Source: Prof. Steve H. Hanke, 5 February 2009.

8. Cumulative economic decline of 44.4 per cent during the period 1997-2007.
9. Low levels of capacity utilization averaging 33.8 per cent.
10. Inability to maintain the infrastructure necessary for agricultural production.
11. Shortages of fertilizers, maize seed and other agricultural inputs.

Causes of the economic crisis

According to the ZCTU's May 2007 Position Paper, the government's explanation of the crisis is that the economy is under sanctions from the West as a result of the land redistribution programme.[5] It also sees profiteering by business and unpatriotic behaviour within certain civil society groups working with the West as primarily responsible for the crisis. Thus, according to this view, the causes of the economic decline and crisis are located externally. This position is articulated in the Millennium Economic Recovery Programme launched in 2000, the National Economic Recovery Programme launched in February 2003, and the ZANU(PF) manifesto, and has characterized most of the speeches given by senior government officials. In the former, the crisis is seen in the context of '… deleterious effects of neo-imperialist machinations aimed at limiting national sovereignty over the redistribution of national assets such as land in favour of indigenous Zimbabweans. These machinations are aimed at frustrating national efforts to transform the Zimbabwean economy so that it cannot reach higher levels of development'.[6]

The alternative explanation traces the crisis to the wrong-headed policies adopted by government since 1997, culminating in the descent into lawlessness and bad governance. That year, 1997, was in many respects a turning point. During the first six months, veterans of Zimbabwe's war of independence organized and demonstrated to urge the government to recognize them for the role they had played in liberating the country. In November, the President awarded each of the estimated 50,000 ex-combatants a one-off gratuity of approximately US$5,000 (Z$50,000) payable by 31 December 1997, and a monthly pension of approximately US$200 (Z$2,000) beginning January 1998. Since these payments had not been budgeted for, the government had to borrow to meet its obligations. This resulted in the massive depreciation of the Zimbabwe dollar on a day afterwards referred to as 'black Friday'. Since when the Zimbabwe dollar has been in free fall.

5   In 2000, the Government of Zimbabwe embarked on a fast-track land redistribution exercise which resulted in the grabbing of white commercial farms by the war veterans and ZANU(PF) militias.
6   (1996) Millenium Economic Recovery Programme. Harare. p. 13.

In August 1998, the government sent Zimbabwean troops to the Democratic Republic of Congo (DRC) to help the Congolese government fight rebels. The DRC war was estimated to cost Zimbabwe US$3 million per month. After the rejection of the government's proposed constitution in the February 2000 referendum, the government deliberately encouraged the occupation of white commercial farms. Since then, there has been a breakdown of the rule of law to an extent that the June 2000 parliamentary and the March 2002 presidential elections were characterized by violence and intimidation.[7]

These political decisions resulted in the budget deficit deteriorating from 5.5 per cent of GDP in 1998 to 24.1 per cent by the end of 2000; it still remains well above 10 per cent.[8] GDP has fallen from US$8bn in 1998 to US$4bn in 2008. Domestic debt, which stood at Z$24.5m in 1995 shot up to Z$347m by end of 2002. External debt was US$5bn in 2008. The country accumulated arrears on its foreign debt repayments in 1999, which rose from US$109m in 1998 to US$1.3bn by December 2002, then to the current level of US$2bn.[9] Inflation has since been labelled the country's 'number one enemy' by Gideon Gono, Governor of the Reserve Bank of Zimbabwe (RBZ), in his first monetary policy statement of 2003. Major factors fuelling inflation since 2000 are excessive money supply growth, a weak parallel market exchange rate, supply bottlenecks arising from the contraction in economic activities, and wage and price spirals. The shortages of foreign currency can mainly be attributed to the destruction of the agricultural sector by the fast-track land reform. The agricultural sector, which five years ago had accounted for 16.5 per cent of GDP and 30 per cent of foreign exchange earnings, was severely crippled; alienation by the international community, and the bruising verbal contest between Zimbabwe, Britain and the United States all contributed to foreign currency shortages. Other contributing factors include recurrent failures by Zimbabwe to settle external debts resulting in the withdrawal of international financial aid, the suspension of balance of payments support, and a marked reduction in aid flows. Banks withheld lines of credit and foreign direct investment shrank. Efforts by the RBZ governor to boost foreign currency reserves in May 2008 by introducing the 'willing buyer willing seller priority-focused twinning arrangement in the foreign exchange market whereby authorized dealers (banks and licensed institutions) will match sellers and buyers of foreign exchange guided by a pre-determined priority list set from time to time by the RBZ'[10], were fruitless as they failed to match parallel market rates.

---

7   Discontent with the *status quo* eventually led to the formation of the Movement for Democratic Change by the Zimbabwe Congress of Trade Unions and other civic organizations in 1999. It is these developments that culminated in the land invasions beginning 2000.
8   CSO (2007), Harare.
9   ZCTU Position Paper, Harare, May 2007.
10 Monetary Policy Statement, Harare, May 2008.

In response to the declining economy, the government has announced a number of policies to address the crisis since 1997. The Zimbabwe Programme for Economic and Social Transformation (ZIMPREST 1996-2000) was launched in 1998, two years behind schedule, to address the shortcomings of the Economic Structural Adjustment Programme. ZIMPREST failed to address the economic problems facing the country. The budget deficit was 10 per cent, inflation way above 50 per cent, unemployment was 60 per cent and foreign currency reserves were depleted.[11] It was against this background that the Millennium Economic Recovery Programme was launched in 2000 with the objective of restoring vibrant economic growth and removing the fundamental causes of inflation. The programme was rendered ineffective due to the withdrawal of support to Zimbabwe by most of the international donor community and international financial institutions. In 2003, the National Economic Recovery Programme was launched to address what the government described as the 'current challenges'; like its predecessors, it failed to address the declining economic performance. Just before the March 2008 elections, the Zimbabwe Economic Development Strategy was announced; its impact is yet to be realized. However, these policies, together with the monetary and fiscal policies, all failed to rescue the economy. The situation was exacerbated by the RBZ Governor taking it upon himself to massively increase the money supply by printing vast numbers of bank notes to finance 'quasi-fiscal' activities. In 2006, Gono remarked, 'We are aware of the inflationary impact of printing money to fund infrastructure development. What good will it do us to have zero inflation and have people dying …'[12] During the June 2008 elections, he said that the RBZ would continue printing money 'as long there are sanctions on Zimbabwe'.

The 2008 elections will be remembered in the history of Zimbabwe as having been conducted during a period when the economy and the social environment were experiencing their worst deterioration. On 25 June 2007, companies were directed to roll back their prices by 50 per cent under the Statutory Instrument 159A of 2007 (Presidential Powers Amending the National Incomes and Pricing Commission Act) after being accused of hiking prices to foment public anger against the government. This policy resulted in bare supermarket shelves. The RBZ made a futile effort to address the shortages by extending cheap finance to companies affected by the price blitz through the Basic Commodities Supply Side Intervention (BACOSSI). The policy was unsustainable and was financed by the printing of even more cash. BACOSSI provided only limited relief in the short-term and worsened the situation in the long-term. The non-availability of basic commodities deepened anger and discontent with ZANU(PF) rule during the electoral period.

11   UNDP (2000) Zimbabwe Human Development Report, Harare.
12   *The Herald*, 16 September 2006.

Social context

These political and economic factors fuelled a social crisis characterized by high levels of poverty; high levels of structural unemployment; a critical shortage of basic commodities; the collapse of the utilities sectors (residents endured months without either electricity or water); conditions of insecurity at all levels leading to growing internal displacements, with economic and political refugees leaving for neighbouring states; a critical exodus of professionals to greener pastures; low disposable income; high levels of malnutrition; and rising inequalities of wealth and incomes. This humanitarian crisis has resulted in high levels of vulnerability among the population.

According to the 2003 Poverty Assessment Survey Report, the number of people living below the food poverty line increased from 29 per cent in 1995 to 57 per cent in 2003 and 69 per cent by 2005. In terms of general poverty, the same study estimated the proportion of the population below the total consumption poverty line to have been at 74 per cent in 1995 and 80 per cent in 2002.[13] These statistics have been rising ever since, and in May 2008 the ZCTU estimated that more than 80 per cent of the population was living below the PDL. In 2008, the country had its worst crop in fifteen years and failed to produce sufficient grain to meet the needs of its people. During the 2007/08 season, only 850,000 tonnes of maize was harvested, against an annual domestic consumption requirement of two million tonnes. The World Food Programme has estimated that 5.1 million people will be food insecure between January and March 2009. Agriculture production shrank by over 50 per cent, and HIV and AIDS infection rates among adults stood at over 20 per cent.

Poverty, and its cousin unemployment, led to an accelerated collapse of the social fabric, increased crime, and endemic levels of corruption, disease and massive starvation. Millions of people in Zimbabwe now work in the informal sector and in precarious jobs with deteriorating conditions of service, earning incomes too low to sustain themselves and their families. Relative to their neighbours in Mozambique, Zambia and Malawi (whom they used to look down upon) Zimbabweans are now worse off and have experienced the humiliation of constituting largest number of refugees in neighbouring countries and outside the region. As already alluded to, it is estimated that over three million Zimbabweans are living in the diaspora with 37 per cent in the United Kingdom, 35 per cent in Botswana, 5 per cent in South Africa and 3,4 per cent estimated to be residing in Canada.[14] According to reports produced by the South African Qualifications Authority,

13 *Zimbabwe Human Development Report,* Harare, 2003.
14 *The Financial Gazette,* 29 May - 4 June 2008.

more than half of the foreign qualifications evaluations done between June and September 2007 were for skilled Zimbabweans seeking work in South Africa. This figure does not account for thousands more who have sneaked into that country without official travel documents.

With poor planning and drought ravaging the farming sector, more than half the population was trapped in grinding poverty, with no respite in sight. Poor agricultural performance can be attributed to the fast-track land reform programme which resulted in the eviction of 4,000 white commercial farmers and culminated in production decreasing by 51 per cent.[15] This economic decline also brought about the collapse of the fertilizer industry and saw a sharp decline in foreign currency earnings from export crops. This was worsened by the government ban of 4 June 2008 preventing humanitarian NGOs from distributing food aid. It is important to note that since the 'No' vote in the 2000 constitutional referendum, ZANU(PF) has viewed the NGOs as an appendage of the Movement for Democratic Change (MDC) and as agents of external actors. As such, a number of government-orchestrated prohibitions were put into place impeding international aid, and efforts were made to ensure that the space for local NGOs to work was closed, including that of allowing humanitarian assistance. The government's justification for suspending NGO operations was an allegation of political meddling aimed at assisting the MDC to effect regime change. According to Human Rights Watch, additional aid agencies were banned from distributing food in several provinces until after the June 2008 presidential election run-off, despite the 78 per cent food deficit in the country and the fact that the situation was worse than it had been after the 1992 drought. At that time, the deficit was 40 per cent, but the situation was alleviated by greater import capacities, international goodwill and human resources.[16] Well before the 2008 ban on humanitarian aid, people in the rural areas had resorted to gathering wild fruits, especially in the drought-prone areas of Masvingo and Matabeleland provinces. To enforce such a ban for political purposes in such a situation was an act of extreme callousness. According to a report in *The Standard* newspaper of 18-24 May 2008, in rural areas of Masvingo province villagers competed with animals for wild fruits and bartered cattle for a few bags of maize. While the true cost per head of cattle in April 2008 was around Z$3tr, desperate villagers were prepared to exchange each head for a bag of grain valued at Z$250bn. The ban on food aid thus put the lives of millions of vulnerable Zimbabweans at risk. Most affected were those with HIV and AIDS, children and the aged.

The 2007/08 agricultural season was a disastrous failure. Indeed, the eviction of productive farmers and the inequitable and irrational redistribution policies destroyed the very foundation of Zimbabwe's economy.

---

15 ZCTU Position Paper, Harare, May 2007.
16 *The Economist*, 17 July 2008.

According to Eric Bloch, an independent economist, agriculture used to provide employment for over 300,000 farm workers, a livelihood for nearly two million people, and food to sustain the whole nation and much of the region. Foreign exchange inflows from agriculture petered out. Notwithstanding the prevailing food deficit following the elections of 29 March, ZANU(PF) militia forced more than 30 of the remaining productive white farmers to abandon their farms.

In addition to the food crisis, the two elections of 2008 were conducted while there was a virtual collapse of the social sector, particularly in health and education. The crisis in these sectors deepened following Statutory Instrument 159A of 2007 which directed that school fees and fees for medical services be approved by the Incomes and Pricing Commission. The effect of this policy was that by the time of the elections, the health and education sectors were barely functional. Teachers, examiners, university lecturers, health professionals, and employees of most parastatals stopped reporting for work citing poor remuneration and an inability to meet the cost of transport to work. In most cases the monthly cost of travel exceeded employees' salaries. Estimates show that the salary for teachers and nurses from January to September 2008 was equivalent to the price of a two-litre bottle of cooking oil. According to the Progressive Teachers Union of Zimbabwe, at least 40,000 teachers left the profession after 2007. Most schools failed to open for the second term of 2008. In addition, in most rural areas the remaining teachers were driven away from schools by ZANU(PF) youth militias, waging a campaign of retribution against those believed to have supported the MDC during the March elections. Officials of the Zimbabwe Electoral Commission (ZEC), many of whom were teachers, were arrested, beaten and intimidated for allegedly violating the Electoral Act and rigging the elections in favour of the MDC. As a result, most teachers fled, leaving headmasters to run the schools. In some instances the latter were also subjected to violence and intimidation. ZIMSEC staff also refused to mark examination papers citing their inability to come to work due to the erosion of their salaries by the harsh economic conditions. Thus the results of the O- and A-level June examinations were disrupted and with this, the future of senior students at high schools.

The health sector was characterized by shortages of drugs, a brain drain of skilled personnel, and a lack of equipment such as X-rays. A study carried out by the Portfolio Committee on Health and Child Welfare in May 2006 revealed that the high attrition of health professionals could be attributed to poor remuneration. The committee observed that as of November 2005, the lowest paid nurse earned Z$2-3m per month, compared with the PDL of Z$12,5m. Qualified health personnel resigned *en masse*, creating a vacancy rate of over 70 per cent and a nurse-patient ratio of 1:40 instead of the desired 1:10.[17] A report by the Zimbabwe Council for

17   Portfolio Committee Report, Parliament of Zimbabwe, Harare, 2006.

Nurses stated that more than 35,000 nurses and 96 doctors had fled from government health institutions since the start of the crisis. This figure doubled in 2008. All government hospitals were non-functional, including the country's biggest referral hospital, Parirenyatwa. The decision by the RBZ Governor to give senior medical staff cars as part of a retention package a few days before the March elections deepened discontent among those who got nothing. The situation in the education sector was mirrored in the health sector, and medical staff and doctors did not report for duty.

The root causes of the economic and social decline are clearly located in policies adopted by the ZANU(PF) government both for short-term political benefits, and as desperate fire-fighting measures in a bid to cling to power and maintain a system of privilege and corruption. Every action undertaken by the ZANU(PF) regime such as the war in the DRC, the farm invasions, and the rewards of hyperinflation, which benefited a small elite, had a seriously negative effect on the livelihoods of the majority of Zimbabweans. This was the context in which the elections of 29 March and 27 June 2008 took place.

The elections

Since 2004, the Southern African Development Community (SADC) and the African Union (AU) had made efforts to resolve the political impasse between the ruling ZANU(PF) and the opposition MDC party led by Morgan Tsvangirai. Following the events of the infamous 11 March 2008 'prayer meeting'[18] organized by the two main opposition parties and civil society organizations, SADC mandated Thabo Mbeki, then South Africa's president, to mediate between ZANU(PF) and the MDC in order to create an environment conducive to free and fair elections in March 2008, and an agreement on constitutional reforms ahead of those elections. The SADC intervention resulted in the amendments to the Electoral Laws Amendment Act 2008, amendments to the Access to Information and Protection of Privacy Act (AIPPA) and Public Order and Security Act (POSA), and the Public Broadcasting Regulations and Constitutional Amendment Number 18. MDC-T dismissed these changes as cosmetic. It is, however, important to note that Zimbabwe was the first southern African country to apply the SADC Principles and Guidelines Governing Democratic Elections.[19] These guidelines are supposed to ensure freedom of association, equal access to

18 On 11 March 2008, the two MDC factions – MDC-T under the leadership of Morgan Tsvangirai and MDC-M under the leadership of Arthur Mutambara – other opposition parties and civil society organizations held a 'prayer meeting' since there was a three-month ban on political rallies. State machinery was used to quell the gathering resulting in the death of one MDC-T youth and the arrest of political leaders and human rights activists.

19 www.sadc.int/archives/read/news/167.

state media, equal opportunity to vote, and the independence and impartiality of electoral institutions. Indeed, between January and March 2008, opposition parties managed to hold rallies in most parts of the country with few instances of violence. In addition, polling took place without any serious problems except in a few rural areas such as Gokwe and Hurungwe where headmen and chiefs instructed people to vote for ZANU(PF) or risk losing food aid.[20] In the March election, it took close to four days for the ZEC to complete the announcement of parliamentary and senatorial results. The results for the House of Assembly stood as follows:

Parliamentary results

Party	Seats
ZANU(PF)	97
MDC-T	99
MDC-M	10

In the senatorial elections ZANU(PF) won a total of 30 seats, MDC-T 24 and MDC-M 6. (Elections in three constituencies were not held due to the death of the respective candidates, hence by-elections were held in June 2008.) For the first time since Independence ZANU(PF) lost control of the House of Assembly. There was a sense of real celebration. Zimbabweans hoped for an end to the eight-year social, economic and political crisis and believed they had achieved this through the democratic process. José Marcos Barrica, head of SADC Election Observer Mission (SEOM), commented that the elections were peaceful, credible and an expression of the will of the people. The results of the presidential poll, however, were withheld. ZANU(PF) accused MDC-T of conniving with ZEC officials to fraudulently reduce Mugabe's tally, and demanded a recount. This strategy, in which votes had to be recounted in 23 constituencies, was intended to reverse ZANU(PF)'s defeat and buy time. On 2 May 2008, the ZEC announced the presidential results, six long weeks after polling, thereby disregarding the Electoral Law Act and the SADC Principles and Guidelines that state that electoral results should be announced after 12 and 24 hours respectively. The prolonged delay in announcing the results meant that very few people were convinced by them, believing instead that Tsvangirai had defeated Mugabe.

According to the ZEC, not one of the four presidential candidates – Robert Mugabe, (ZANU(PF)), Morgan Tsvangirai (MDC-T), Simba Makoni

20   *The Independent,* 24 April - 1 May 2008.

(Independent) and Langton Towungana (Independent)[21] – had received the outright majority required by the Electoral Act. Accordingly, a run-off election was held on 27 June between Tsvangirai and Mugabe. The period leading to the run-off was characterized by politically motivated violence resulting in loss of life, internal displacements mostly of rural people by the ruling party loyalists, damage to property and serious injury. The Zimbabwe Association of Doctors for Human Rights treated over 300 cases of injury resulting from organized violence and torture; 3,000 families were displaced; 500 people were hospitalized and, as of April, ten had been murdered.[22] In addition, many rallies were banned and over 400 opposition party supporters were arrested – Tsvangirai alone was arrested five times in June, and Tendai Biti, Secretary General of MDC-T, was arrested on treason charges. A convoy of British and American diplomatic staff investigating reports of election violence in Mashonaland Central was not spared when their vehicle tyres were slashed and one of their drivers beaten for allegedly interfering in the affairs of a sovereign country.

Claude Ake[23] contends that the 'critical aspect of true democracy is not multi-party elections but the assurance of popular participation within African political systems'. ZANU(PF) failed to embrace this important aspect of true democracy; freedom of assembly and movement were heavily restricted and rural areas virtually sealed off from the opposition. Indeed, the ZANU(PF) campaign was laden with threats of war: statements such as 'Zimbabwe was won through the bullet and not through the ballot' were common. Although the government never accepted responsibility for the violence, it openly encouraged it with rhetoric invoking depictions of the MDC-T as a group of 'traitors of the liberation struggle' and as 'puppets' of Britain and the USA.[24] *The Herald*,[25] the state-controlled daily newspaper, constantly referred to the MDC-T as 'stooges of white imperialist interests' (see Chapter 3). In Harare, residents were frog-marched to rallies and all-night vigils not dissimilar to the *pungwes* of the liberation war. Residents were told to remove their satellite dishes, which provided them with access to alternative perspectives, in an operation dubbed 'burutsa dish rako' (take away your dish). The police banned prayer meetings, accusing pastors of using them to conduct political gatherings without the clearance which

---

21 Simba Makoni was a former ZANU(PF) politburo member who defected five weeks before the electoral race citing a lack of succession plans and a lack of economic and political reforms within the party. Many people regarded him as a ZANU(PF) mole. Langton Towungana was little known to the electorate although he said that he was compelled by God to participate. Morgan Tsvangirai secured 47.9 per cent of the votes, Robert Mugabe 43.2, Simba Makoni 8.3 per cent and Langton Towungana 0.6 per cent.

22 *The Economist*, 22 April 2008.

23 Ake, Claude (1996) *Democracy and Development*. The Brookings Institution, Washington DC.

24 The *Independent*, 23-30 April 2008.

25 The only daily paper in Zimbabwe since the banning of the independent *Daily News* in 2006.

police claimed was required under POSA. Three main church bodies were affected by this ban: the Evangelical Fellowship of Zimbabwe, the Catholic Bishops Conference and the Zimbabwe Council of Churches. Before the 29 March elections, they had held prayer meetings at which they pleaded for divine intervention to ensure a free and fair election, the election of a leader with respect for human rights, and a return to the rule of law.

Everyone acknowledged the existence of politically motivated violence, but opinions differed over its causes and origins, nature and extent, and impact on the electoral process.[26] The scale of the violence was such that a week prior to the presidential run-off, Mbeki made spirited efforts for the election to be cancelled, urging the two parties to start negotiating for a Government of National Unity. His sentiments were echoed by many African luminaries, including Kofi Annan and Desmond Tutu. On 22 June, however, Tsvangirai announced that he was withdrawing from the run-off, citing the escalation of political violence and intimidation, and his fear for their lives and livelihoods of his supporters.

Notwithstanding his withdrawal, on 27 June a one-man election took place. Voter turn-out was poor in urban areas and a high number of ballot papers were spoiled. ZESN's October 2008 Election Report noted 39,975 spoilt ballots in the March election and 131,481 in June; many carried messages such as 'God bless this country', 'Let there be free and fair elect-ions' and 'No to dictatorship', as well as derogatory and obscene statements which expressed the electorate's dissatisfaction with the way in which the elections had been conducted.

Unlike the March results, the 27 June results were speedily released. Indeed, within 24 hours, Mugabe was sworn in, claiming to have 'won' with 2,150,269 votes, while Tsvangirai, who had withdrawn, received 233,000 votes. However, the process leading to the run-off did not conform to the SADC Principles and Guidelines. Reports by observers from the Pan-African Parliament, Botswana and SADC roundly condemned the election process and outcome as 'not representing the will of the people of Zimbabwe', and not conforming to SADC Principles. Virtually no government recognized the results that gave Mugabe this landslide victory. The United Nations Security Council denounced the violence perpetrated by the ZANU(PF) militia both before and after the June elections, while the European Union and the G8 declared the final result to be illegitimate. On 22 July, the EU extended its list of targeted sanctions to include companies linked to the Mugabe regime, although a Security Council resolution to impose multi-lateral arms, travel and financial sanctions had been vetoed by China and Russia on 11 July. However, according to the International Crisis Group, although the AU, SADC and the Pan-African Parliament observer missions declared the poll not credible, they did nothing to translate their statements into official censure or punitive action against the Mugabe regime.[27]

26 SEOM Preliminary Report, June 2008, p. 5.
27 'Negotiating Zimbabwe's Transition', Africa Briefing No. 51, May, 2007.

Conclusion

The 29 March and the 27 June elections were conducted within a social, political and economic crisis with no end in sight. The year 2008 will be remembered in the history of Zimbabwe as one in which the state of the economy and the social, political and economic environment experienced a steep decline that will take years to reverse. Zimbabweans continue to face economic turmoil and corruption, severe food shortages and the collapse of vital services. The government's sticking-plaster approach, including removing ten zeroes from the Zimbabwean dollar in August 2008, has not helped the economy nor Zimbabweans. Zimbabwe's 29 March 2008 elections opened a new chapter in the country's long-running political crisis when the MDC-T won control of parliament from ZANU(PF); Mugabe and his hardliners, however, blocked any possibility of democracy running its course by withholding the presidential results and launching a vicious, punitive, intimidatory countrywide crackdown on the opposition ahead of the controversial 27 June presidential run-off election.

2

The Quest for Change
Public Opinion & the Harmonized
March Elections

Anyway Chingwete Ndapwadza
& Ethel Muchena

Introduction

Public opinion was significant in Zimbabwe's 29 March harmonized elections because it related directly to immediate political activity. In order to tap into public opinion and make predictions about the elections, the Mass Public Opinion Institute (MPOI)[1] conducted three surveys in the first quarter of 2008. The January and February surveys had a sample size of 1,000 and the March survey sampled 1,200 Zimbabweans. The use of 1,000 cases gave a margin of error of plus or minus 3.5 per cent with a confidence level of 93 per cent, whilst a sample size of 1,200 translated to a plus or minus 2.5 per cent margin of error. Table 1 shows the achieved demographics for the surveys.

Table 1: Respondents Demographics

Socio-demographics of respondents	Per cent of respondents
Place of residence Rural Urban	 63 37
Age 18-30 31-50 51+	 49 33 18
Gender Female Male	 51 49

---

1 MPOI is a non-profit non-governmental organization established and registered in January 1999 to undertake, publish and discuss research into public opinion.

Apart from the surveys, the Institute conducted two rounds of Focus Group Discussions (FGDs), in August 2007 and February 2008.[2] A total of thirteen FGDs were completed in the first round and six in the second. Targeted participants were brought together for interactive discussion. For both rounds, participants were unfamiliar with each other but had similar characteristics. Accordingly the FGDs were stratified by age, gender, place of residence, employment status, level of education and ethnicity. This allows for an in-depth analysis of the variables.

The challenge of research in Zimbabwe

The political volatility of the country posed a challenge, especially in ZANU(PF) strongholds, which have always proved resistant to the conduct of research and data collection. Consequently, for the safety of field researchers and to avoid data being tampered with, the Institute was forced to substitute highly politicised areas with others. Districts such as Mudzi, Chipinge, Mount Darwin, Rushinga and Bindura urban are virtually closed communities and heavily politicized and sensitized against opposition politics, urbanites, researchers or strangers. During previous research conducted before the 2002 presidential elections, for example, questionnaires were confiscated in no-go areas such as Chipinge, Bindura urban and Mudzi; researchers were beaten in Rushinga. So it has become a norm for MPOI to avoid these areas. Thus, for the surveys in question, Chipinge rural was substituted with Chimanimani, Mount Darwin rural with Mazowe, and Bindura urban with Glendale. The January and February surveys did not include Mashonaland Central province. The March survey cautiously sampled Mazowe and Glendale, in a few relatively quiet districts.

The conduct of our social science research was also threatened by the fear factor as rural people in particular are afraid to be interviewed or invited to attend FGDs, due to the hostile environment and the question of personal security. Recruiting FGD participants proved to be a huge task due to the effort required to convince participants why they should attend.

Defying the winds of change: March 2008 election irregularities

The MPOI quantitative and qualitative survey results depict a shift in support from ZANU(PF) to the larger faction of the MDC led by Morgan Tsvangirai (MDC-T) and reveal consistent irregularities in the election administration, delimitation process, voter registration and voter education.

2   These have been published in Mass Public Opinion Institute (MPOI) *Desperate for Change, Zimbabweans Discuss the Country's Economic, Political and Social Crisis,* (Report of Focus Group Discussions), Harare. August 2008.

Sound election administration is critical in building political party confidence in the conduct and fairness of elections. However, the delays that accompanied the release of election results – the presidential results, in particular, which were released over six weeks – have a bearing on the spirit of democracy in Zimbabwe.

A new delimitation exercise was conducted in advance of the 29 March election, and there was insufficient time for people to identify their constituency boundaries and register – or re-register in cases where boundaries had been shifted. Further, a preliminary delimitation report was not tabled expeditiously, as envisioned in the electoral law, in order to provide an opportunity for formal input by the political parties. Instead, the final delimitation report was tabled in Parliament very late in the electoral process with little or no time to educate the public on changes to ward and constituency boundaries.

The process of voter registration and the inspection of the voters roll had restrictive requirements that resulted in failure by many people to register. Some potential voters were not accorded the opportunity to register because they failed to produce the required documentary evidence reasonably proving where they live. In the FGDs, one female participant from Matabeleland South said the registration process was difficult: 'I was told to go and get a reference letter from the chief who stays in a different area. I could not get transport and could not meet the deadline on the just ended mobile registration.' Voter registration ought to be an ongoing process. Indeed, in June 2007, there was a mobile registration exercise but unfortunately most people were not aware of the process, which was inadequately publicized. We repeatedly heard in Mashonaland Central province that 'we only heard about it when it was already over'.

The Electoral Act obliges the Zimbabwe Electoral Commission (ZEC) to conduct voter education and also clearly states that the Commission must commence a programme of voter education not later than 90 days before the polling day. However, in the 2008 elections, voter education began late and was little in evidence by the time of the March elections. Voter education was also compromised by resource constraints, inadequate training of voter educators, insufficient or incorrect information on the electoral process (especially the delimitation exercise), the manner in which the harmonized elections would be conducted, the practical implications on the voter, the number of ballot boxes, the number and colour coding of ballot papers, and contradictory information on how voters requiring assistance would be treated.

Public opinion on the 29th March 2008 harmonized elections

In September 2007, ZANU(PF) and the two MDC formations unanimously agreed to amend the Constitution of Zimbabwe for the eighteenth time, seeking to harmonize presidential, parliamentary, senatorial and council elections which were to be held on 29 March 2008. Many looked forward to these harmonized elections, hoping that they would bring sanity to the country's polity. However, the popular expectations of an MDC-T victory reflected in the research findings, did not translate into reality due to the aforesaid electoral irregularities. These predictive polls were crucial as they informed the different political players. This chapter discusses the major findings of the MPOI research, from voter registration to political party and candidate preferences.

Voter registration

To establish the percentage of citizens that had registered to vote, the questions asked were: 'Are you a registered voter?' or 'have you registered to vote for the 2008 harmonized elections?' The results presented in Figure 1 show that the number of registered voters rose to 86 per cent by mid-March. The surge in registrations which took place in February may be attributed to the stimulus of Simba Makoni's entrance into the political race.[3] As Alex Magaisa commented, Makoni's presidential bid caused a 'large amount of excitement both within and outside Zimbabwe. It has certainly injected some life to the electoral processes'.[4] However, the specified figures in the table outnumber the actual registration rate of 63 per cent.[5] Such a discrepancy can be accounted for by the margin of error as well as the fact that survey respondents wanted to associate themselves with 'normality', i.e. participating in an election rather than distancing oneself from it.

Intention to vote

The number of people who turn out to vote in an election is always of interest to the public and to prospective MPs. These statistics also reflect positive or negative support for the political system as a whole. Apathy does not reflect well on the health of the body politic. A willingness to vote

3   Simba Makoni, the President and Founder of the Mavambo/Kusile/Dawn movement formed on 5 February 2009, due to agitation with the then ruling party ZANU(PF) and its party leader, President Robert Mugabe.
4   The *Zimbabwe Independent* 8-14 February 2008. p. 7.
5   ZESN Report 'Zimbabwe 29 March Harmonized Election and 27 June 2008 Presidential Run-off', August 2008.
6   It should be noted that as a high percentage of the population now depend on informal cross-border trading for their survival, the decision to stay at home in order to vote was an important statement.

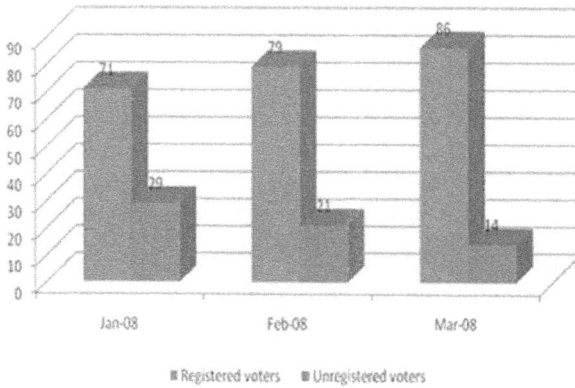

Figure 1: Voter registration
Question: Are you a registered voter?

Figure 2: Reasons for not voting
Question: If no, (i.e., not intending to vote), why aren't you going to vote?

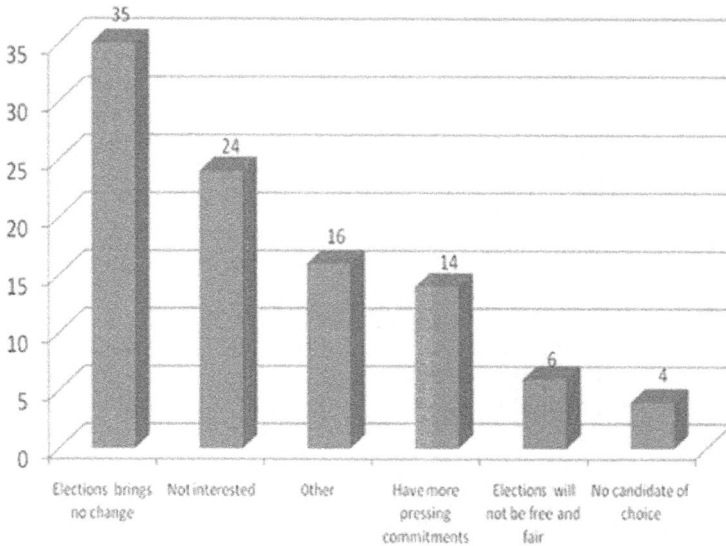

was not only portrayed by those who remained in the country at the election period,[6] but there was a burning desire among exiles as well. It should be pointed out that while some exiles returned home to vote, the electoral law does not allow postal voting by its citizens living outside the country. Some Zimbabweans wished to return home and vote because their exile experience has been so bad. Tawanda Muronda, for example, lamenting his life experience in South Africa, said, 'I have lived here for six years. Look at the holes in my shoes. Life is not that good. ... I feel I need to go back home and remove the person who has done all this damage to many people here.'[7] Nonetheless, although MPOI statistics suggest that 86 per cent of voters had registered and wanted to vote, official ZESN statistics show a voting rate of 47 per cent.[8] Whilst some might have failed to cross the border to cast their ballot, other aspiring voters were turned away because they were allegedly in the wrong ward or their names were missing from the voters roll.[9]

MPOI surveys suggest that though some Zimbabweans express a considerable desire to vote, fewer people take the necessary steps to make their intention a reality.[10] The January 2008 survey revealed fewer (71 per cent) registered voters than those who intended to vote (83 per cent), a gap of 12 per cent. In February, the pre-election survey recorded 79 per cent registered voters against 84 per cent intending to vote, a 5 per cent gap. The challenges associated with registration in Zimbabwe have always deterred voters. Supporting this notion, one elderly Bulawayo participant said, 'When I went to register, I was told (that) they (ZEC officials) wanted my proof of residence, so I was frustrated. It's difficult to register'.

Further analysis from the January survey reveals that 14 per cent said they would not vote, 3 per cent were indifferent, and a large majority, 83 per cent, had resolved to participate in the elections. In any election, as in any business, a rational person will employ a cost-benefit analysis. Voter apathy is a direct indication of the excess cost of participating in an election. Asked to provide reasons why they had decided not to vote, 35 per cent thought elections would not bring the change they so desired; 24 per cent were simply not interested; 14 per cent had more pressing commitments; 6 per cent reported that elections 'will not be free and fair', and 4 per cent (as depicted in Figure 2) said that the pool of candidates did not provide them with the choice they required.

Indeed, participants doubted the credibility of Zimbabwe elections. All processes of egalitarianism were blocked. A snap survey conducted by the *Zimbabwe Independent* reveals similar sentiments: those polled suggested

---

7   *The Standard*, 16-22 March 2008.
8   ZESN Report 'Zimbabwe 29 March Harmonized Election and 27 June 2008 Presidential Run-off', Harare. August 2008.
9   *The Standard*, 30 March - 5 April 2008.
10   Professor Eldred Masunungure *et al.*, 'Report on the Zimbabwe Electoral Processes and Reform, an Impact Study', December 2007.

Table 2: Factors affecting voting

	Correlation coefficient
Secrecy of the ballot	0.228**
Freeness and fairness of the 29 March elections	0.074*
Registration	0.036
Importance of the elections	0.013

that the elections would not bring about leadership change and that 'whether Mugabe, Makoni or Tsvangirai wins, there will be no benefit for me'.[11] Many FGD participants believe the ballot does not provide an answer to leadership change in Zimbabwe. In support of this notion, one elderly male participant in Masvingo said, 'Voting is a problem. The ballot will not change anything.'[12] Voicing the same sentiment, a young man from Mashonaland Central had this to say: 'Change is inevitable, but not through voting.'[13]

Further analysis of the factors affecting voting revealed some positive correlations between participation in the 29 March elections and the election environment, the level of importance attached to the elections and its variegated dimensions (Table 2).

Voters indicated a willingness to participate in an election if guaranteed a secret ballot. The relationship between these two variables is highly significant at 1 per cent. Voters could also be persuaded to vote if they believed the elections would be free and fair. This confirmed our findings (above) where 6 per cent of the respondents said they would not vote because 'the harmonized election would not be free and fair'. Above and beyond these considerations, the survey also revealed an association between voter registration and voting. In any election, registration must precede voting; being denied access to register means being denied a vote. Whilst all these qualifying factors are of significance, in our view they did not undermine the importance of an election in which many Zimbabwean voters participated, thus indicating the importance they attached to it. Official statistics recorded an increase in voter turnout for the 29 March parliamentary and presidential elections, from 20 per cent, witnessed in the senatorial elections to 42.7 per cent,[14] a 22.7 per cent increase. Nonetheless, we must ask, what had Zimbabweans to say in relation to secrecy of their ballot? Did they also perceive the election process as free and fair? A majority, 91 per

---

11 The *Zimbabwe Independent*, 29 February - 6 March 2008, p. 7.
12 MPOI report, 'Desperate for Change, Zimbabweans Discuss the Country's Economic, Political and Social Crisis', August 2008, p. 35.
13 Ibid.
14 The Zimbabwe Electoral Supervisory Commission Report on the March and June 2008 elections.

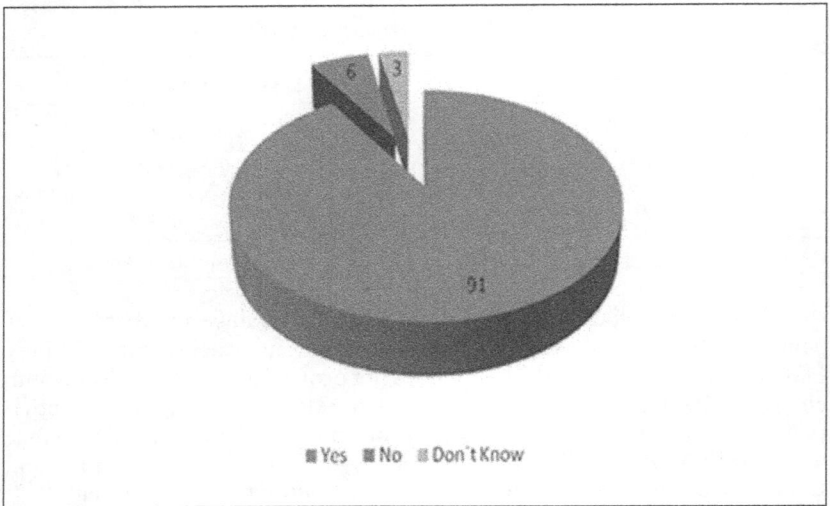

Figure 3: Secrecy of the ballot

Question: Do you think that your vote is your secret?

Figure 4: Free and fair, March 29 harmonized elections

Question: Do you think the 2008 elections will be free and fair?

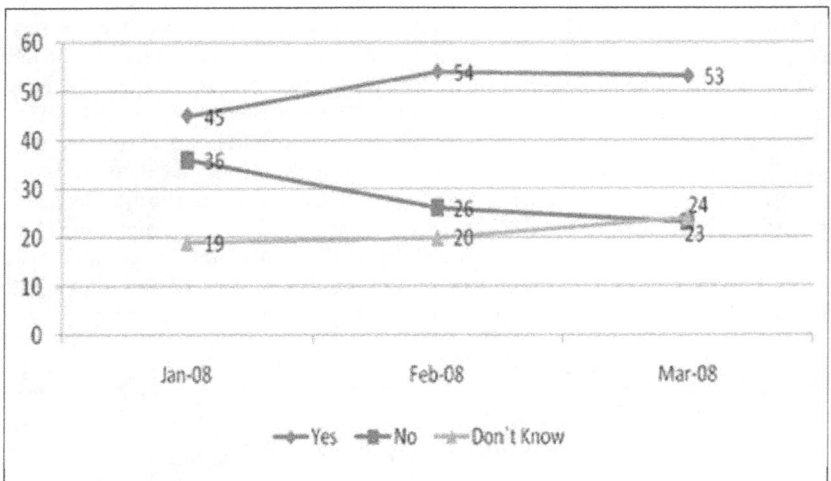

cent, believed their vote to be secret, 6 percent reported a non-secret ballot, whilst 3 per cent did not have an opinion to share (Figure 3).

On freeness and fairness of the harmonized elections, 45 per cent of the respondents thought the elections would be free and fair, 36 per cent refused to respond to the survey question, and 19 per cent professed ignorance. More grew optimistic as we moved closer to the elections, with 54 per cent in February and 53 per cent in March predicting credible elections (Figure 4).

Judging opinions on political violence, 85 per cent of the respondents in January 2008 confirmed having not witnessed any political violence since October 2007, 1 per cent reported minor cases, 4 per cent major cases and 1 per cent did not have any opinion on the issue. Even when a comparison was made to the March 2005 parliamentary elections, the majority, 74 per cent, had observed a reduction in cases of political violence, with only 6 per cent reporting an increase and 15 per cent thinking that the political atmosphere had remained static.

Voting preference

House of Assembly party preference

The purpose of pre-election surveys was to ascertain voters' preferences. Who, and which political party, would Zimbabweans vote for? Specifically the survey sought answers to the following question: 'If you were to vote for a Parliamentary candidate of your choice today, which party would he/she belong to?' Table 2 reveals a loss of popularity for the ruling party. Zimbabweans desire change, especially a change in leadership. Shifts in party allegiance are revealed in a survey conducted in May 2007 where ZANU(PF) garnered support of 33 per cent, against 21 per cent for the MDC-T and 1 per cent for the MDC-M. By December 2007, the former ruling party's support had dwindled to 19 per cent, and the MDC-T gained an additional 4 per cent (Table 3). However, of much concern is the proportion that either refused to respond, or hid within the 'my vote is my secret' category. In January 2008, the survey recorded 41 per cent against 31 per cent for March 2008. Because of fear of retribution, most opposition supporters can hardly disclose their political allegiance. Many who have done so have suffered political persecution.

While the above surveys reflected the MDC-T victory, one conducted by Dr Joseph Kurebwa (Lecturer and Chairman, University of Zimbabwe Department of Political and Administrative Studies) predicted that Mugabe would win most of the House of Assembly seats. According to his survey, 'Mugabe would clinch 41 Senate seats and 137 House of Assembly seats, ensuring another two-thirds majority in the next Parliament.'[15]

15   *The Herald*, 28 March 2008; *The Standard*, 30 March - 5 April 2008.

Table 3: January survey

House of Assembly Preference	May 2007	December 2007	January 2008	March 2008	March 2008: Only valid per cent rate*
ZANU(PF)	33	19	21	21	36.1
MDC-T	21 (-12)	25 (+6)	30 (-9)	31 (+10)	54.5
MDC	11	1	3	5.2	
Independent candidate			3	2	3.6
Refused to say	21	28	17	8	
My vote is my secret	11	15	24	23	
I will not vote		4	2	5	
Don't know			1	2	
Other parties	13	7	2	5	

*These disregard all invalid percentages from 'my vote is my secret', 'I will not vote', 'other' and refusals.

Question: 'If you were to vote for a Parliamentary candidate of your choice today, which party would he/she belong to?'

It further projected that Morgan Tsvangirai's faction would win 13 Senate seats and 53 House of Assembly seats. Contrary to this, political scientist Eldred Masunungure argued in an article in the *Zimbabwe Independent* that 'no party will be able to gain a two-thirds majority in the House of Assembly'.[16]

Preferred Presidential candidate

When people were asked which Presidential candidate they would vote for, 35.5 per cent said Mugabe, and 49.4 per cent Tsvangirai.[17] Another 15 per cent chose Makoni, and only 0.1 per cent Mutambara. Dr Kurebwa's survey, which was dismissed as 'phony' by some political analysts, predicted an overwhelming percentage for Mugabe (56-57 per cent) ahead of Tsvangirai (26-27 per cent) and Makoni (13-14 per cent). However, many Zimbabweans expressed deep scepticism about the these findings: 'Kurebwa's surveys are designed to justify manipulation and rigging of elections by the state'.[18] Masunungure predicted the possibility of a run-off: 'All things being equal, no one will gain over 50 per cent of the vote in the first round and a run-off is almost certain.'[19]

The need for political change

Results from the two FGDs depicted eager anticipation for change, with a body of opinion feeling that the only way to speak to power is through elections. 'Change will come through elections,' said a rural participant, a young female from Matabeleland South. Elections should form a cornerstone of democracy if conducted freely and fairly. However, the Zimbabwean election, despite being endorsed by SADC as free and fair, failed to some extent to follow the laid down principles governing democratic elections. There were significant irregularities on the election day, 29 March. 8,500 ghost voters were discovered in Harare North constituency (Ward 42); a significant proportion of voters were turned away either because their names were not on the voters roll or they were trying to vote in the wrong ward; there was a shortage of ballot papers in Kariba, Makoni North and Rusape; for the Harare North constituency where ghost voters were discovered, ZEC printed 50 per cent more ballot papers than there were registered voters.[20] Indubitably, the democratic wind that ought to have prevailed was blocked when other eligible voters failed to participate in the election.

However, some Zimbabweans are yearning for leadership change, as

16 The *Zimbabwe Independent* 14-20 March 2008.
17 A question on presidential choice was only asked in the March 2008 survey. Percentages given are valid votes only.
18 The *Zimbabwe Independent,* 28 March - 3 April 2008.
19 Ibid. 14-20 March 2008.
20 The *Standard,* 30 March - 5 April 2008.

the February 2007 focus group discussions revealed. A young man from Harare Province: 'The change needed is government first, there must be new blood.'[21] Participants believe the ZANU(PF) government has to step down since they 'have stayed in power for too long'. One middle-aged female from Mashonaland West said, 'Leadership should change and we should not let a leader be in the same position for 20-30 years.'[22] A middle-aged man from Matebeleland North said, 'There is need to change the President and his subordinates. They don't tell him the truth. The tractor must go with his trailers so that we can get effective change.'[23]

In a snap survey conducted by the *Zimbabwe Independent*, Fibion Gumisai said the current government has failed dismally to serve the people over the past 27 years '... and there is need for the electorate to go out and vote for change.' He urged Zimbabweans not to be 'apathetic but [to] exercise their right to vote to bring democratic change in the country.'[24] In the same survey, a resident from Mufakose said, 'I am going to vote. My vote may make the difference. I just hope that all the people who registered to vote will go and vote. We need change of leadership in this country. Life has become unbearable.'

The FGD results showed a preference for the MDC-T in nearly all provinces. Generally, participants held them in high regard. This could be due to the party's 'change' message. Participants said this faction's strength lies in its pledge to fulfil the people's will by bringing about the long-awaited change, a new constitution as well as economic upturn, thus building a new Zimbabwe.

Asked to express their views about ZANU(PF), participants in two FGD rounds gave downbeat opinions. The party scored very low and its perceived weaknesses far outweighed its strengths. It has failed to fulfil its promises, which explains why many Zimbabweans live in gloomy poverty. It is blamed for being 'selfish, not people-oriented and not principled'. Some participants identified the pivotal role the party played in the liberation struggle which brought about the country's independence. However, this they believe is now history and cannot justify the current torment being experienced in the country. Many people from Manicaland, Masvingo, Mashonaland Central and Harare provinces could not ascribe any success to the party; instead, they heavily criticized it for abusing power, using state machinery to crush the opposition and for failing to meet the people's demands and expectations.

> ZANU(PF) has all the authority and power; is failing to fulfil what they promised (to the people), is good at carrying out their evil; not people oriented;

21   MPOI report: 'Desperate for Change, Zimbabweans Discuss the Country's Economic, Political and Social Crisis', August 2008, Harare p. 34.
22   Ibid.
23   Ibid.
24   The *Zimbabwe Independent*, 29 February - 6 March 2008.

not principled; wants to annihilate the country as a whole; has failed to meet the demands of the nation; manipulates everything by force; rigs every election conducted in the country; internally divided; lacks support from the majority; vandalizes and devastates every good effort of national building; always heads for a downfall.[25]

Unable to resuscitate the economy of Zimbabwe, autocratic, they keep on basing decisions on past experience which is irrelevant, no democracy, pulling down economy, very violent, abusive, and aggressive.[26]

The second round of the FGDs was consistent with this, most participants favouring MDC-T. Several had invested their trust in the party and its leader: 'he is still young and still has the chance to run around in search for foreign aid'.[27] Some commended him for his consistency in the struggle to liberate Zimbabweans:

(I would vote for the) MDC led by Tsvangirai, we look at where we have come from with him, spearheading the struggle for survival, the improvement of living standards, the liberation of the people from dictatorship and corruption, I think he is one of the few Zimbabweans who has managed to challenge Mugabe, highlighting his failures.[28]

There was, however, a notable shift of party affiliation in the Midlands participants. When asked which party they trusted, they said they trust the MDC party led by Morgan Tsvangirai. They 'no longer trust ZANU(PF)', which is what was said in Round 1; '[I] do not know of Dr Makoni and do not understand what Prof. Mutambara, leader of the other MDC splinter group is really after.' These participants believe the MDC-T is best positioned to bring change to Zimbabwe. But this was not the case in Matabeleland and Bulawayo provinces where there is a strong feeling that the MDC-T cannot revolutionize the country. '[L]ook at the government and the confusion in the MDC-T, and let us try something new. Maybe Simba Makoni will do, he is an economist and knows how to deal with the economy.'[29]

To further understand participants' views of political parties and their leaders, there was an exercise which allowed participants to express what comes to mind at the mention of certain leader's names. As in Round 1, Mugabe received harsh words from almost all participants. Makoni, who only stood as a candidate after the first round of FGDs, was positively identified by some in Matabeleland provinces and was described as someone 'who has foresight, brave thus deserves to be given a chance to try'.[30] Mutambara's public support of Makoni in the presidential vote may explain such affirmative descriptions. Tsvangirai was acclaimed in all

25 FGD. Young males, Mashonaland Central rural, tertiary education.
26 FGD. Young females, Harare urban, tertiary-level students.
27 FGD. Middle-aged females, Midlands rural, secondary education.
28 FGD. Young males, Harare urban, at least secondary education.
29 FGD. Middle-aged female, Bulawayo, at least secondary education.

other provinces, where Makoni was seen by the participants as 'a traitor working on a ZANU(PF) ticket, a failure, who failed as a minister and is confused'. The general opinion of Tsvangirai was that he is someone who has concern for the people, is a better leader and is courageous; some participants even used Biblical allusion: 'He is on a mission to deliver God's people from Egypt to Canaan.'[31] Although Mutambara was not in the race for the presidency, participants depicted him as one who is 'unable to rule, not organized, there to divide and confuse voters'.[32] Some participants from a Mashonaland East FGD went on to say that, '...he is just there to cause confusion. He is the one who caused the split of the MDC. He is not organized.'[33] A participant from Mashonaland Central agreed: 'He is a hypocrite, does not have direction, doesn't know what he wants and is not yet politically mature.'[34]

In consultation with the two main political parties, MPOI obtained from each a catchy message that they believed could entice people to vote for them. The ZANU(PF) message read: 'ZANU(PF) are the true sons of the soil and our liberators. They fight to protect the sovereignty of Zimbabwe and defend us against those who would turn our country back into a colony. ZANU(PF) also works for the empowerment of black Zimbabweans through the redistribution of land and support for black ownership of businesses in key sectors, such as mining and manufacturing.' Many disapproved of this message as stale and out of tune with the present realities; most participants emphatically rejected the notion that the ruling party alone liberated the country. The FGDs were of the opinion that 'Zimbabwe's independence was not brought about by ZANU(PF) alone, as they claim, but rather by the people of Zimbabwe who tirelessly worked together to free the nation from colonial bondage.' Several believed ZANU(PF) to be oppressing people merely on the grounds that they fought the liberation struggle. A middle-aged female from Manicaland province had this to say: 'ZANU(PF) worsened our situation even though they liberated us. They also need to note that everyone played a role in the liberation struggle.' Similarly, a participant from Harare province said:

> I wasn't impressed where they say they are the true sons of the soil. They are not true sons of the soil just because they are ZANU(PF). Zimbabweans are the true sons of the soil and not ZANU(PF) and ZANU(PF) are not our liberators; it is our fathers who fought the liberation struggle and not ZANU(PF).[35]

Apart from showing disapproval of the ZANU(PF) statement, participants further confirmed a strong feeling of dislike for the leader of the then ruling

30 FGD. Middle-aged female, Bulawayo.
31 FGD. Young female, Harare.
32 FGD. Middle-aged females, Midlands rural.
33 FGD. Elderly males, Mashonaland East rural, secondary education.
34 FGD. Young male, Mashonaland Central rural, secondary education.
35 FGD, Young male, Harare, secondary education.

party in both rounds of the FGDs. They used harsh words to describe his personality. Many were of the opinion that he is 'a dictator, blinkered and rules with an iron fist'. Such sentiments were particularly strong amongst participants from Harare, Mashonaland Central, Masvingo, and Mashonaland West provinces. The President is even portrayed as a 'hard hearted man, a destroyer' and a 'rigid person' who does not consider people's rights and interests. However, there remained a few loyalists who were of the opinion that he is 'intelligent, clever, understanding, trying to develop the nation, and is strong, apart from being the best orator in southern Africa'. The MDC-T message read:

> The MDC believes that Zimbabwe needs a new beginning. They have a vision for a prosperous New Zimbabwe that will finally complete the ideals of the liberation struggle. MDC is committed to freedom and equality for all and a law-abiding, democratic government. The party's priority will be to fix the economy, so that Zimbabweans can return to a dignified life with access to land, jobs, food, health and education.

It was a message that resonated with many participants, particularly the idea of 'a new beginning' that offered hope and inspiration. Supporting this perception, Alex Magaisa suggested that, 'if Zimbabwe needs anything at this juncture, it is the stabilization in all areas of life. A leadership that is capable of providing stability should find favour among the people.'[36] Indeed, it is this view that explains the mileage that the MDC-T received from people in need of hope and a new future. The party campaigned on a platform of economic stabilization, restoration of law and order and constitutional change. It pledged to tackle unemployment and boost the economy. Participants regarded the leader of the larger MDC faction with great honour, some describing him as 'a saviour for the future Zimbabwe; has the people at heart; caring; courageous; outspoken; has a vision; the voice of the oppressed; has people at heart'.[37] Others paid tribute to the MDC-T statement as focusing on the future. A young female from Harare province said, 'I respect the MDC-T vision very much for they base it on our present life and the future. We cannot just continue to look back; we appreciate the past but what of the future?'

Conclusion: predicted election outcome versus the actual outcome

Based on people's expressions and feelings towards candidates and messages, it was overwhelmingly clear who was going to win the elections. The MPOI research findings revealed a loss of popularity for ZANU(PF) and President Mugabe. The opinions displayed by the discussions are similar to those expressed in the outcome to the elections (Table 4). There has been

36 The *Zimbabwe Independent*, 8 - 14 February 2008, p. 7.
37 FGD. Young females, Harare, University students.

Table 4: Zimbabwean parliamentary and senatorial elections, 2008

(All 210 seats in the House of Assembly of Zimbabwe and 60 (of the 93) seats in the Senate of Zimbabwe).

Leader	Morgan Tsvangirai MDC	Robert Mugabe ZANU(PF)	Arthur Mutambara Faction of MDC	Independent
2005, after MDC split	House of Assembly (HoA): 27 seats Senate: 0 seats	HoA: 78 seats Senate: 43	HoA: 14 seats Senate: 7	HoA: 1 seat Senate: 0
Seats won (2008)	HoA: 100 seats Senate: 24 seats	HoA: 99 seats Senate: 30	HoA: 10 seats Senate: 6	HoA: 1 seat Senate: 0
Seat change	HoA: +73 seats Senate: +24 seats	HoA: +21 seats Senate: -13	HoA: -4 Senate: 7	HoA: 0 Senate: 0
2008 Actual results (% of total votes)	HoA: 42.88 per cent Senate: 43.29 per cent	HoA: 45.94 per cent Senate: 46.15 per cent	HoA: 8.39 per cent Senate: 6.72 per cent	HoA: 2.25 per cent
Predictions - March 2008 Survey	HoA: 54.5 per cent	HoA: 36.1 per cent	HoA: 5.2 per cent	HoA: 3.6 per cent

Table 5: Zimbabwe presidential election, 2008
(29 March and 27 June 2008)

Candidate	Robert Mugabe ZANU(PF)	Morgan Tsvangirai MDC	Simba Makoni Independent	Langton Towungana Independent
Actual, after 29 March Presidential election	43.2 per cent	47.9 per cent	8.5 per cent	0.6 per cent
Predictions from the March 2008 Survey	35.5 per cent	49.4 per cent	14.9 per cent	0.1 per cent

a distinct shift of support from ZANU(PF) to the MDC-T. In the March 2005 elections to the House of Assembly, ZANU(PF) won 78 of the 120 directly elected seats; the MDC, established in 1999 and led by Morgan Tsvangirai, won 41 seats. The MDC was later divided over whether to participate in the November 2005 Senate elections. Tsvangirai called for a boycott of the election; the MDC Secretary General, Welshman Ncube, participated in the vote. This gave birth to the smaller, pro-Senate MDC faction, referred to as the MDC-M after the party leader Arthur Mutambara. The MDC-T thus remained with a total of 27 House of Assembly seats and the splinter MDC party, led by Mutambara, acquired 14 seats. The final 2005 Senatorial results gave 43 of the 50 directly elected seats to the ZANU(PF) and 7 to the MDC-T.

Constitutional Amendment No. 19 increased the number of members of the House of Assembly from 150 to 210 and the Senate was enlarged from 50 to 93. Of the 93 senatorial seats, 60 were contested; two were reserved for the president and deputy president of the Chiefs' Council, 10 for the provincial governors, 16 for the chiefs, and 5 for presidential appointees. According to the final 2008 House of Assembly election results – including by-elections in Gwanda South, Pelandaba/Mpopoma and Redcliff – ZANU(PF) won 99 seats, the MDC-T 100, MDC-M 10 and there was one independent seat. ZANU(PF) won 30 of the Senate seats, the MDC-T 24 and MDC-M 6. The elections results seem to corroborate the public opinion polls that were conducted prior to the elections which showed the MDC-T to have gained support even in former ZANU(PF) strongholds.

The same picture is reflected in the presidential election. Following a 2005 change in the Electoral Act, the winner needed to win a majority of the vote, with a second round if necessary within 21 days, contrary to the first-past-the-post system previously in place. In the first poll, Tsvangirai won 47.9 per cent, Mugabe 43.2 per cent, Makoni 8 per cent and Towungana the remainder. Predictions from the March 2008 Survey were close to the mark, especially for the MDC-T (Table 5).

Similarly, in the parliamentary elections, ZANU(PF) was struck a heavy blow as many people shifted their allegiance to the MDC-T. In 2002, Robert Mugabe won by 56.2 per cent against Tsvangirai's 42 per cent, although most voters believe these elections were not free and fair, and were marred by political violence. The 2008 harmonized election reflected a 13 per cent loss in votes for Mugabe.

The MPOI's surveys, revealing a loss of popularity for ZANU(PF) and its president candidate, were clearly mirrored by the 2008 elections results. However, popular hopes for the 2008 harmonized elections were shattered by the need for the successful presidential candidate to garner at least a 50 per cent of the votes plus one vote. Thus, the much needed democratic dispensation was blocked.

The research is validated by having provided best projections about the future and the direction of the country. Undoubtedly, in predicting political developments, people can sincerely rely on public opinion.

3

The Media Environment Leading up to Zimbabwe's 2008 Elections

Andrew Moyse

Introduction

Ever since the birth of meaningful political opposition to the ruling ZANU(PF) party in Zimbabwe, elections have become a battleground. The political struggle of the newly formed MDC and civil society against the political hegemony of ZANU(PF) initially manifested itself in the Constitutional Referendum of February 2000, which witnessed the first and only official polling defeat for ZANU(PF) – prior to the 29 March harmonized elections of 2008. In that referendum Zimbabweans resoundingly rejected a draft constitution presented by the government that proposed to extend the Executive's authoritarian grip on power. But this singular electoral victory for the people of Zimbabwe proved to be an unimaginably costly rebellion against the authority of the ruling party.

With a parliamentary election less than four months away – in June of that year – extreme and repressive measures were taken by the ZANU(PF) government to assure electoral victory and to ensure that a defeat at the polls would never happen again. The result has been a relentless crackdown on Zimbabweans' civil and political liberties to an extent that now only a small vestige of that democratic space remains.

Among the greatest casualties has been Zimbabweans' constitutionally guaranteed right to freedom of expression and their subsidiary rights to receive and impart information without hindrance. In many ways the constitutional referendum of 2000 defined the nature of today's media landscape, as civil society, in collaboration with the independent press, and particularly the relatively new *Daily News*, overcame a tidal wave of propaganda in the government-controlled media campaigning for acceptance of the draft constitution.

An ironic consequence of that referendum result was that it not only provided government with a useful tool to measure increasing public resentment to its rule, a timely warning of the drastic action that it would need to take to retain power – it also allowed government to identify the most dangerous threats to its political survival: a vibrant civil society which had just given birth to a massively popular political opposition – and an increasingly effective private media.

A nation deprived

Apart from the country's pending total economic collapse (see Chapter 1) that crippled the operations of most domestic media institutions and the capacity of the public to access them, a host of blatantly unconstitutional and repressive laws were enacted that effectively emasculated the independent media and deprived the nation of its rights to freedom of expression, including the right to be informed. At least four newspapers were closed under these laws and scores of journalists harassed, arrested, detained and thrown out of work. One was even murdered.[1]

At the same time, the government hijacked the national public broadcasting corporation (ZBC) and used it relentlessly to disseminate propaganda discrediting the opposition and enhancing the image of the ruling party. Despite the fact that the Supreme Court declared ZBC's monopoly of the airwaves unconstitutional more than nine years ago,[2] government has not permitted any independent electronic media organizations to operate. The Broadcasting Services Act[3] (BSA) ostensibly allows for other broadcasting entities. But despite the fact that the Supreme Court struck down the monopoly on radio and television broadcasting held by ZBC, the BSA contains so many restrictive clauses that it is virtually impossible for private investors to establish independent broadcasting companies.

Today, ZBC still enjoys a *de facto* monopoly of the airwaves, which ZANU-(PF) has relentlessly exploited to malign the political opposition and its critics, particularly at election time. Although the Broadcasting Authority of Zimbabwe went through the motion of inviting applications for more broadcasters more than four years ago, none of the applications were ever approved.[4]

The extent of this bias is well illustrated in the following statistics compiled by the Media Monitoring Project Zimbabwe of the coverage of the

1 The battered body of retired ZBC cameraman, Edward Chikomba, was found dumped in a bush near Darwendale. The discovery was first reported by Zim Online on 05/04/07.
2 *Capital Radio (Private) Limited v. Minister of Information, Posts and Telecommunications*, Judgment No. S.C. 99/2000, Constit. Application No. 130/00.
3 Chapter 10:26.
4 *The Herald* (29/04/05) reported BAZ acting chairman Pikirayi Deketeke announcing that it had turned down all applications for radio broadcasting licences because the applicants all 'failed to meet the requirements of the Broadcasting Services Act'. Although there was some debate about the Munhumutapa African Broadcasting Company owned by James Makamba, which had applied for a television licence, it too was turned down 'because the applicant had failed to demonstrate that it had the funds to operate a television station' (*Zimbabwe Independent* (16 September 2005).

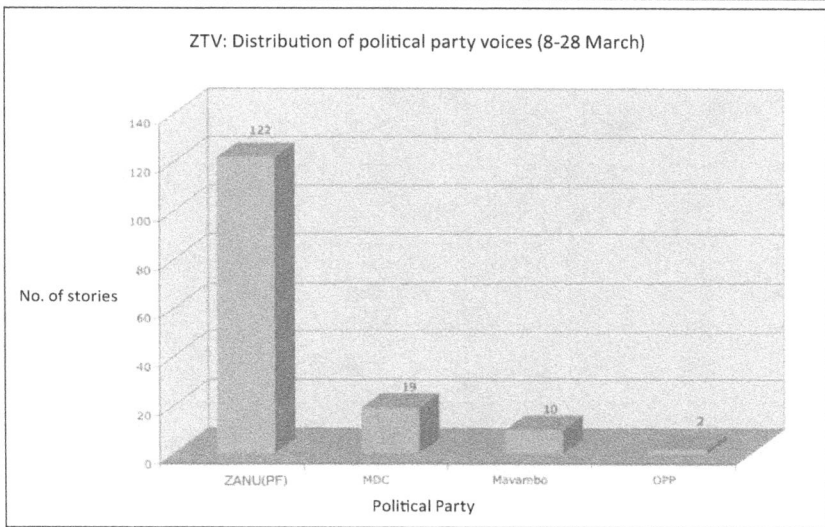

Figure 1

political contestants by the ZBC in the last three weeks of the election campaign leading up to polling day for the 29 March harmonized elections.

ZBC election campaign coverage, 8-28 March 2008

Despite ZBC's publicized promise to abide by the Zimbabwe Electoral Commission's (ZEC) media regulations (see below) demanding fair, equitable and accurate coverage of the contestants in the 21 days ahead of the March election, its coverage of the contesting parties showed a complete disregard for these provisions.

For example, out of the 153 stories ZTV (Zimbabwe's sole television station) devoted to the parties' campaigns in the three weeks before the poll, 122 (80%) were allocated ZANU(PF) and nineteen (12%) to the two MDC factions. Former Finance Minister Simba Makoni's *Mavambo* project was given ten stories or (7%) and the small parties were covered in two reports (1%) (Figure 1).

ZTV's sourcing pattern also reflected its overwhelming pro-ZANU(PF) slant. Of the 148 voices from the contesting parties, 127 (86%) were ZANU(PF) and only eight (5%) were MDC. This is despite the fact that the party was contesting almost all the constituencies that ZANU(PF) was. *Mavambo* was quoted nine times (6%), while small parties were cited four times (3%) (Figure 2).

It adopted a similar trend in its coverage of the presidential candidates'

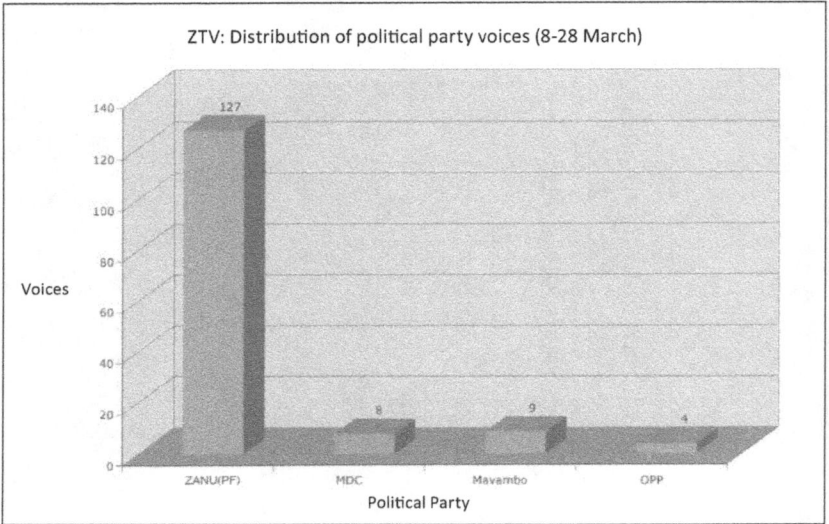

ZTV: Distribution of political party voices (8-28 March)

Figure 2

Figure 3

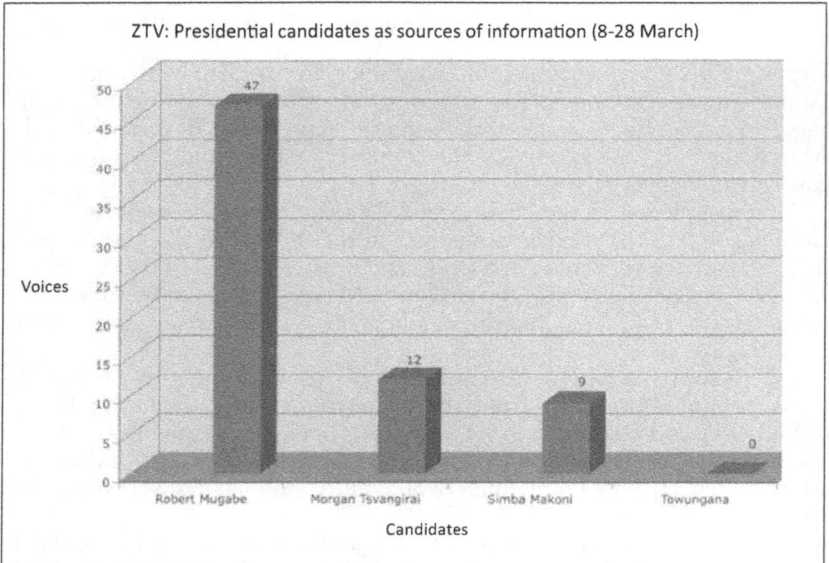

ZTV: Presidential candidates as sources of information (8-28 March)

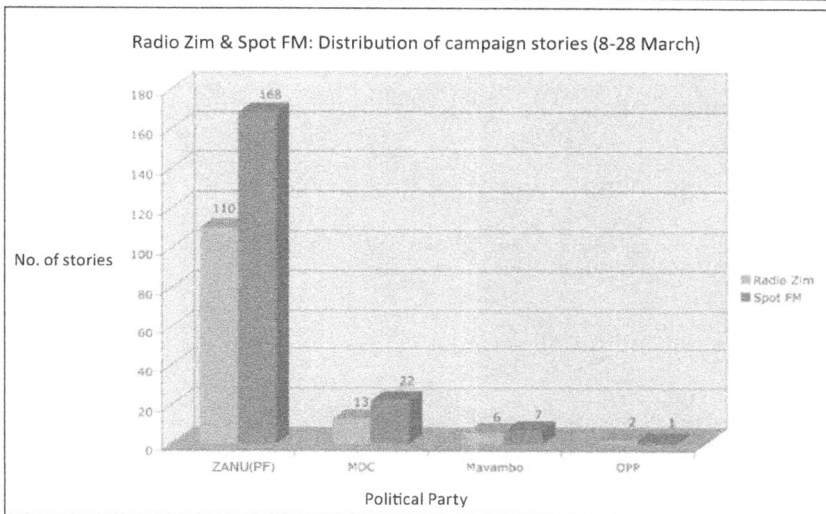

Radio Zim & Spot FM: Distribution of campaign stories (8-28 March)

Figure 4

voices. Robert Mugabe was cited 47 times (69%) out of the 68 presidential voices the station quoted, while his two rivals shared the remaining 31% between them: Morgan Tsvangirai twelve voices (18%) and Makoni nine (13%). The other presidential candidate, Langton Towungana, was not quoted (Figure 3).

ZBC's two main domestic radio stations also displayed their contempt for the ZEC's regulations governing media coverage of political parties and their contestants. Out of 131 campaign stories Radio Zimbabwe aired in the 21 days ahead of the elections, 110 (84%) were on ZANU(PF) while only thirteen (10%) were on the MDC. *Mavambo* was covered six times (5%), while two stories (1%) were devoted to minor parties. Spot FM's coverage was similar. Of the 198 campaign stories it broadcast in the same period, 168 (85%) were on ZANU(PF) and the rest (15%) on the MDC and other contestants. Of these, 22 (11%) were on the MDC, seven (3%) on *Mavambo* and only one per cent on other small parties.

Almost all the stories on the MDC and *Mavambo* were either brief pieces on the parties' activities buried in the bulletins or were reported in the context of discrediting their policies and their leaders (Figure 4).

The stations' disproportionate coverage of the parties in its bulletins was also reflected by the sources they cited in their news reports. For instance, of the 91 political parties' voices cited by Radio Zimbabwe, 73 (82%) were ZANU(PF), twelve (13%) the two MDC formations and four (5%) minor parties. None were *Mavambo*. Likewise, there were no *Mavambo* voices out of the 127 political parties' sources cited by Spot FM. Of these, 114 (90%) were ZANU(PF) and only twelve (9%) were from the two MDCs.

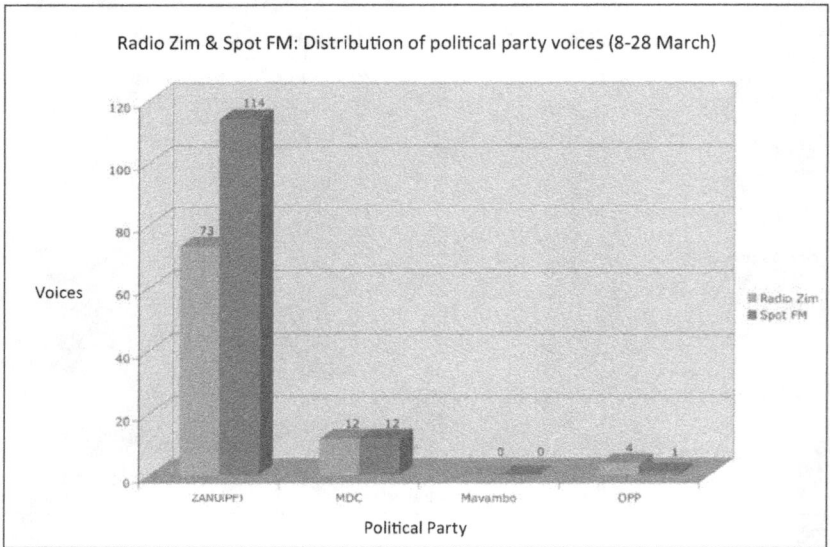

Figure 5

Figure 6

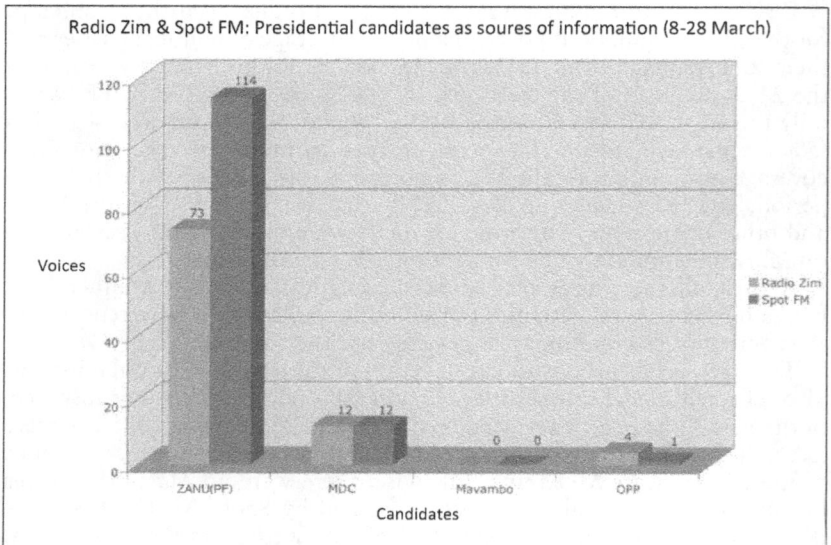

The other opposition parties were quoted once (Figure 5).

Their unbalanced sourcing was also extended to their coverage of the presidential candidates. Mugabe's voice constituted 80% of the 62 presidential voices Radio Zimbabwe cited against six (10%) each for his rivals Tsvangirai and Makoni. Towungana was not quoted. On Spot FM, Mugabe was cited 44 times (83%) out of the 53 presidential voices the station carried, while Tsvangirai was cited four times (8%) and Makoni six times (9%). To make matters worse, Mugabe's opponents were hardly given sound bites but had their campaign statements recounted by the broadcaster's reporters, who then negatively qualified them (Figure 6).

Such open support for ZANU(PF) and its presidential candidate also resulted in ZTV giving more airtime to ZANU(PF)'s electoral preparations in its news bulletins. For example, of the nine hours and twenty minutes ZTV devoted to reporting the parties' campaign activities in its main news bulletins (7 a.m., 6 p.m. and 8 p.m.) between 1 March 2008 and the eve of voting (28 March), eight hours and 44 minutes (93.5%) of this was favourable coverage of ZANU(PF)'s activities. The remaining 36 minutes were divided among the ruling party's opponents, including both factions of the MDC, Makoni and other minor political contestants.

In short, ZBC transformed itself into a private broadcaster for ZANU(PF) and the government during the March election campaign at the expense of all other political opinion.

But this appalling performance is nothing new, for it reflects exactly the same bias of ZBC's news output in all previous election campaigns that MMPZ has monitored. In fact, the figures on ZBC's coverage of political parties reflect a consistent trend in its daily coverage of political events even between elections.

It should be noted that MMPZ was unable to produce any coherent statistics of ZBC's coverage of the presidential candidates' campaigns leading up to the 27 June presidential election run-off (from which the MDC-T candidate, Morgan Tsvangirai eventually withdrew following a nationwide campaign of state-sponsored political violence) because Tsvangirai's campaign activities were completely censored in all of ZBC's radio and television news bulletins. In contrast, ZBC's bulletins gave saturation coverage to President Mugabe and his party's campaign to have him re-elected.

Similarly, the government seized the mainstream national newspapers that were once protected by a nominally independent trust, to promote the image of the ruling party and to persecute individuals and organizations critical of government. The main daily and Sunday newspapers of the Zimbabwe Newspapers Group, whose editorial content is directly controlled by the Department of Information, were used regularly in 2008, as they had been in the country's three previous elections since the turn of the millenium, to disseminate hate messages, often racist, threatening and insulting, against those considered to be 'enemies' of the state. The intention of this campaign appears to have been to dehumanize these people and organizations to such an extent as to imply they no longer deserved to have their basic rights protected. This extreme and dangerous practice represented an intolerable abuse of the publicly-owned media. In most democracies the public media have a mandate to provide fair and accurate coverage of events and issues affecting the interests of the people.

The public media in Zimbabwe did not merely fail to live up to this duty, they were manifestly used to misinform and confuse the public, especially during election campaigns. For example the government-controlled media, have, in past elections, been used to raise confusion over what documents are required to vote, or to register as a voter (also see Chapter 7).

The government-controlled media's understanding of its responsibilities towards enlightening the public over relevant electoral issues and events – voter education – in 2008 remained distinctly limited and appeared to reflect the government's attitude towards this important issue. Voter education and the inspection of the voters roll leading up to the 2008 elections received only sporadic and inadequate publicity. The same could be said of the delimitation of the country's political boundaries under constitutional changes introduced in 2007. The amendments had expanded the number of constituencies from 120 to 210. This important exercise was conducted almost totally out of view of the public and without their consultation. It was merely presented as a *fait accompli* and no effort was made by the state-controlled press to investigate or explain the frequently bizarre new boundaries that gave rise to the suspicion of gerrymandering.

Voter education, too, was restricted to the exclusive authority of the government-appointed ZEC, thus suffocating the expertise of civil society and rendering their initiatives to inform the public about their constitutional rights and duties to clandestine and risky exercises that carried criminal penalties. For example, the ZEC ordered the national broadcaster to remove the voter education advertisements flighted on its radio and television broadcasts by the civic election watchdog, the Zimbabwe Election Support Network (ZESN), on the grounds that they had not been cleared by the ZEC prior to broadcast and were thus illegal. Applications to the ZEC to clear the material met with no response.[5]

The privately-owned media (with no such national obligation) did significantly better than the government-controlled media in informing the public about their electoral rights and electoral issues, especially in collaboration with civic organizations. But the banning of *The Daily News* in September 2003, the only independent daily source of information readily available to the public that provided an alternative to the otherwise dominant government-controlled media, represented a great loss to Zimbabwean society. This loss was exacerbated by the absence of any independent radio stations operating from within the country.

The only readily accessible sources of alternative information following the daily's banning were three independent weekly newspapers that still operate today, two of them aimed generally at the business commu-

5   See Chapter 8.

nity and a Sunday family paper.⁶ But although they continued to provide some assistance in servicing the public with credible alternative information, they remained weekly publications with severely limited circulations and therefore incapable of providing most Zimbabweans with their daily information needs.

This information drought gave rise to the emergence of two overseas-based radio stations run by Zimbabweans broadcasting news about Zimbabwe into the country for two or three hours every evening during the week, and to a phenomenal growth in web-based on-line agencies reporting exclusively on Zimbabwe. However, the government has admitted to jamming the broadcasts of the short-wave stations using Chinese supplied equipment, and the on-line agencies are only accessible to the very tiny fraction of the public that have access to the internet.

Just after the March 2005 parliamentary elections a fourth weekly paper, *The Zimbabwean*, and later its sister Sunday paper, both published in South Africa to avoid the restrictive publishing laws in Zimbabwe and imported into the country, joined this small group of independent news organizations and have become, by a large margin, the country's most popular newspapers.

Even so, while these news services have managed to narrow the 'information gap', they remain a poor substitute for the critically important alternative daily news service of a domestic independent daily paper or radio station.

As a result, the government-controlled media at the time of the 2008 elections overwhelmingly dominated the airwaves and the daily print media market and were harnessed by ZANU(PF) to disseminate and propagate official government doctrine virtually unchallenged. The vast majority of Zimbabweans were obliged to depend on them for news about the country (and, for that matter, world events). This situation exposed the average citizen not only to misinformation about important national issues, but also to potentially harmful disinformation.

Since the closure of *The Daily News* the government-controlled media have been able to set the national agenda by determining what news and issues are reported and how they are packaged for public consumption. Inevitably, this gave rise to grossly biased accounts in every sphere of Zimbabwe's social, political and economic development, reporting news and opinion that reflect only positively on government decisions and policies. No criticism was tolerated and the socio-political and economic crises that have afflicted the country since the turn of the millennium were only reported in the context of the ruling party's official perspective – that they have been caused by Western imperialist machinations to recolonize Zimbabwe.

In the campaigns of the two elections in 2008 the government-owned

6 The *Zimbabwe Independent*, *The Financial Gazette* and *The Standard*. Remarkably, *The Financial Gazette* displays considerable editorial independence despite a significant portion of the shares of the publishing company being effectively held Mugabe affiliate, Gideon Gono, or his proxies and possibly elements within the state security body.

public broadcaster and newspapers used this unchallenged advantage relentlessly to malign and disparage the political opposition.

Zimbabwe's political leadership and the journalists working for the government media employed unacceptably offensive, false and intolerant language, first to persuade the electorate not to vote for those people and organizations challenging ZANU(PF)'s political dominance and then to threaten them, most particularly in the June presidential election run-off.[7]

Although the political opposition was allowed limited direct access (advertising) to the government media in the March elections, as media regulations require,[8] their activities and statements were censored or deliberately distorted in order to present them in a negative light. In addition, those accused of 'undermining the country's sovereignty' and otherwise impugned and maligned in the columns of the government newspapers or on ZBC, were never given the chance to respond to the allegations.

By abandoning these basic principles of ethical journalistic practice, these institutions declared themselves to be undisguised instruments of ZANU(PF)'s propaganda. In other words, apart from the advertising content submitted by the political opposition, the news content of these institutions remained as biased and distorted as they have ever been against ZANU(PF)'s political challengers.

Following the March elections, and contrary to media regulations, the MDC was denied all access to the government media[9] and the daily hate campaign conducted in the government media against the MDC's presidential candidate became a tidal wave of venomous insults, threats and false allegations.[10]

The nationwide wave of state-sponsored violence that preceded the June 2008 presidential run-off has a precedent in the June 2000 general elections when the government pursued its so-called 'fast-track' agrarian reform programme – and the persecution of its political opposition, the Movement for Democratic Change. But unlike 2008, the excesses of the government in the 2000 election campaign also gave rise to a bitter media war.

While the government media were enlisted to portray the violent seizure of white-owned farmland as a natural reaction to a recalcitrant and racist farming community who had betrayed the revolution by supporting a Western-sponsored political opposition in the hope of retaining their land, *The Daily News* and the independent weekly press reported the appalling human rights abuses and other excesses of government activity that occurred in the months following the referendum.

At that time *The Daily News* provided a critical service providing the

7   See the 'hate speech' quoted below.
8   See further below.
9   See for example Zim Online 07/05/08 *Mugabe's Govt Wants Monopoly of Airwaves* and *The Zimbabwe Times* 13/06/08 – *Government Bans MDC Adverts* available at http://www.thezimbabwetimes.com.
10 See *The Language of Hate – Inflammatory, Intimidating and Abusive Comments of Zimbabwe's 2008 Elections*, Media Monitoring Project Zimbabwe (MMPZ), forthcoming, 2009.

public with a readily accessible and credible source of alternative information to the propaganda disseminated by the prevalent government media, reporting news of the violence and providing an alternative perspective on the motives for the land invasions.

In the 2008 elections the public had no such access to alternative sources of information, although the privately-owned weekly press and the niche market radios and on-line agencies helped to bring to the world's attention the extent of the violence, terror and killings that swept through the country in the run-up to the presidential election run-off.

In the 2000 elections the Media Monitoring Project of Zimbabwe documented the emergence of the use of 'hate speech' in the government media,[11] which was specifically directed at destroying the political opposition's support base and discrediting the MDC by accusing them of being 'puppets of the British' whose intentions were to resist the land reforms and surreptitiously 'recolonize Zimbabwe' through the political opposition.

However, in spite of the state media bias, the endemic violence and the electoral chicanery of the government, the 2000 election result, where a party barely nine months old won nearly half the seats in Parliament, reflected the important role the private press played in providing sufficient information for the electorate to make up their own minds.

The presidential election campaign of 2002 was essentially a similar story, although the hate campaign against the MDC had been refined and intensified to unprecedented extremes and the independent media had themselves become targets for violent attack.

Soon after that election the government introduced the notoriously repressive Access to Information and Protection of Privacy Act[12] (AIPPA) that effectively imposed controls on who would be allowed to practice journalism – and punitive criminal penalties for those individuals and media organizations that failed to comply with them. *The Daily News* fell foul of this law. Subsequent legislation reinforced AIPPA's 'chilling effect' on independent media activity and provided government with sufficient legal instruments to suffocate the expression of independent thought and criticism in the mainstream domestic media. Ever since that time the government media have enjoyed an unrivalled dominance.

Such was the scenario for the 2005 parliamentary and municipal elections, which witnessed an inevitable decline in the activity of the private media, particularly in its role as an independent electoral watchdog. With the election management under the full control of government institutions loyal to the ruling party (see Chapter 7) and no significant alternative daily media to counter government dogma, there appeared to be little motive to indulge in the same levels of hate propaganda against the opposition that had been deployed in previous elections.

The result of that election, where the opposition lost its parliamentary

11 MMPZ (2000) *Media War: A Report on the Election Coverage of the 2000 Parliamentary Elections*. Harare.
12 Chapter 10:27.

ability to block constitutional change, appeared to confirm this.[13] It also allowed the government media to convince themselves and those loyal to the ruling party that public support for the MDC was indeed waning significantly.

That result might well have influenced the way ZANU(PF) initially approached the March 2008 harmonized elections. The party evidently felt sufficiently confident to agree to electoral undertakings that guaranteed that the results of the poll would be made public immediately after the tally at each polling station. And in its efforts to appear to be complying with SADC accords on the conduct of elections which provided that the opposition be given 'equitable' access to the 'public' media, the two MDC parties and the presidential contenders were also granted unprecedented – though still unequal – advertising space on radio and television and in the pages of the dominant government-controlled papers.[14]

But that was as far as the concessions went. Despite the fact that amendments were made (at the beginning of 2008) to the electoral laws relating to the media, including AIPPA, the Broadcasting Services Act and even the Public Order and Security Act,[15] as a result of SADC mediation that attempted to democratize the electoral environment, they were utterly ineffective in improving the bleak media landscape as the country approached the landmark elections of 29 March.

Most notably, the government – and the media they controlled – were responsible for this situation by simply ignoring the regulations that provided for fair and equitable coverage of election contestants and selectively applied laws controlling media activity without reference to any of the amendments intended to ease these restrictions.

It might be instructive to explore these laws and regulations here.

Electoral laws and international treaties affecting the media

International Treaties

While international treaties and covenants are not automatically incorporated into Zimbabwean law, violation of these treaties is obviously a transgression by the government of its international obligations. They also provide an important yardstick by which all parties to such treaties can evaluate compliance with democratic norms.

The *SADC Principles and Guidelines Governing Democratic Elections*, adopted by SADC countries, including Zimbabwe, in Mauritius in August 2004, provide that all parties should have equal opportunity to access the state media. In addition to the SADC electoral guidelines, the SADC Parliamentary Forum's Electoral Norms and Standards for Democratic

---

13 A vote of two-thirds of members of parliament is required to pass a constitutional amendment.
14 See SADC Principles and Guidelines Governing Democratic Elections, Article 2.1.5.
15 Chapter 11:17.

Elections have provided a minimum standard for staging elections in the SADC region since their adoption in March 2001. Zimbabwe is a signatory to this protocol too.

Both documents are similar in relation to their observations and recommendations on the role of the media in elections. Most particularly they note that most SADC countries (including Zimbabwe) have committed themselves to upholding universal human rights and freedoms, including the freedoms of association and of expression. Of these two freedoms, however, it is remarkable that the SADC guidelines only specifically refer to freedom of association.

Both documents also recommend that governments holding elections have a responsibility to safeguard and protect all human and civil liberties. They further recommend that all political parties have equal and agreed-upon space in the state-owned media to publicize their announcements, messages and advertisements. Notably, however, neither of the guidelines specifically recommends the impartial, fair and accurate coverage of the contesting parties in the state-owned media.

Instead, they appear to accept the inevitability of biased coverage in favour of the ruling party in the publicly-owned media and recommend the strengthening of the private media as a means of countering the imbalance this causes in the media landscape.

Thus the Parliamentary Forum's guidelines recommend that:

> ... governments should take the emergence of private media as a healthy development in the institutionalization of the democratic process (and) the conduct of the elections, and should therefore refrain from taking decisions and actions that thwart the development of a strong private media. There should therefore be a domestic information law that reaffirms the existence of private media.

These guidelines note that the government-controlled media often create an imbalance in the election playing field caused by its 'biased' and 'selective' reporting.

One problem that does not appear to have been directly addressed by either of these documents is the need to ensure that public officials, particularly the police and election officials, are obliged to respond promptly and adequately to inquiries by the media. The failure of the police in Zimbabwe to fulfil this important public duty, particularly in relation to the private media, is a matter of public record. Without access to official comment, media organizations are obliged to rely on unsubstantiated evidence. Such a situation reduces the transparency and credibility of the electoral process and erodes public confidence in the media.

Most surprisingly, neither of the documents refers to the African Commission on Human and People's Rights' Declaration of Principles on Freedom of Expression and the Media adopted in 2002 considerably strengthening Article IX of the African Charter dealing with freedom of expression.

It must be assumed that this important declaration of principles on freedom of expression in Africa, which has been so massively violated in Zimbabwe, is recognized by these guidelines.

Certainly, the SADC guidelines note that SADC countries are committed to:

promote the development of democratic institutions and practices... and (to) encourage the observance of universal human rights as provided for in the Charter and Conventions of the African Union.

This is the guarantee that should protect media freedom and diversity in SADC countries but which has been ignored in Zimbabwe.

Zimbabwe's laws

Zimbabwe's laws governing media coverage of elections are contained in the Zimbabwe Electoral Commission Act.[16] For the 2008 elections, government expanded upon the requirements of the Act through the Zimbabwe Electoral Commission (Media Coverage of Elections) Regulations of 2008.[17]

Apart from requiring the public broadcaster to 'afford all political parties and independent candidates contesting an election... free[18] access to their broadcasting services,' the Act stipulates[19] that during an election both the broadcast and print media's news coverage shall ensure that:

(a) All political parties and candidates are treated equitably in their news media, in regard to the extent, timing and prominence of the coverage accorded to them.

(b) Reports on the election in their news media are factually accurate, complete and fair.

(c) A clear distinction is made in their news media between factual reporting on the election and editorial comment on it.

(d) Inaccuracies in reports on the election in their news media are rectified without delay and with due prominence.

(e) Political parties and candidates are afforded a reasonable right of reply to any allegations made in their news media that are claimed by the political parties or candidates concerned to be false.

(f) The news media do not promote political parties or candidates that encourage violence or hatred against any class of persons in Zimbabwe.

(g) News media avoid language that:
  (i) encourages racial, ethnic or religious prejudice or hatred; or
  (ii) encourages or incites violence; or
  (iii) is likely to lead to undue public contempt towards any political party, candidate or class of person in Zimbabwe.

With respect to direct access the Act provides that while the media were 'not obliged' to air or publish political adverts, it recommends that when they carry such material:

(a) They shall offer the same terms and conditions of publication, without

16   [Chapter 2:12] [as amended by the Electoral Laws Amendment Act, 2007 (No. 17 of 2007)].
17   Statutory Instrument 33 of 2008.
18   In the sense of 'unhindered' rather than 'without charge'.
19   In section 16F.

discrimination, to all the political parties and candidates contesting the election; and

(b) The price it charges for publication shall be at the lowest rate it offers to publishers of commercial advertisements; and

(c) Every such publication shall be identified clearly as an advertisement.[20]

In principle, the regulations and the stipulated mechanism to monitor the media's adherence was a great improvement on the previous practice where the standards were only formulated for ZBC, which was given the sole responsibility to enforce them. For example, in 2002 the broadcaster drafted its own '10 Golden Rules' governing direct access and political advertising during the presidential elections – and then went on to ignore them.

Similarly, the responsibility for enforcing the Broadcasting Services (Access to Radio and Television During an Election) Regulations[21] for the 2005 elections also lay with ZBC itself and the Broadcasting Authority of Zimbabwe, whose board was then unilaterally appointed by government.

Even so, although regulations governing the media's coverage of elections for 2008 appeared to be commendable in theory, the manifest failure of the ZEC as the authority responsible to ensure that the media adhered to these laws[22] completely undermined their value. The ZEC's evident failure to stop the proliferation of hate language in the public media during the 2008 elections, and its failure to even mention the existence of extreme bias and inequitable coverage of the election participants in these media, provides a good illustration of how laws in Zimbabwe are selectively applied – and indeed ignored – in the service of ZANU(PF).

The main instrument that was still being used to gag the independent media in the country at the time of Zimbabwe's two landmark 2008 elections remained the Access to Information and Protection of Privacy Act. This patently unconstitutional piece of legislation essentially turns the business of gathering and disseminating news – the very essence of free expression – into a privilege controlled under the Act by excessively restrictive clauses that carry heavy criminal penalties including custodial sentences for any violation.

This law was used to close down the country's most popular daily newspaper *The Daily News*, (and confiscate its equipment) for what should have been regarded as the petty administrative offence of failing to register with the government-appointed Media and Information Commission (MIC). Its sister Sunday paper suffered the same fate, and another weekly newspaper, *The Tribune*, was also forced to close in June 2004 for similarly trivial reasons. A Bulawayo-based paper, *The Weekly Times*, was forced to close in February 2005 within weeks of its launch.

These closures were enforced by the MIC, a creation of AIPPA, which

---

20 Section 16D.
21 Statutory Instrument 22 of 2005, which were repealed and replaced for the 2008 elections.
22 Section 16G of the Zimbabwe Electoral Commission Act.

was plainly not independent. It was ostensibly set up to 'regulate' the media and promote media diversity. The Commission's chairman was appointed by the Minister of Information and had wide powers of control and restriction, which were used effectively to close newspapers and to control who was allowed to operate as a publisher and a journalist.

In January 2008, amendments[23] were made reconstituting the nature of the Commission and establishing a media council[24] (again as a result of SADC's mediation in its efforts to democratize Zimbabwe's electoral process). The new legislation provided that the MIC was disbanded and replaced by the Zimbabwe Media Council. Significantly, the members were now to be chosen from a list of twelve submitted by a parliamentary committee. The authorities simply ignored these changes. The chairperson of the disbanded MIC, Tafatona Mahosa, continued to act as if he retained his powers, and the authorities continued to have scores of journalists harassed and arrested, using provisions (some of which had been repealed by the amendment) that are clearly undemocratic and violate international covenants on freedom of expression, as well as SADC's Principles and Guidelines on Democratic Elections.

Legal challenges to the MIC's decisions, particularly journalists' constitutional challenges to the requirement to register before being allowed to work as a journalist, were initially unreasonably delayed in the courts and then the subject of a controversial Supreme Court ruling[25] declaring that the Zimbabwe Constitution protects the fundamental right to freedom of expression but *not the means* of exercising it. This ruling was possible only because the clause in Zimbabwe's Constitution protecting freedom of expression does not specifically include the protection of the media.

Other, equally repressive laws also affect freedom of expression and the operations of the media. For example, the Public Order and Security Act (POSA), primarily aimed at restricting freedom of assembly and association, also provides severe sentences for those ridiculing the presidency and the uniformed forces.

In 2005, another law forced through Parliament (despite an adverse report from its own legal committee declaring that a number of clauses violated the Constitution) makes provision for a jail term of up to twenty years for simply 'communicating' 'material' falsehoods.

The Criminal Law (Codification and Reform) Act[26] makes it a criminal offence to communicate to any other person a statement which is wholly or materially false with the intention or realizing that there is a real risk or possibility of: inciting or promoting public disorder or public violence or endangering public safety; or adversely affecting the defence or economic interests of Zimbabwe; or undermining public confidence in a law enforce-

---

23 Act 20 of 2007.
24 See section 42A of the amended Act.
25 *Association of Independent Journalists & Others v The Minister of State for Information and Publicity in the President's Office & Others* SC-136-02.
26 Chapter 9:23, Section 31.

ment agency, the Prison Service or the Defence Forces of Zimbabwe; or interfering with, disrupting or interrupting any essential service.

This truly draconian piece of legislation not only makes it extremely difficult for the media to report these important issues, but also silences potential sources of information who will be terrified of falling foul of the law by 'communicating' information that they cannot substantiate. Journalists, and publishers too – at least those operating inside Zimbabwe – are extremely wary of publishing any story that is disputed for fear of risking lengthy jail terms.

And then there is the Interception of Communications Act, which extends this fear to private e-mail and telecommunications, as well as the post.

Faced with such repressive instruments, the few remaining independent media have little chance of fulfilling their role as watchdogs of government activity. And they run great risks in reporting adequately on the partisan activities of the police force and other security agencies, which continue to persecute the political opposition and critics of government.

These laws clearly all serve to silence reporting on any evident abuse of power, and experience has shown that a vindictive government will not hesitate to persecute those brave enough to challenge them: during 2008, more than twenty foreign and local media workers were subjected to harassment, assault, censure and arrest by the security services and ruling party supporters or other shadowy quasi-government agencies.[27]

Such incidents clearly illustrate the vulnerability of the private media, the political opposition and activist members of civil society who continued to be on the receiving end of hate messages disseminated by the so-called 'public media' aimed at dehumanizing all those who dared to publicly criticize government.

More than any other factor, the public 'hate' campaign in the government-controlled print media created an atmosphere of fear and anxiety, undermined public faith in the media to inform them fairly and accurately, and threatened the very fabric of society with its divisive invective.

Most troubling is the role government officials played in spreading this dangerous propaganda that undermined the political stability and political tolerance clauses that appear in Zimbabwe's own electoral regulations as well as in the SADC's guidelines.[28]

President Mugabe and the leadership of ZANU(PF) set the trend for these offensive and inflammatory comments and encouraged the government media's columnists and presenters to follow suit. Several examples of this unacceptable language denigrating the MDC and its leadership and threatening the electorate are provided here in an attempt to give some indication of the state media's electoral reporting:

> 'ZANU(PF) fought for you, for our rights, land and a bright future. This legacy should not simply be vanquished by the stroke of a pen at the ballot just because

---

27 See MMPZ (2008). *Report on the Journalists Arrested and Victimised in 2008*. Harare.
28 Article 2.1.3.

I am not getting basic goods... Otherwise a simple X would have taken the country back to 1890. The Third Chimurenga can't just die because of an X. All those who died in the struggle will turn in their graves.' President Mugabe, *The Sunday Mail* (15/06/08)

'This is up to you; if you want peace, you should vote for us. If you vote for the MDC, we will go to war.' Samuel Mumbengegwi, former Finance Minister, *The Financial Gazette*, (19/06/08)

'MDC is a creation of our former colonizers who are using faction leader Morgan Tsvangirai as their puppet to further their interests of imposing an illegal regime change in Zimbabwe.' Editorial, *The Chronicle* (11/06/08)

'Voting for Tsvangirai, an imperial puppet, is the same as voting for homosexuality.' Ruggel Nyatsvimbo, war veteran, *The Chronicle* (13/06/08)

'Tsvangirai is confused... what they are doing is no different from engaging in prostitution.' Grace Mugabe (wife of the President), *The Chronicle* (14/06/08)

'Tsvangirai is a traitor. I came here to warn you about the machinations of the Rhodesians and their imperialist allies who we dislodged through the protracted armed struggle, but now they intend to come back using one of our fellow Zimbabweans, Tsvangirai, as their running dog – *chimbwasungata*. If you vote for Tsvangirai on June 27, you are voting for the former Rhodesians and thus you are voting for war.' Vice-President Joseph Msika, *The Manica Post* (20/06/08)

'Our comrade Robert Mugabe will romp to victory. We say so because we have no apology to make to any house nigger and puppets.' General Constantine Chiwenga, head of the Zimbabwe Defence Forces, *The Herald* (23/06/08)

President Mugabe's comments threatening war if the electorate again chose to vote for the political opposition manifested a political intolerance that was often reported without comment by the state media. Coupled with statements by military commanders that they would not recognize any leader who had not fought in the liberation war[29] (a clear reference to Tsvangirai) the effect was clearly to terrorize the public – the media included.

Conclusion

These conditions in Zimbabwe's media landscape made a mockery of the country's own regulations and of the regional and international covenants Zimbabwe has signed – including the SADC Principles and Guidelines – guaranteeing freedom of expression and association and electoral integrity. The only certainty this restrictive media climate guaranteed is that there could not have been free and fair national elections of any sort in March 2008, whatever the verdict of the few 'friendly' observer missions who were allowed to attend and who judged it a generally free and fair exercise.

---

[29] 'I'll only salute Mugabe, not sell-outs: Chiwenga'. *The Standard*, 9 March, 2008.

4

Voting For Change
The 29 March Harmonized Elections
Eldred V. Masunungure

Introduction

The first half of 2008 was a momentous period in Zimbabwe's political history. Between March and June of that year, two critical but sharply contrasting elections were held and their outcome has determined Zimbabwe's trajectory, triggering a political transition in which the country is locked at the time of writing. The 29 March elections are commonly referred to as the 'harmonized elections', a reference to their consolidating all national and local government elections; the second election, held on 27 June, was consequent upon the inconclusive 29 March presidential election and is commonly referred to as the 'run-off' election. The March elections were the most peaceful (and even enjoyable) since the genesis of Zimbabwe's mega-crisis in 2000 while the June elections will go down in history as the bloodiest since independence. This chapter dissects the two sets of elections in terms of the roles played (or not played) by the pivotal domestic political and security actors during the watershed elections, particularly in the inter-election period.

The 29 March harmonized elections

The synchronized elections of 29 March were for: (1) the office of executive president; (2) the 210 House of Assembly seats; (3) the 60 elective seats in the 93-member Senate; and (4) the 1,958 local council seats. The institutional and electoral frameworks in which these elections were held are discussed elsewhere in this book. The newly enacted Constitutional Amendment No. 18 provided for the harmonized elections and offered the first occasion that Zimbabwe held all four elections simultaneously. The elections were all held on one day rather than over two or three days as had been the electoral tradition, and they were conducted against the backdrop of the SADC-mediated political negotiations between the then ruling ZANU(PF) party and the two opposition formations of the Movement for Democratic Change (MDC). The latter point speaks to the fact that Zimbabwe was already in the process of negotiating its political transition from authoritarianism to a more tolerant and democratic political dispensation.

Following the sitting of nomination courts on 15 February 2008 in the country's ten provinces, a total of 4,406 candidates successfully filed their papers to contest the elections as follows: Presidential candidates 4, House of Assembly candidates 774, Senatorial candidates 197 and local authority-candidates, 3,431. A total of 413 candidates filed their papers unopposed: 411 for local authority elections, one for the House of Assembly and one for the Senate. Elections were suspended in three House of Assembly constituencies following the deaths of the candidates after nomination.[1] As a consequence, 206 House of Assembly seats, 59 Senatorial seats and 1,541 wards were contested. More than a dozen political parties and several independent candidates contested in the polls.

Contestants: political parties

The March 29 elections attracted substantial interest among Zimbabwe political parties and independents with seventeen of them contesting the parliamentary elections, mostly for the lower house, the House of Assembly (Table 1, see over).

A total of 773 candidates – including a record 104 independents – contested the 210 House of Assembly seats and 196, including 20 independents, the 93 Senate seats.[2] Though the electoral arena appeared crowded, more than two-thirds of the parties were essentially fly-by-night political entities that only emerge at election times and quickly wither away soon after. Essentially, the parliamentary contest was between the three best-known parties, ZANU(PF), MDC-T and MDC.[3] Even the results of the elections reflect this triangular distribution of power. At the close of nomination courts, ZANU(PF) had won two constituencies when its House of Assembly and Senate candidates were nominated unopposed in Mashonaland Central and had also won 392 council wards unopposed in various parts of the country.

1 The vacancies were later filled through by-elections held concurrently with the controversial Presidential run-off election on 27 June.
2 Most of the independent candidates were aligned to Makoni's Mavambo political project.
3 These were also the only three parties engaged in political dialogue under the auspices of the SADC-appointed mediator, former South Africa president Thabo Mbeki.

Table 1

Party	Party Leader	No. of Candidates Fielded	
MDC-T	Morgan Tsvangirai	204	61
MDC	Arthur Mutumbara	151	36
ZANU(PF)	Robert Mugabe	219	61
UPP	Daniel Shumba	49	11
PAFA	Abel Ndlovu	6	
ZANU-Ndonga	Wilson Kumbula	2	1
FDU	Paul Siwela	7	1
ZPPDP	Tafirenyika Mudavanhu	8	
ZDP	Kisinofi Mukwazhe	9	2
PUMA	Leornard Nkala	7	7
CDP	William Gwata	2	
ZAPU-PF	Sikhumbuzo Dube	1	1
ZURD	Madechiwe Collias	1	
VOP	Moreprecision Muzadzi	1	
ZiYA	Moses Mutyasira	1	
UPC			
Independents		104	20
TOTAL		**773**	**196**

Key: MDC-T: Movement for Democratic Change-Tsvangirai (MDC-T); MDC: Movement for Democratic Change (MDC);[4] ZANU(PF): Zimbabwe African National Union-Patriotic Front; UPP: United People's Parties; ZPPDP: Zimbabwe Progressive People's Democratic Party; PUMA: Patriotic Union of Matabeleland; FDU: Federal Democratic Union; ZANU-Ndonga: Zimbabwe African National Union-Ndonga; ZDP: Zimbabwe Democratic Party; CDP: Christian Democratic Party; ZiYA: Zimbabwe Youth Alliance; PAFA: Peace Action is Freedom for All; ZURD; ZAPU-FP: Zimbabwe African Peoples Union; VOP: Voice of the People; and UPC: United People's Congress.

4   The Movement for Democratic Change was formed in September 1999 but split into two factions in October 2005 mainly over the virtues of participating in elections for the newly recreated upper chamber, the Senate, which had been abolished in 1987. The larger body of the opposition party remained with founding President Morgan Tsvangirai while the splinter faction was led by Professor Arthur Mutambara. For avoidance of voter confusion, the former faction became known as MDC-T while Mutambara's formation contested as the MDC though it is now commonly referred to as 'MDC-M'.

The presidential contestants

On paper, the presidential election was a four-cornered contest but in fact it was a triangular fight between Robert Mugabe of ZANU(PF), Morgan Tsvangirai of the MDC-T and Mugabe's erstwhile finance minister and fellow politburo member, Simba Makoni, who stood as an independent. The real battle was between incumbent president Mugabe and his long-term political rival Tsvangirai; virtually all Zimbabweans and other observers regarded these two as the real combatants.

Robert Mugabe: Mugabe is the only leader Zimbabwe has known since its independence in 1980 when he assumed the post of Prime Minister. When this office was abolished and fused with that of Head of State in 1987 to create the executive presidency, Mugabe became the first, and so far the only, occupant of the post. He contested and in each case controversially won successive presidential elections in 1990, 1996, 2002 and was in 2008 seeking a fourth presidential term of office.

Mugabe launched his re-election campaign on 29 February and presented his party's election manifesto. ZANU(PF)'s theme was: 'Defending our Land and National Sovereignty: Building Prosperity through Empowerment'. Its campaign style and message centred on the party's leadership of the 1970s liberation struggle, its deliverance of social services in the 1980s, and of land since 2000, and promises to deliver economic empowerment and indigenization of the economy by capturing majority shares in mining and other foreign-owned companies after the elections. The party manifesto identified twelve key areas, notably land and sovereignty; busting sanctions; completing and consolidating land reforms; rehabilitating, upgrading and expanding infrastructure; resolving the energy crisis; economic prosperity through indigenization; small to medium enterprises development; science and technology; youth and women empowerment; and building alliances with progressive partners in the world.

Mugabe was trumpeted as someone 'tried and tested' and the party vowed to win the elections 'resoundingly so that the British can feel the heat'.[5] Despite its official call for a 'peaceful, democratic, sovereign Zimbabwe,' ZANU(PF)'s violent streak was not far from the surface. Mugabe's campaign slogan was 'vote for the fist', and his portraits had him wearing an olive-green military-type shirt and holding a clenched fist, all of which symbolized the party's militancy to which the MDC responded with a newspaper advert asserting that: 'The war is over. We cannot feed people with clenched fists.'[6]

---

5   *Zimbabwe Independent*, 14 March 2008.
6   Cris Chinaka, *Mail and Guardian*, 'Mugabe's iron fist: War veterans and green bombers', 20 March, 2008. Chinaka also noted that for some of Mugabe's loyalists, the image of their

Mugabe urged delegates gathered at the launch to 'go fighting' to ensure victory for ZANU(PF): 'Go fighting, not physically, but through word and deed,' he said. He was very confident of triumphing on 29 March:

> Victory is certain, but the size of the victory is what we are aiming at. We are not aiming at victory because we have won already. All we want now is the enhancement of that victory. We want a big, big, big victory, a thunderous one.[7]

As if to publicly demonstrate the abuse of state media, the occasion was broadcast live on the state-controlled Zimbabwe Broadcasting Corporation (ZBC) TV and radio, in stark contrast to that of Tsvangirai's faction of the MDC, which took place at Sakubva stadium in Mutare.

Mugabe also warned against Kenya-style violence, in reference to the post-election political violence that engulfed Kenya in early 2008, saying the security forces stood ready to crush such protests. 'If Tsvangirai and his [MDC] group have such plans, they must stand warned... That will never happen here, never, never. We will never allow it. We have enough security forces to handle that.'[8]

Mugabe routinely disparaged his presidential challengers as stooges of the West. Makoni was dismissed as worse than 'a political prostitute', and a frog with 'an inflated ego'. 'He is like a frog trying to inflate itself up to the size of an ox. It will burst.'[9] Tsvangirai was referred to as a puppet of Western imperialism led by Britain who 'will never rule this country.'[10] Such hate-filled and intemperate language was to be the hallmark of Mugabe's campaign.

Morgan Tsvangirai: Since the formation of the MDC in September 1999, Tsvangirai has been Mugabe's mortal enemy. His party was the key partner in a coalition of forces that delivered ZANU(PF)'s first electoral defeat in the February 2000 constitutional referendum. A former trade union leader, Tsvangirai has come closest to ousting Mugabe in previous elections[11] and on 11 February he announced that he would stand as presidential candidate for his MDC faction.

On 23 February he launched his campaign and presented his party's

6 (cntd) leader's clenched fist is still a call to war and that members of the youth brigades – known as 'green bombers' because of the military-style clothes they wear – who act as security guards at ZANU(PF)'s rallies are seen in the rural areas as 'the party's eyes, ears and fists.'

7 *The Herald*, 'ZANU(PF) Launches Manifesto' 1 March 2008.

8 Reuters, 'Mugabe warns over Kenya-style violence' 21 March 2008.

9 Cris Chinaka, 'Mugabe belittles opponents as frog and puppet' Reuters, 23 February 2008.

10 Chinaka, 'Mugabe's iron fist'. See also Ofeiba Quist-Arcton's 'Mugabe Faces Strong Challenge in Zimbabwe Vote' 27 March 2008, http://www.npr.org. On Mugabe's campaign strategy, Norma Kriger commented: 'Mugabe campaigns as if Britain is his electoral opponent because, he insists, it seeks to re-colonise Zimbabwe' in 'Understanding Zimbabwe's Election' *Africa Policy Forum*, 24 March 2008.

11 Tsvangirai narrowly lost the 2002 presidential election that was widely condemned, nationally and internationally, as rigged.

election manifesto, promising total transformation rather than partial change. The MDC marketed its leader as not only a change agent but also a 'man of the people, man for the people, man of peace'. The party's manifesto revolved around five key issues:

1. *people-centred governance* meaning a new 'people-driven' constitution, respect for human rights, democracy and rule of law;
2. *people-centred land and agrarian reforms* with attention to transparency, sustainability, productive land use, food security and job creation;
3. *people-centred economy* 'that guarantees growth, food security, investment and job creation';
4. *people-centred social agenda* with emphasis on 'affordable and quality health care and education for all'; and
5. *national integration and reconciliation*.

Tsvangirai dismissed Mugabe as 'one of the greatest tyrants of the 21st century'[12]. He also dismissed Makoni as 'old wine in a new bottle', because of his long association with Mugabe and ZANU(PF) and because he merely wanted to 'reform an institutionalised dictatorship'.[13] Like Makoni, he accused Mugabe of ruining Zimbabwe's once vibrant economy and transforming the country from a breadbasket into a basket case. Tsvangirai promised hope and change.

Simba Makoni: Makoni's presidential candidature was a product of serious and long-simmering fissures inside ZANU(PF), centring on leadership succession. These divisions burst into the open over the party's Central Committee decision in March 2007 to again field Mugabe as its candidate in the 2008 elections. This announcement widened and deepened succession and leadership struggles within the party, which was compelled to convene an Extraordinary Congress in December 2007, presumably to settle the leadership and candidature question 'once and for all'. It was later announced by the party's chairman, John Nkomo, that Mugabe had been selected to be the party's 2008 presidential candidate by acclamation and that the party Congress had 'fully and unreservedly' backed the decision.

On 5 February 2008, this façade of unity within ZANU(PF) was removed when, less than a week before the presidential nomination date, Makoni announced his presidential candidature:

Let me confirm that I share the agony and anguish of all citizens over the extreme hardships that we all have endured for nearly 10 years now. I also share the widely held view that these hardships are a result of failure of national leadership and that change at that level is a prerequisite for change at other levels of national endeavour.[14]

12 Chinaka, 'Mugabe belittles opponents as frog and puppet.'
13 'Tsvangirai rules out pact with Makoni' AFP, 11 February 2008.
14 Fanuel Jongwe, 'Ex-minister takes on Mugabe' The *Times* (South Africa), 5 February 2008.

He was immediately dismissed from the party[15] and was also threatened by war veterans.[16] To his discredit, he continued to insist on being ZANU(PF), and certainly that he was not anti-ZANU(PF). It was clear then that Makoni and his supporters wanted to see leadership renewal within the party. Though he had held several high-profile positions in Government, in ZANU(PF) and was Executive Secretary of the Southern African Development Community (SADC) for ten years, he had never held an elected position.

Makoni launched his campaign on 13 February 2008 and also presented 'elements' of his election manifesto which centred on a '10 Point Plan for Quick Turnaround': 'we promise to deliver to the people of Zimbabwe a quick economic turnaround through national political dialogue and healing; the strengthening of our economic sectors; and harnessing international goodwill.' His campaign slogan was: 'Let's Get Zimbabwe Working Again!' Makoni derided Mugabe's campaign symbol of a fist by saying 'the fist has become a hammer smashing the country.'[17] Makoni's entry into the presidential race energised many Zimbabweans who had previously made up their minds not to vote; most of his supporters were urban and educated classes.[18]

On 15 February 2008, four candidates registered for the presidential race: Mugabe, Tsvangirai, Makoni and little known Langton Towungana; Arthur Mutambara, leader of the splinter faction of the MDC, announced that he would not stand but would instead support Makoni.[19] There had been speculation that the opposition would field one candidate in order to enhance their chances of defeating Mugabe but talks to reunite the two MDC factions had collapsed in early February. Although Mutambara pledged his support for Makoni, Makoni stressed that he was running alone and was 'not in an alliance with anyone. I am an independent candidate and I am standing alone.'[20]

15 The party's legal secretary said Makoni had automatically 'self-expelled himself.' On 1 March, former Interior Minister and politburo member Dumiso Dabengwa and former Speaker of Parliament Cyril Ndebele defected to join Makoni.

16 Joseph Chinotimba, deputy leader of the Zimbabwe National Liberation War Veterans Association chillingly warned: 'Traitors should know ZANU(PF) has a history of dealing harshly with their kind' (Quoted in BBC 'Zimbabwe war vets threaten Makoni', 7 February 2008).

17 Chinaka, 'Mugabe's iron fist'.

18 After the founding independence election in 1980, there was a growing tendency towards electoral apathy, a process that was somewhat reversed in the 2000 and 2002 parliamentary and presidential elections respectively. However, the failure of both elections to deliver a decisive victory leading to a transfer of power led to a recidivism in political apathy that was also reflected in people's reluctance to register to vote. Most people felt that the outcome of the March 2008 elections was predetermined and decided not to vote. The entry of a new and respectable political player changed the scenario, leading to a surge in voter registration.

19 Three other candidates had their candidatures rejected for varying reasons. Mutambara stood for a parliamentary seat in Chitungwiza but lost heavily.

20 'Zimbabwe presidential candidates confirmed', AFP, 16 February 2008.

The pre-poll arena

The pre-29 March environment is described and analysed in many of the contributions to this volume, particularly the constitutional, legal and institutional framework governing the elections and some of the changes – albeit modest and even cosmetic – instituted by the Constitutional Amendment No. 18 that received bi-partisan support. The impaired integrity of electoral institutions (especially the Zimbabwe Electoral Commission (ZEC), but also the Electoral Court) and the asymmetrical media terrain are also discussed elsewhere. This chapter highlights other developments that cumulatively vitiated the democratic credentials of the harmonized elections.

Later sections of this chapter outline some of the unsavoury pronouncements made by senior security chiefs to the effect that they would not recognize the election of anyone other than their preferred candidate, Robert Mugabe. These statements, which had an uncanny resemblance to those made just before the 2002 presidential election, had the intended effect of intimidating prospective voters and were clearly in violation of both the spirit and letter of the law.

A constant in ZANU(PF)'s election strategy is the use of state-financed patronage. There were widespread reports of abuse of state resources in the ruling party's election campaign. Most disturbing was the politically motivated distribution of food aid to starving voters, especially in the rural areas. Traditional and community leaders were also mobilized to deliver the rural vote in exchange for perks such as vehicles, electrification of their homes, and, most critically, the privilege to allocate scarce and highly valued food aid, farm inputs and equipment. There were also salary hikes to uniformed forces and civil servants and pension increases for ZANU(PF)'s storm-troopers, the war veterans. For the elite loyalists, promises of shares under the indigenization and empowerment legislation were meant to glue them to the party. Other sectors and professionals also benefited: vehicles for doctors, promises of houses for health institutions and buses for rural districts, were all designed to induce the beneficiaries to vote in a favourable manner.[21]

Equally disturbing were the selective invitations to foreign observers and foreign media. The government refused to invite 'unfriendly' foreign observers or to accredit foreign journalists, preferring instead to invite 'friendly' countries, organizations and media houses. The United States, the European Union, and even some SADC and African Union organizations and media were barred, including the Electoral Institute of Southern Africa (EISA), e-TV, and the SADC Parliamentary Forum.

---

21 The central bank (Reserve Bank of Zimbabwe) was heavily involved in the financing, procurement and distribution of these patronage goods.

Also noteworthy was the disenfranchisement of voters in the diaspora. Zimbabwe allows for postal votes but restricts this to those serving in diplomatic missions and those on state duty outside their voting districts and these mostly comprise police, soldiers and civil servants. For the March harmonized elections, it was alleged – and not denied – that ZEC had printed some 600,000 postal ballots when only 30,000 had been applied for. This generated considerable tension and suspicions that the extra ballots were going to be used to rig the elections. There were also allegations that ZEC had ordered the printing of nine million ballot papers when the total number of registered voters was less then six million.

It was also a matter for deep concern that the ZEC did not acquit itself in the critical area of voter education. The 29 March elections were a new experience for virtually all Zimbabweans and more so for first-time voters; they were also complex elections. And yet many voters were not adequately advised about voter education, inspection of the voters roll, location of polling stations, time of voting, and more critically, that voting for all four elections would take place on the same day. Many voters thought the four elections would be held on four separate days. There were also entirely new electoral constituencies and boundaries but many voters were not appraised of this. Shockingly, despite not having the capacity to mount an effective civic and voter education campaign, ZEC proceeded to ban civic education organizations – Zimbabwe Elections Support Network (ZESN), Civic Network (CIVNET) and others – from carrying out this important function.

There were also deep concerns about the state of the voters register, a perennial issue in Zimbabwe's elections. There were credible reports that the register was inflated with ghost voters and fictitious names. According to ZEC, there were more than five and a half million voters registered as at 15 February 2008 (Table 2, right), a figure that is difficult to accept given the massive out-migration since 2000. The statistic suggested that virtually every adult out of about twelve million Zimbabweans had registered to vote, an outcome that is clearly unfathomable given the levels of apathy among the population and the scale of emigration.

The biggest source of worry was pronouncements made by some senior military officials that clearly vitiated the democratic character of elections as arenas of choice. One of the defining features of constitutional democracies, and a hallmark of democratic politics, is the non-partisanship of the military and security organs of the state. This does not necessarily mean soldiers and those who command them are political eunuchs; it does mean that soldiers are not partisan political animals. They serve the state, and not political actors, whether these are individuals or parties. In Zimbabwe's case, a bit of background is necessary.

In Zimbabwe's complex political scenario, and because of the history of the protracted liberation struggle of the 1970s, there is symbiosis between the military elite and the political elite that is mediated by ZANU(PF), the

Table 2: Voter's Register, House of Assembly Constituencies
& Polling Stations

Province	No. of registered voters	No. of constituencies	No. of polling stations
Bulawayo	313,459	12	207
Harare	766,478	29	379
Manicaland	709,664	263	79
Mash. Central	448,477	18	1,150
Mash. East	624,630	23	774
Mash West	582,989	22	1,100
Masvingo	699,199	26	1,202
Mat. North	345,264	13	545
Mat. South	342,280	13	528
Midlands	739,510	28	1,289
TOTAL	5,571,950	210	9,132

political vehicle that drove the armed struggle. When ZANU(PF) captured the state in 1980, it deliberated proceeded to construct the state in the image of the party by fusing the two. In this endeavour, the liberation war fighters became the new soldiers in a new state; their commanders became part of Zimbabwe's military elite. Those who were part of the political wing of the liberation struggle became the new political elite. What unified the political and the military elites is the ZANU(PF) party.

In this new party-state, many who constitute the military and security elite have found it difficult to dissociate themselves from the party. This is particularly so because their erstwhile commander-in-chief during guerrilla days is also their commander-in-chief in post-liberation Zimbabwe. In this complex scheme of things, when the party is in trouble, it is incumbent on the soldier class to come to the party's aid. Political forces that threaten the party's hold on power *ipso facto* threaten the state. It has been difficult, if not impossible, for the military to insulate itself from ZANU(PF)'s partisan politics. This is the context in which the role of the military and security organs should be understood in Zimbabwe's electoral politics. Some incidents of such partisan involvement are highlighted below. They illustrate that the involvement of the military was more covert than explicit but nonetheless an abrogation of its proper role in a democracy.

Six months before the harmonized elections a senior army officer, Brigadier-General David Sigauke, was quoted as allegedly threatening any government not led by Mugabe and ZANU(PF):

As soldiers, we have the privilege to defend this task (of guaranteeing Mugabe and ZANU(PF) rule) on two fronts: the first being through the ballot box, and second being the use of the barrel of the gun should the worse come to the worst. I may therefore urge you as citizens of Zimbabwe to exercise your electoral right wisely in the forthcoming election in 2008, remembering that 'Zimbabwe shall never be a colony again'.[22]

Little imagination was needed to interpret the message. After all, 'Zimbabwe shall never be a colony again' was a ZANU(PF) slogan.

Three weeks before the poll, the Commander of the Zimbabwe Defence Forces (ZDF), General Constantine Chiwenga, warned that he would not tolerate Mugabe losing to 'sell-outs and agents of the West.' Speaking to *The Standard* newspaper, he was more than emphatic:

Elections are coming and the army will not support or salute sell-outs and agents of the West before, during, and after the presidential elections. We will not support anyone other than President Mugabe who has sacrificed a lot for this country.[23]

Few harboured any doubts about the allegiance of the ZDF and how it would behave should an 'undesirable' outcome occur.

As for the police, the Zimbabwe Human Rights NGO Forum summarized their partisanship in a report just before the 29 March elections:

A highly politicised police force has been employed [by ZANU(PF)] as one of its instruments of repression, backed up by the intelligence service [the Central Intelligence Organisation (CIO)] and the army. The police force has largely abrogated the right of freedom of assembly for opponents of government. It has freely allowed meetings and demonstrations by ruling party supporters, but has frequently disallowed and brutally broken up meetings and demonstrations by the opposition and by organisations that are critical of the Mugabe administration. The police have arrested on spurious charges large numbers of opposition supporters and critics of the government and, in many instances, have subjected them to torture.[24]

On the eve of the synchronised elections, the Police Commissioner General, perhaps expressing his personal rather than institutional opinion, warned the police force and people of Zimbabwe against voting for what he referred to as 'stooges of the British':[25] 'We will not allow any puppets to take charge.'[26] However, the institutional position of the Zimbabwe Republic Police (ZRP) was for 'Zero Tolerance' and a 'Violence-Free Election'. To this extent, it actually held anti-political violence marches in Harare suburbs on the eve of the elections.

The Zimbabwe Prison Services (ZPS) was not immune to the partisan

22   *The Herald*, 'Army urged to defend Zim's sovereignty,' 25 September 2007.
23   *The Standard*, 9 March 2008.
24   Zimbabwe Human Rights NGO Forum, 'Can the elections in Zimbabwe be free and fair in the current environment?', Harare, 18 March 2008, pp. 4-5. The Forum's answer to the question was that 'it is not possible to hold free and fair elections under the prevailing conditions.'
25   ZANU(PF) deliberately and routinely dismisses the MDC as a western front for 'regime change'. It has labeled the MDC 'a puppet of the British and Americans'.

virus. A month before the elections, the Commissioner of Prisons, retired Major-General Zimondi, said he would not salute opposition presidential candidates Makoni and Tsvangirai should either of them happen to win the presidential election: 'If the opposition wins the election, I will be the first one to resign from my job and go back to defend my piece of land. I will not let it go.' Zimondi was addressing a passing-out parade of prison officers whom he then ordered to vote for Mugabe: 'We are going to the elections and you should vote for President Mugabe. I am giving you an order to vote for the President.' For the avoidance of any doubt, he added: 'I will only support the leadership of President Mugabe. I will not salute them [Makoni and Tsvangirai]'.[27] The message to voters and the opposition presidential candidates was unambiguous.

The CIO is also headed by a retired ZDF senior officer, retired Major-General Happyton Bonyongwe. The intelligence service steered clear of any public statement of support to Mugabe. However, Bonyongwe was forced to refute media allegations that he was linked to Makoni's presidential bid. He defended himself and the CIO as non-partisan:

> In my case and as far as the service is concerned, we are a professional service. I was appointed by H.E. President Mugabe. I am serving the President and through him my country.

> I serve one master and the master is the President. The fact is no faction which can claim ownership of me means I am doing my job impartially. ... We are professional and principled and we will not abandon our task to protect the security of Zimbabwe, national interest and our leader, the President. Basically that is the CIO.[28]

On Friday, 28 March, a day before the elections, the security service chiefs held a joint press conference. They called – commendably – for the upholding of peace and tranquillity as the nation voted. However, in a thinly-veiled warning to the MDC-T, the security chiefs said:

> May we remind everyone that those who think and do evil must fear, for the defence and security forces are up to the task in thwarting all threats to national security. Also those who may have been breathing fire about Kenya-style violence should be warned that violence is a poor substitute for intelligence and that it is a monster that can devour its creator as it is blind and not selective in nature. Such misguided elements should stop this dangerous dreaming where they start to commend themselves, measure themselves by themselves, and compare themselves among themselves forgetting the Constitution and our existence. Doing so is not wise.[29]

---

26 Zimbabwejournalists.com 14 March 2008
27 *The Herald*, 'I'll not salute Tsvangirai, Makoni – Defence chief', 29 February 2008.
28 'Zimbabwe: I've No Ties With Makoni – CIO Boss', *The Herald* 15 March 2008.
29 See *The Sunday Mail*, 30 March - 5 April, p.7. While it may have been necessary, in full memory of the Kenyan scenario, to make such a joint statement, some quarters interpreted the statement as having been tailor-made to pre-empt any possible reaction by the opposition MDC-T to potentially flawed elections.

From the above, it is clear that the security organs – at least their bosses – shared pro-regime political preferences and were generally hostile to an MDC-T victory. However, there was no evidence of an institutionalised insistence on who to support. If anything, there were reports that the rank and file of the military and police were sympathetic to the opposition MDC-T and that many voted for it. There is no doubt, though, that the top military and security commanders openly displayed their sympathies for ZANU(PF).

The political campaign itself pleasantly surprised many by being peaceful and relatively free.[30] Political parties and candidates were able to carry out their business almost unhindered and their supporters tolerated each other amazingly well. There was a remarkable reduction in inter-party violence, intimidation and harassment and supporters moved freely to and from rallies, freely wore their party regalia and even mingled among themselves.[31] Formerly 'no-go' areas like Mashonaland Central and East were accessible to opposition parties and candidates. The police also conducted themselves professionally – unlike in previous elections when they were justifiably accused of being a partisan arm of ZANU(PF) – and adopted a 'zero-tolerance' approach to political violence and publicised this stance. Even the MDC acknowledged the professional conduct of the police during the campaign.

There were some events that spoiled the above positive picture and these were a relic of the past. For instance, some politicians, especially from ZANU(PF), continued to use inflammatory language at rallies and in the state-controlled media. Some traditional leaders – perhaps as a mark of gratitude for the state-provided vehicles, scotch carts, ploughs, and wheelbarrows – openly campaigned for ZANU(PF) and threatened their subjects with eviction, beatings and denial of food. Until the last two weeks of the campaign, the state media certainly did not acquit themselves in a manner that complied with the SADC Principles and Guidelines. However, in the last two weeks preceding the elections, there was a significant if not dramatic improvement in the state media's conduct.

On balance, it is fair to say the pre-election environment was relatively peaceful and sufficiently conducive to the free expression of the people's will in the ballot box. It is also fair to say that, with a few exceptions,

---

30 Given that 'Zimbabwe's politics are profoundly shaped by violence,' (Alexander and Tendi, 2008, p. 5), many observers and analysts (including this writer) were justifiably puzzled by this 'anomaly' and wondered whether it was not a case of calm before the storm.

31 EISA, one of the SADC election monitoring organizations that was not accredited to observe the elections but nonetheless sneaked in and managed to do so also rendered a positive assessment. It commended 'an atmosphere of calm and tranquillity in which candidates, parties and people from diverse political backgrounds were able to operate' and that 'unlike in previous elections, freedom of assembly, freedom of association, freedom of movement and freedom of speech could be generally exercised without undue hindrance' (EISA Interim Statement on the Zimbabwe Election 2008). Most observer groups made similar findings and conclusions.

Figure 1: Parliamentary results*

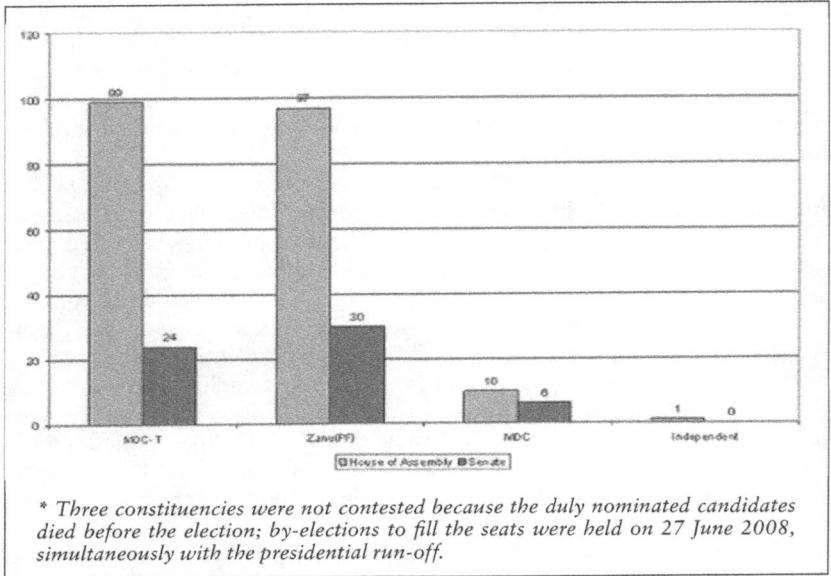

Three constituencies were not contested because the duly nominated candidates died before the election; by-elections to fill the seats were held on 27 June 2008, simultaneously with the presidential run-off.

activities on polling day were conducted in an efficient, orderly and profess-ional manner and, most importantly, to the satisfaction of all contestants. However, and as a consequence of poor and inadequate voter education, a significant number of people were turned away, either for not being on the voters roll, being aliens, being in the wrong ward or not having the national identity card – which was the only acceptable form of voter identity, unlike past elections when a driver's licence was also deemed acceptable.

Vote counting and declaration of polling station results were also above board, with ZEC being commended for doing a professional job. Unlike in previous elections, votes were counted at polling stations and results posted outside the polling station for everyone to view. Constituency results were also publicly posted by Constituency Elections Officers and that very act constituted the declaration of the results at that level. This was the case for all elections, but the declaration of the presidential result was the only one for which the Chief Elections Officer had the prerogative of announcing after collating and verifying all results from all constituencies; this was done at the National Command Centre in Harare.

The vote count showed that out of an estimated (but most likely inflated) 5,571,950 registered voters, 2,537,240 (43 per cent) turned out to vote. There were nearly 40,000 spoilt ballots (1.6 per cent). The House of Assem-bly and Senatorial results are shown in Figure 1.

Even before the official parliamentary results had been released, many observer groups had made public their interim findings and almost all were uniformly positive. For instance, the Pan-African Parliament (PAP) was impressed by the independence and transparency of ZEC and concluded: 'On the overall, the basic conditions of credible free and fair elections as contained in the OAU/AU Declaration on Principles Governing Democratic Elections in Africa (2002) were reflected in the Zimbabwe Harmonised Election, thus far.'[32] The SADC Elections Observer Mission (SEOM) also concluded that 'the elections held in Zimbabwe on 29 March 2008 have been a peaceful and credible expression of the will of the people of Zimbabwe.'[33] The uninvited Electoral Institute for Southern Africa rendered a more restrained verdict, finding that 'the 2008 Harmonised Elections in Zimbabwe were partly free' but that the electoral process was 'severely wanting in respect of fairness'.[34]

The accolades showered on ZEC for organizing a comparatively credible poll quickly gave way to deep anxiety and scepticism at the manner in which it publicized the parliamentary results. Despite the fact that the results were posted at polling and constituency centres throughout the country, it took ZEC 36 hours to start announcing them. The body seems to have abandoned the simple and straightforward procedure which it had advertised before the elections; instead, it took five days to announce the House of Assembly and Senate results and it did so in a suspicious manner. From that point onwards, the credibility, autonomy and professionalism of the ZEC was seriously interrogated and whatever confidence and faith people had invested in it was eroded.

After announcing the parliamentary results, ZEC went into hibernation and froze the results of the presidential election for 32 days before announcing them on 2 May 2008 (Table 3). The MDC appealed to the courts on several occasions to have the results released; SADC convened an extraordinary summit on 12 September calling for the 'expeditious' release of the results, but to no avail; the United Nations Security Council made similar futile efforts, as did the G8, which called for 'speedy, credible and genuinely democratic resolution of this situation.'[35] In the meantime ZEC was lackadaisically re-counting, re-collating and re-verifying the votes.

Although according to the contested official results Tsvangirai garnered the most votes in the presidential election, he did not achieve the required legal threshold to capture the presidency and this necessitated a run-off election. The legal technicalities involved are discussed by Greg Linington (Chapter 6).

32 *The Herald*, 1 April 2008.
33 *The Herald*, 31 March 2008.
34 EISA Interim Statement.
35 G8 Foreign Ministers' Statement on Zimbabwe, 17 April 2008.

Table 3: Presidential Poll Results – 29 March 2008 Harmonized Elections

Candidate	Number of votes	Actual percentage
Makoni, Herbert Stanley Simba	207,470	8.3%
Mugabe, Robert Gabriel	1,079,730	43.2%
Towungana, Langton	14,503	0.6%
Tsvangirai, Morgan	1,195,562	47.9%
Spoiled ballots	39,975	
Total votes cast	2,537,240	
Percentage poll		42.7%

Source: Zimbabwe Election Support Network [ZESN], report on the Zimbabwe 29 March harmonized election and 27 June 2008 presidential run-off, August 2008.

Analysis of the 29 March election results

The first salutary lesson from the 29 March elections was that ZANU(PF) was a fractured party, and its traditional rural stronghold weakened. A provincial breakdown of the results clearly demonstrated that the party had lost significant support even in its heartland provinces of Mashonaland West, East and Central. Most poignantly, the historical divide between the rural and the urban electorates was closing. ZESN put is thus:

> Clearly evident from these election results is that while the opposition urban support base is relatively secure, this is no longer the case for the ruling party in its traditional strongholds. The opposition challenge which in the past was largely confined to the urban areas and had given the impression that rural areas were the unchallenged political enclaves of the ruling party has since been busted. The contestation that was initially confined to urban areas has since shifted to rural areas.[36]

The MDC-T won seats in all ten provinces, had a clean sweep in Bulawayo and won all but one of the 26 House of Assembly seats in Harare.

The results reflected a seismic movement, a silent revolution depicted in the massive swing of political support from the 45-year old ZANU(PF) to the nine-year old opposition movement. The results were testimony to a dramatic drop in ZANU(PF) support in just three years:[37] In the March 2005 parliamentary elections, the party won 78 (65 per cent) of the 120 contested seats and 59.6 per cent of the vote, compared to the MDC's 41 seats (34 per cent) and 39.5 per cent of the vote. In the March 2008 elections, ZANU(PF)'s share of the House of Assembly vote dropped to 46 per

36 ZESN, August 2008, p. 42.
37 The result was also testimony to the vastly improved political atmosphere – especially in relation to politically-motivated violence and intimidation – compared to previous elections.

cent and its 99 seats translated to 47 per cent of the 210 seats. On the other hand, the combined MDC formations captured 51 per cent of the House of Assembly vote and 52 per cent of the seats, a remarkable recovery indeed.

Of major significance is that in 2005, ZANU(PF) could count on 30 indirectly elected members of the then 150-member single-chamber Parliament and, with a combined total of 108 seats, the party exceeded the two-thirds majority required to amend the Constitution. In the 2008 elections, ZANU(PF) lost not only this two-thirds majority; it also lost even the simple majority needed to drive legislation through parliament. In short, and for the first time in post-independence Zimbabwe, ZANU(PF) lost its political hegemony in parliament and the electorate; it became a minority party. This was an electoral *chimurenga* (uprising) of sorts, a silent and non-violent uprising based on the ballot box rather than the gun.

A second cardinal lesson from 29 March is that the revolutionary shift in political allegiances was a consequence of the disconnect between ZANU(PF) and its social base, especially the peasant class. This disconnect was rooted in the real world of economics, the material world of human existence. The protracted and deep economic crisis and the poor policy responses had taken their toll.[38] For the first time since 2000, Zimbabwe witnessed the convergence of economic well-being and political allegiance. Economic discontent translated into political discontent via the medium of the ballot box, marking the intersection of electoral politics and economics.

Another lesson from 29 March is that the ZANU(PF) message had lost its salience and no longer resonated with the masses as it used to. The message of liberation war, of sovereignty, of 'the land is the economy and the economy is land,' of ZANU(PF) being the only custodian of the revolution, and of 'the fist', failed to connect with the masses – rural and urban. Or the message was not as effectively communicated as in the past. It could also be that the opposition's message was more effective, a view suggested by Jocelyn Alexander and Blessing Miles Tendi:

> On the campaign trail, Tsvangirai drew huge crowds. His party's slick and positive advertising campaign, with its emphasis on political change, economic recovery, and promises of compensation and truth-telling about past state atrocities, held a wide appeal. It stood in stark contrast to ZANU(PF)'s name-calling and threats and the ubiquitous pictures of a fist-waving Mugabe. ZANU(PF) promised – as it had for years – that 'Zimbabwe will never be a colony again.' ZANU(PF) would 'punish and forever silence puppet sanctions-mongers.'[39]

The elections were testimony to the political polarization of the Zimbabwe

---

38 The most devastating policy failure, and one which had spectacularly perverse consequences, was the ill-advised and poorly executed Operation Reduce Prices of mid-2007. It can be contended that this single policy thrust drastically eroded ZANU(PF)'s support base and bridged the rural-urban political polarization.

39 Alexander and Tendi, 'A Tale of Two Elections: Zimbabwe at the Polls in 2009' *Concerned Africa Scholars, Bulletin* No. 80, Winter 2008, p. 5.

population. In the House of Assembly election ZANU(PF) got 46 per cent of the vote to the combined MDC's 51 per cent, a difference of only five percentage points. In the Senate elections, ZANU(PF) again received 46 per cent of the vote and the MDC factions 50 per cent. The presidential election results reflected the same trend. It was thus evident that Zimbabwe is a politically divided society.

Perhaps the last lesson was that both political patronage and propaganda have their limits. As noted above, the ZANU(PF) government – with the aid of the Reserve Bank – dispensed patronage on a massive scale. The propaganda of the state-controlled electronic and print media seemed to have lost its potency, having reached saturation point. Certainly the nationalist discourse and liberation war narratives were losing their vibrancy. The law of diminishing efficacy seems to be at work in respect of both patronage politics (and attendant economics) and political propaganda.

It is not clear how far the above lessons were understood by ZANU(PF) and whether or not there was any political learning. If there was, it appears that ZANU(PF)'s interpretation of the results was that they were a result of one missing ingredient in the party's electoral repertoire: violence.[40] It is this lesson – that violence pays –that was deployed in the run-up to the 27 June presidential election.

Conclusion

The 29 March 2008 harmonized elections were the closest to 'normal' that Zimbabwe has held in a decade. It was as if they were directed at discrediting Alexander and Tendi's characterization of Zimbabwe politics as 'profoundly shaped by violence.'[41] They were elections with a choice. For the first time since 2000, Zimbabweans were accorded a real opportunity to speak to power and make their voice heard via the ballot box. 29 March was a moment of hope and jubilation. Regrettably, the moment of jubilation was soon turned into a Hobbesian state of nature as ZANU(PF) fought back to regain lost ground and did so with all the coercive resources it could muster. Chapter 5 addresses the Hobbesian state of nature that unfolded between 29 March and the 27 June second round elections, a run-off that proved to be an election without a choice.

40 Alexander and Tendi assert that: 'It is not too much of an oversimplification to argue that violence has been an essential glue for ZANU(PF), necessary to both the maintenance of party discipline and electoral success ...' Ibid., p. 6.
41 Ibid., p. 5.

5

A Militarized Election
The 27 June Presidential Run-off

Eldred V. Masunungure

Introduction

In this chapter we seek to dissect the second tale of the 2008 elections, the 27 June presidential run-off election. Chapter 4 discussed the key features and actors in the 29 March harmonized elections that, by most accounts, were reasonably free and fair and produced plausible results. Though there were petitions filed by both ZANU(PF) and the MDC-T challenging some of the results, the 29 March election results have been recognized as representing the genuine expression of the voluntary will of the people. Those results – especially the parliamentary results – were subsequently adopted as the benchmark and formula for the allocation of executive power under the 15 September 2008 power-sharing agreement.

This chapter demonstrates the brazenly intrusive and expansive role of the military/security complex in the run-off election and the consequent omnipresent fear that enveloped the whole country. The systemic violence and intimidation was so intense as to force one of the presidential candidates to withdraw, paving the way for a one-horse election. The run-off election degenerated into a typical Zimbabwean election, one without a choice.

The oddities of Zimbabwe's run-off election

As is evident in Greg Linington's contribution, the law provided for a 'second election'[1] to decide the presidency in the event that the first election

---

1   This second presidential election came to be referred to as the 'run-off' election, a usage that we adopt in this book.

proved inconclusive, i.e. with no candidate obtaining 50 per cent +1 of the valid votes. The law also provided for 21 days for such a presidential run-off to be conducted after the first election.[2] Zimbabwe's run-off election, however, was marked by several peculiarities. First, this was the first time in the history of elections in both pre- and post-independence Zimbabwe that the country was holding a run-off. In previous presidential elections, Mugabe would romp to victory, though very controversially in respect of the 2002 presidential election when he won by 56 per cent of the vote to Tsvangirai's 42 per cent.[3] In addition, Mugabe did not even consider a run-off, let alone coming second to his long-time adversary. After casting his vote on 29 March, Mugabe said a second round would not be necessary as he was going to knock out all his opponents and conquer them in the first round:

> We are not used to boxing matches where we go from round one to round two. We just knock each other out. That's how we have done it in the past. That's how we will do it this time.
>
> It's a constitutional requirement that there may be a re-run, but it won't be necessary.[4]

The second peculiarity was the inordinate delay in announcing the results of the first round presidential election held on 29 March; the results were frozen for five weeks, well beyond the timeline for holding the run-off election. A third oddity was the time it took after the announcement of results on 2 May to announce the run-off date. When the date was finally announced on 16 May, it was two days after the government had first extended the period for the second round election from 21 days to 90 days after the announcement of results. Due to a combination of all the above, it is virtually impossible to determine when the presidential run-off campaign actually started. However, it appears fair to suggest that it began as soon as ZANU(PF) got wind of the results, which must have been soon after 29 March, i.e. in early April.

For instance, on 3rd April, long before the results of the presidential election had been announced, the Deputy Information Minister said: 'ZANU(PF) is ready for a run-off, we are ready for a resounding victory.

---

2   Legal controversy erupted as to when the first election ended and the 21 days began to take effect. Was it 21 days after voting day of 29 March, or 21 days after the announcement of the results on 2 May? The election body later decided to settle the matter unilaterally. On 14 May, a Special Government Gazette extended the period for the run-off election from 21 days to 90 days after the announcement of the results. Two days later, ZEC announced that the run-off would be held on 27 June 2008.

3   The controversy had several sources: the unequal electoral landscape, the partiality of the public media and election officials, the politicization of the electoral body, alleged rigging, and mismanagement of the voting process, especially the unfair distribution of polling stations between urban areas (Tsvangirai's stronghold) and rural areas (the heartland of Mugabe's support.).

4   'Mugabe confident no need for a re-run,' *The Sunday Mail*, 30 March 2008.

In terms of strategy, we only applied 25 percent of our energy into this campaign. ... (the re-run) is when we are going to unleash the other 75 percent that we did not apply in the first case.'[5]

Then on 4 April, 2008 the ZANU(PF) Politburo held an extraordinary meeting that sought among other things to carry out a post-mortem of what in law was still an incomplete election process and plan a way forward. After the meeting, ZANU(PF) Secretary for Administration, Didymus Mutasa, announced that the party had decided that Mugabe would participate in a run-off. 'It's definite there will be a re-run. We are down but not out', he said and added: 'Absolutely, the candidate will be Robert Gabriel Mugabe – who else would it be other than our dear old man?'[6] This shocked many people who strongly suspected that ZANU(PF) had gained advance knowledge of the results and the defeat of its presidential candidate and therefore was already planning for a run-off.

Further, on the very day the ZANU(PF) Politburo was meeting, veterans of Zimbabwe's guerrilla war were marching through the capital; according to Sapa-AP, 'while they were silent, there was little doubt they were out to intimidate President Robert Mugabe's political opponents.'[7] This chapter reflects on how the winds of democratic change were defied, paying particular attention to the leading role of the military/security sector in this process.

The military/security factor in the run-off election

The April to June 2008 election interregnum was a militarized moment. A ZANU(PF) that had been de-stooled as the ruling party in parliament was not prepared to be dislodged from State House. A pivotal player in the militarized elections was the Joint Operations Command (JOC), a military/security body comprising the heads of all security organs (army, air force, prison service, intelligence, and police) which, according to Jocelyn Alexander and Blessing Miles Tendi, 'decided within days of the (29 March) election to deploy a strategy of delay and violence in order to hold onto the all-important executive'.[8]

The militarization of the 27 June election was part of the militarization of the state that had started several years before with the onset of what ZANU(PF) and the government termed the 'third Chimurenga', a reference to the often violent take-over of white-owned farms from 2000 onwards.

---

5 'Robert Mugabe emerges as Zimbabwe 'crackdown' begins', the *Daily Telegraph* (UK), 7 April 2008.
6 'Robert Mugabe will contest Zimbabwe presidential run-off', ibid. 7 April 2008.
7 'War veterans march, Zimbabwe opposition factions vow to work together for possible runoff', Sapa-AP, 4 April 2008
8 Jocelyn Alexander and Blessing Miles Tendi, 'A Tale of Two Elections: Zimbabwe at the Polls in 2008', *Concerned Africa Scholars, Bulletin,* No. 80, Winter 2008.

This metamorphosed into a 'governance-by-operations' militaristic style of policy implementation. Alexander and Tendi note that since 2000,

> Zimbabwe's state has been described as increasingly 'militarised', with military men being appointed in key positions throughout the state, and an expanding range of decisions and actions being taken by the military, from political strategy to the formulation and implementation of agrarian and economic policy.[9]

The increasing penetration of the military/security sector is closely associated with the party-state phenomenon. In practice, a party-state means the ruling party is fused to the state; party and state structures at all levels are conflated. Moreover, in the party-state duality, the party is supreme over the state. All formal organs of the state – including the military and security services – are closely linked to the party without being officially integrated into it. Bratton and Masunungure characterize the Zimbabwe case as a 'politicised party-state'.[10]

The militarization of Zimbabwe politics in the service of the ruling party became evident at the turn of the millennium and towards the June 2000 parliamentary elections. Some commentators then were already alluding to this militarization. For instance, constitutional expert and activist Brian Kagoro was perturbed by 'early signs of militarisation, orchestrated by the government' while academic Brian Raftopoulos was more categorical:

> ...it is quite clear that President Robert Mugabe's real strength is the coercion which comes out of the army and the liberation war veterans. He is using it to the full and the militarisation will be to his benefit even if the opposition does well in any elections which might take place.[11]

To Michael Bratton and Eldred Masunungure, the year 2000 'was a turning point in civil-military relations. With the emergence of the MDC challenge, the military's involvement in political life became increasingly open'.[12] The militarization of the state took the form of a growing number of senior military officers being appointed to lead strategic state institutions including the Zimbabwe Prisons Service (ZPS) the Zimbabwe Republic Police (ZRP), the Central Intelligence Organization (CIO), the Zimbabwe Electoral Commission (ZEC), and parastatals such as the National Oil Company of Zimbabwe (NOCZIM), the Grain Marketing Board (GMB), National Railways of Zimbabwe (NRZ) and The Department of National Parks and Wildlife.

In their analysis of Zimbabwe's blocked democracy, Bratton and Masunungure characterize Mugabe's post-independence regime as 'a militarized form of electoral authoritarianism' which has come to rest on 'the interpen-

---

9 Ibid.
10 Michael Bratton and Eldred Masunungure, 'Zimbabwe's Long Agony', *Journal of Democracy*, Vol. 19. No. 4, 2008, p. 44.
11 Quoted in Alex Duval Smith, 'Parliament disolved as "creeping coup" looms', The *Independent* (UK), 12 April 2008.
12 Bratton and Masunungure, 'Zimbabwe's Long Agony', p. 48.

etration of two key organs of authority: the ruling party and the security forces.' This perspective can be extended to the analysis of Zimbabwe's two elections. This chapter argues that both 'organs of authority' were important in the two elections but that their visibility and significance differed fundamentally between them. In the lead up to the March elections, it was the party – as was the case in previous elections – that played a critical and prominent role in the campaign while the military and other security branches played a background, more-or-less subdued, and more rhetorical than physical role. ZANU(PF) fought for power against its opposition rivals and did so more or less politically. The political leadership of the regime campaigned for power and did so without directly and physically bringing the men and women in uniform into the fray. The military leadership of the regime occasionally revealed its partisan sympathies but there was no wholesale and systematic political mobilization of the security/military sectors as institutions. It can thus be fairly asserted that the march to the 29 March elections was a political march and not a military march. The campaign was a political campaign; though the military/security may have lurked rather menacingly in the background, their claws remained sheathed.

Unlike the pre-29 March period, the campaign afterwards was a visibly militarized one. The security forces, rather than the ruling party, were in the forefront, spearheading the march to the 27 June run-off. Available evidence suggests that the governing regime came to the conclusion that the party had failed in the march to 29 March and therefore that military should lead the march to 27 June. Here is how the ZANU(PF) president described his party's 29 March performance when he addressed the party's Central Committee in mid-May:

> We went to the elections completely unprepared. We went to the elections completely unprepared, unorganised and this against an election-weary voter. Our structures went to sleep, were deep in slumber in circumstances of an all-out war.

> [The structures] were passive; they were lethargic, ponderous, divided, diverted, disinterested, demobilised or simply non-existent. It was terrible to see the structures of so embattled a ruling party so enervated.

> As leaders, we all share the blame: from the national level to that of the branch chairman. We played truant; we did not lead, we misled; we did not encourage, rather we discouraged; we did not unite, we divided; we did not inspire, we dispirited; we did not mobilise, we demobilised. Hence the dismal result we are landed with ('Unite for victory: President.') [13]

Prior to this rare, candid and public declaration of the 'dismal' performance of the party, Mugabe was reported to have told his ZANU(PF) Politburo in early April 2008 that in order to win the presidential election run-off, the party must establish a warlike and military-style leadership to campaign for him. The *Zimbabwe Independent* quoted one of the documents as follows:

13 *The Herald*, 17 May 2008.

[Mugabe] said the party must establish an almost military/warlike leadership which will deliver. The president and first secretary said the party must mobilise massively to achieve a resounding victory in the run-off. He said party members must understand this was a sink-or-swim election.[14]

Mugabe is said to have come up with this 'warlike' strategy after meeting his JOC advisors before the April Politburo meeting. The import of this was to reduce the run-off contest to a battle between the bullet and the ballot. In this battle, ZANU(PF) was making it starkly clear that in its political world, the bullet is supreme and the ballot is subservient to it. This philosophical line dates back three decades to when, in 1976, the ZANU president and ZANLA commander-in-chief articulated his party's militaristic conception of the source of political authority:

...our votes must go together with our guns; after all any vote ... shall have been the product of the gun. The gun, which provides the votes, should remain its security officer, its guarantor.[15]

This thinking is itself the supreme vitiation of elections as an expression of democratic choice because if the ballot produces a result that is incongruent with the expectations of the gun-wielders, then the bullet will shred the ballot. For ZANU(PF), elections are a continuation of war by other means. A senior army officer made this unambiguously clear in the run-up to the run-off when he publicly declared that ZANU(PF) captured power after a bitter and protracted war and would not surrender the country unless it was defeated by the MDC in a war. In the words of Major-General Engelbert Rugeje: 'This country came through the bullet, not the pencil. Therefore, it will not go by your X of the pencil.' Rugeje also chillingly promised his Masvingo audience of villagers that on his return after the vote, 'the helicopter will be full of bullets.[16] In the northern part of the country in Mashonaland West, soldiers reportedly handed out bullets to villagers and told them: 'If you vote for MDC in the presidential run-off election, you have seen the bullets; we have enough for each one of you, so beware.'[17]

Mugabe, the soldiers' Commander-in-Chief, endorsed this view. At one of his election rallies, he warned: 'We fought for this country, and a lot of blood was shed. We are not going to give up our country because of a mere X. How can a ballpoint fight with a gun?'[18] Mugabe's Commander of the Defence Forces then put the matter to rest by predicting a resounding electoral triumph for his political boss: 'Our comrade, Defence Forces chief, our leader President Mugabe and comrade-in-arms will romp to victory.

14 'Mugabe Orders "warlike" campaign', the *Zimbabwe Independent*, 23 May 2008.
15 Mugabe, R. *Our war of Liberation: Speeches, Articles, Interviews*. Gweru, Mambo Press, 1981, p. 100.
16 'Politicians threaten to wage post-election war', *The Financial Gazette*, 19 June 2008.
17 'Mugabe's brutality to force election victory revealed', *The Independent* (UK), 9 June 2008.
18 Robert Mugabe warns Zimbabwe's voters: 'How can a pen fight a gun?' *The Times*, 17 June 2008.

We say so because we have no apology to make to any house nigger and puppets.'[19]

The military factor in the run-off election was so dominant and visible that to many critical observers, the military had covertly taken over and had become the arbiter of Zimbabwe's fate. There were reports of a 'military coup by stealth', with Mugabe being 'beholden to his senior generals to hold office' but more as the regime's titular leader.[20] A Human Rights Watch Zimbabwe specialist, Tiseke Kasambala, noted an 'increasing militarisation of the state' and that evidence pointed to 'an increasing role by the army in state affairs.' According to her, 'The army is no longer just in barracks, waiting to protect the country. The army is out there, taking a role in the day-to-day government of the country'.[21] In early June 2008 Tsvangirai himself claimed that 'the country has witnessed a *de facto coup d'etat* and is now effectively run by a military junta.'[22]

The period between 29 March and 27 June 2008 gave the strong impression that the ZDF were little more than ZANU(PF) in uniform. For instance, a month before the run-off election, Army Chief of Staff Major-General Martin Chedondo made this unambiguously clear when he addressed soldiers:

> The Constitution says the country should be protected by voting and in the 27 June presidential election run-off pitting our defence chief, Cde Robert Mugabe, and Morgan Tsvangirai of the MDC-T, we should, therefore, stand behind our Commander-in-Chief.
>
> Soldiers are not apolitical. Only mercenaries are apolitical. We have signed and agreed to fight and protect the ruling party's principles of defending the revolution. If you have other thoughts, then you should remove that uniform.[23]

As if not to be outdone by the gun-wielders, members of ZANU(PF)'s political class echoed the same militaristic sentiments, and just and as chillingly. The then Finance Minister Samuel Mumbengegwi was reported to have equated an MDC victory with a declaration of war. Addressing school heads in Masvingo province, he admonished: 'This is up to you, if you want peace, you vote for us. If you vote for the MDC, we will go to war.' The same function was addressed by then Masvingo Resident Minister and Governor, Willard Chiwewe, who bluntly decreed that Zimbabweans had no choice but vote for ZANU(PF). 'This is a choice with no choice. It's either you vote for war or peace.'[24]

More fundamentally, the above statements betray two radically differ-

19 'President will win run-off poll hands down: Chiwenga', *The Herald*, 23 June 2008.
20 'Zimbabwean generals have taken Robert Mugabe's power', the *Daily Telegraph* (UK), 6 June 2008.
21 Ibid.
22 'Zimbabwe Opposition Leader Says Country Run by Military', Voice of America, 10 June 2008.
23 'Rally behind President in runoff, soldiers told', *The Herald*, 31 May 2008.
24 *The Financial Gazette*, 19 June 2008.

ent conceptions of the sources of power and legitimacy. In the ZANU(PF) political world, legitimacy and power flowed from the barrel of the gun – and also from God, in the case of Mugabe[25] – and not from the ballot. On the other hand, the MDC-T continued to invest faith in the ballot as the only viable source of power and legitimacy. The 27 June moment was therefore a contest between these two conceptions and, as it turned out, the ZANU(PF) conception 'won' the game.

The political environment: the reign of fear

By all accounts, the inter-election period was one of the most traumatic and abnormal political situations in the country. Richard Joseph's observation in February 2008 that 'the notion of an electoral process in Zimbabwe with Mugabe at the controls can only be described as Orwellian'[26] was more apt in respect of the run-off election. Terence Ranger sums up the 'abnormal' period:

> It is hard to comprehend how abnormal the situation in Zimbabwe has been between the March and June elections. Zimbabwe has had no parliament although all the MPs have been elected. The new parliamentarians have not met to elect a Speaker. Several MDC MPs have been arrested on charges ranging from child abduction to organising violence; many others are in hiding. There have been no functioning city councils or mayors even though a full slate of councillors was elected in March. The elected councillors in Harare met on private premises and chose themselves a mayor, but the only – and terrible – result of that was that his wife was abducted and brutally killed. Not surprisingly, no mayors have been elected elsewhere. Zimbabwe cities have been 'in commission.' Zimbabwe has hardly had a functioning civil society. Its human rights bodies have been raided and all non-governmental organisations have been prevented from operating in rural areas. Journalists have been beaten, arrested and killed. Churches have been under pressure, as Mugabe has declared his desire to see every church answerable only to Zimbabweans leaders and committed to the Zimbabwean revolution.[27]

The pre-election context is also well summarized by Craig Timberg:

> In three months between the 29th March vote and the June 27 runoff election, ruling-party militias under the guidance of 200 senior army officers battered the Movement for Democratic Change, bringing the opposition party's network of activists to the verge of oblivion. By election day, more than 80 opposition supporters were dead, hundreds were missing, thousands were injured and

---

25 A week before polling day, Mugabe declared that 'only God' could remove him from office and that the MDC 'will never be allowed to rule this country – never ever.' He was addressing a group of Bulawayo business people when he thundered: 'Only God who appointed me will remove me – not the MDC, not the British.' 'Only God can oust me, Mugabe declares', AFP, 21 June 2008.

26 Joseph, Richard, 'Challenges of a "Frontier" Region', in *Journal of Democracy*, 19, 2, April 2008, p. 105.

27 'Will normality return to Zimbabwe?' *The East African* (Kenya) 7 July 2008.

hundreds of thousands were homeless. Morgan Tsvangirai, the party's leader, dropped out of the contest and took refuge in the Dutch Embassy. [28]

Timberg revealed that the brutal campaign was code named CIBD, an acronym for Coercion, Intimidation, Beating, and Displacement. In fact, the vicious campaign went beyond CIBD to include murder. The campaign was code-named 'Operation Makavhotera Papi' (Operation Who Did You Vote For?). It began in the rural areas, and within them, in the three Mashonaland provinces of Mashonaland West, East and Central. Incidentally and ironically, these were ZANU(PF) strongholds. The party won sixteen of the eighteen House of Assembly seats in Mashonaland Central, its best performance country-wide. In Mashonaland East, ZANU(PF) won nineteen of the 23 contested House of Assembly seats and yet it recorded the highest level of violence. From Mashonaland the violence spread to other provinces and from the rural areas the violence spread to the urban centres. In a tragic sense, the whole country was unified, in violence, and its pattern was the same, indicating a central point of organization and execution.

The bloody crackdown was reportedly orchestrated and systematically executed by soldiers,[29] police, state security agents, ZANU(PF) militia and veterans of the liberation war. The violence took the form of intimidation, kidnapping, torture, arson and murder of opposition or suspected opposition leaders, activists and supporters.

Many domestic and international observers documented the horrors attendant on the run-off, where Zimbabwe was reduced to a Hobbesian state of nature, in which life became 'solitary, nasty, brutish and short'. Human Rights Watch captured the litany of sordid incidents in its June 2008 report:

> There is overwhelming evidence that the organised pattern of abuses have been replicated throughout the provinces. In nearly all the areas affected by violence, victims and eyewitnesses told Human Rights Watch that it was usually conducted at night and was characterised by abductions, beatings and the looting and burning of huts and other property.
>
> ZANU(PF) officials and 'war veterans' are beating and torturing suspected MDC activists and supporters in hundreds of base camps established across the provinces as local centres of operations. ZANU(PF) supporters, government officials, 'war veterans' and state security forces are conducting brutal daily 're-education' meetings in which they beat and at times torture local residents to force them to denounce the MDC and swear allegiance to ZANU(PF). Further, ZANU(PF) and its allies have gone on a campaign of widespread destruction

28 The *Washington Post*, 5 July 2008.
29 The Government denied involvement and instead blamed the MDC for instigating the violence. The military, for instance, issued a statement denying involvement: 'The Zimbabwe National Army wishes to raise concerns over articles being published in the print and electronic media on allegations relating to the alleged political violence, assaults, harassment and robberies perpetrated by men in army uniforms. The army categorically distances itself and any of its members from such activities' (IRIN, 'Zimbabwe: Hunger drives post-election violence, deepens poverty'. 9 May 2008).

of property and looting, including the burning of homesteads that has led to thousands of people being internally displaced. There has been a spate of abductions and killings of known MDC activists by suspected agents of the state, ZANU(PF) supporters and 'war veterans' in the province of Mashonaland East and Harare. [30]

The Zimbabwe Election Support Network (ZESN), a local elections watchdog, was equally blunt:

> When the results were finally released on 2 May 2008, it took almost two weeks to have the run-off date announced on 15 May 2008 during which the run up to the run-off degenerated into a run over leaving in its wake a trail of destruction, houses burnt down, many people displaced and homeless, many children orphaned, and community relations torn asunder. Freedom of assembly and movement were heavily restricted with rural areas virtually sealed off from opposition rallies, the opposition leadership subjected to sporadic arrests and detentions, their campaign activities under total blackout on national electronic and press media. Hate speech, incitement of violence, and threats of war characterized electoral campaigns, with the ruling party presidential candidate threatening to go back to war if he lost the election to the MDC presidential candidate, whom he considered a puppet of the West. [31]

The observations by ZESN were confirmed by field reports from other domestic observers, notably the Catholic Commission for Justice and Peace (CCJP), a much respected defender and advocate of human rights and social justice dating back to before independence. The CCJP was one of the organizations that decided to observe the run-off election but 'under protest' given the unpropitious conditions obtaining in the post-harmonized elections period.

The following field observations from CCJP graphically capture some of aspects of the pre-election environment:

> The June 27 run-off election was characterised by a wave of intimidation, torching of houses, beatings, abductions, ceaseless meetings and many other forms of violence. The pre-election period to this election left the people of Gokwe in total fear and psychological stress.

> The MDC was not allowed in any form to hold a meeting or any form of gathering. If by any chance they attempt to meet, they (meetings) were either broken away by the Police, Army or the Zanu PF Youth Militia.

> In some villages, people who were known to belong to the opposition had their names written down by kraal heads and ruling party leaders – for the purpose of identifying them and dealing with them later in form of murdering them or beating them, denying them food handouts and above all, as a threat *(CCJP: Diocese of Gokwe).*

> This Pre-Presidential period (29 March to 27 June 2008) was the most violent

30 Human Rights Watch, '"Bullets for Each of You": State-sponsored Violence since Zimbabwe's March 29 Elections', New York, June 2008, p. 19.
31 ZESN, 'Report on the Zimbabwe 29 March Harmonised Elections and 27 June Presidential Run-off', Harare, August 2008, p. 9.

and bloody of all post-colonial elections that we have witnessed as an observer group. The most primitive and uncivilised methods and tactics were used in this supposedly modern day election.

Only ZANU PF rallies were witnessed throughout the Diocese. The rallies were not attended out of one's choice or free will. People were forced to go to rallies in all the rural areas of Masvingo.

Violence was intense. It was manifested in four major ways: intimidation, beatings, killings and arson. All forms of threats were used from verbal to physical threats. Youth (ZANU PF) and militia established bases which in other words could be termed as torture camps *(CCJP: Diocese of Masvingo)*.

The superficial and negative peaceful environment that prevailed prior to the harmonised 29th March Election has been turned into a turmoil of direct and open violence, torture, beatings, arson, abductions, kidnapping and mass displacement, initiated and spearheaded by government agencies, security forces (military junta), war veterans, youths militias and Zanu PF supporters.

The period between March 29 2008 and June 27 2008, the date set for the run-off elections thus can be described as 'days of Armageddon' for the Zimbabwean populace *(CCJP: Manicaland)*.

Two weeks before polling day, the CCJP was compelled to issue a stinging press statement on the pre-run-off environment.

The reign of violence that has been unleashed on the country, especially in the rural areas and former commercial farming areas, is unacceptable. Base camps from which militias terrorise defenceless rural populations must be disbanded as a matter of urgency. People are being force-marched to political re-orientation meetings and are told that they voted 'wrongly' in the Presidential poll on 29 March 2008 and that on 27 June 2008, they will be given the last opportunity to 'correct their mistake', else the full-scale shooting war of the 1970s will resume. It is in this context that despicable atrocities are being committed by members of both contesting parties, ZANU PF and MDC.[32]

Many other observers – regional and international, friend and foe – of Zimbabwe's post-harmonized elections scene arrived at the same verdict. For instance, the Pan-African Parliament Observer Mission which arrived in the country on 14 June 2007 to observe the run-off warned that 'violence is at the top of the agenda of this electoral process' and that it had received 'many horrendous stories. The election is a far cry from what we had [in March].'[33] Tanzanian Foreign Minister Bernard Membe, speaking on behalf of the SADC Organ on Politics, Defence and Security lamented the dim prospects for a free and fair election: 'There is every sign that these elections will never be free nor fair.'[34]

Across the Atlantic both the United States and the United Nations expressed their deep anxiety with Condoleezza Rice, then United States

---

32 Zimbabwe Catholic Bishops' Conference, 'Press Statement on the Current Crisis in Our Country', 12 June 2008.
33 'Harare cuts back on election observers', the *Financial Times* (UK), 19 June 2008.
34 'Zimbabwe vote cannot be fair, say African ministers', Reuters, 19 June 2008.

Secretary of State, accusing the Mugabe regime of having given up 'any pretence that the 27 June elections will be allowed to proceed in a free and fair manner'.[35] Five days before polling, the UN Security Council unanimously condemned the politically motivated violence: 'The Security Council regrets that the campaign of violence and the restrictions on the political opposition have made it impossible for a free and fair election to take place on 27 June.'[36]

The environment was such that Tsvangirai went into self-imposed exile for six weeks soon after the March 2008 elections for fear of assassination attempts.[37] He returned to Zimbabwe on 24 May but his campaign was consistently blocked or frustrated; he was arrested or detained on several occasions until he gave up the fight.

These were the conditions in which the run-off election was to be conducted. It is evident that the prevailing conditions were inimical to a fair, free and credible election. It should be noted that ZANU(PF) not only rejected allegations of state-instigated violence and its central role in it but actually blamed the MDC for the violence. Mugabe and his security chiefs constantly warned the MDC against perpetrating violence. Genocide Watch, a human rights group, calls this phenomenon 'mirroring' and describes it as 'a strange but common psychological mechanism of denial used by mass murderers.'[38]

For instance, in late May 2008, the Police Commissioner General Augustine Chihuri said: 'The nation is facing a myriad of challenges and machinations by external forces and their internal sympathisers, who I normally call puppets. Its very existence and survival is threatened by these puppets and their handlers.'[39] But what motivated the ZANU(PF) regime to behave in the manner it did? Various explanations can be offered.

Towards explaining the scorched-earth campaign

As already noted, ZANU(PF) lost its parliamentary majority for the first time since the watershed independence elections and its leader personally lost a presidential contest, coming second to his arch-rival Morgan Tsvangirai, the man he publicly despised for his modest education. Mugabe must have felt a sense of grievous personal loss and humiliation and his power base – the military/security establishment – also got angry on his behalf. The loss had to be avenged, and those who had caused it – the MDC in

35 Ibid.
36 'Security Council Urges Zimbabwe to Halt Violence', the *New York Times*, 24 June 2008.
37 Tsvangirai was a target of increasing criticism for staying out of the country while his supporters were attacked, tortured and killed.
38 Quoted in 'Violence approaching political mass murder' http://www.thezimbabwetimes.com, 25 June 2008 (accessed 4/1/09).
39 'MDC chief tallies cost of post-poll mayhem', Reuters, 28 May 2008.

particular and the voters in general – had to be 'disciplined' for their 'delinquent' conduct on 29 March 2008.

But why target ZANU(PF)'s own support base and strongholds? For ZANU(PF), it was more hurtful to lose a single seat in its traditional strongholds than to lose all seats in the 'enemy's'. So, while it was understandable for the party to lose all seats, as it did, in Bulawayo, it was unforgivable to lose two out of eighteen seats in Mashonaland Central, or four of the 23 seats in Mashonaland East. This partly (if not largely) explains why the epicentre of the strategy of 'electoral cleansing'[40] was in the Mashonaland provinces, and within them in those constituencies where it lost or won marginally. Even in constituencies where it won, the brutal campaign visited those areas whose polling stations had recorded a loss for the party or where a large opposition vote had been recorded.[41] ZANU(PF) treated those who voted for the opposition in its traditional backyard as stray voters, who, like stray animals, had to be brought back into the kraal, but after some whipping. They had to be taught not to go astray next time. A party politburo member provides evidence of this line of thinking when, quoted anonymously, he warned the 'stray voters': 'We're giving the people of Zimbabwe another opportunity to mend their ways, to vote properly ... this is their last chance.'[42]

This line of agument was earlier articulated by Bratton and Masunungure:

> The objective was to kill MDC officials and polling agents, displace qualified electoral officials such as teachers, and punish known MDC supporters. The targets of intimidation were not so much the solid MDC strongholds in the cities and the southwest, but politically contested areas in the country's middle belt and northeast where, in the first round of the election, voters had swung away from ZANU(PF) and toward the MDC.[43]

Bratton and Masunungure contend that the object of electoral cleansing was to create 'no-go zones' 'where the ZANU(PF) monopoly could be enforced at the local level through the direct and demonstration effects of violence'.[44] To reinforce this, the regime banned the operations of virtually

---

40 The term is used by Bratton and Masunungure, 2008, p. 51.
41 As discussed elsewhere, an innovation of the March harmonized elections was the publication and posting of results at the polling station. It greatly enhanced transparency of the results but had the unintended effect of exposing MDC strongholds. On this, Human Rights Watch observed that 'ZANU(PF) supporters and their allies have not found it necessary to prove that a person voted for the MDC before meting out 'punishment.' Instead they have examined results posted outside polling stations to identify areas where people voted for MDC in large numbers, even if the MDC lost to ZANU(PF) in those areas.
42 Bratton and Masunungure, 'Zimbabwe's Long Agony', p. 44.
43 Ibid. p. 51.
44 Ibid. pp. 51-2. The potency of the demonstration effect is best captured by Sun Tsu's often quoted saying 'Kill one, frighten a thousand' (cited in Stiff, Peter, *Cry Zimbabwe*. Alberton, Galago Publishing, 2000, p. 22.)

all NGOs operating in rural areas, especially those delivering humanitarian relief. The consequent human suffering was comprehensive and unprecedented; it was a scorched-earth policy which was comparable in its ferocity and objectives to the Gukurahundi campaign of the early 1980s. It was as if the regime was guided by Emperor Caligula's philosophy: 'Let them hate as long as they fear.' The fear was guaranteed to deliver victory for Mugabe, and the party was emphatic about this. For instance, one senior ZANU(PF) leader told Robyn Dixon of *The Los Angeles Times*: 'There is no way we are to lose the runoff. We are going to make sure of that. If we lose the runoff, then the army will take over. Never be fooled that Tsvangirai will rule this country. Never.'[45]

Associated with the above reasons is a deeply rooted sense of ZANU(PF) entitlement to rule, and to do so for eternity. The top ZANU(PF) political generation and its allies in the military/security establishment have an 'end of history' perspective to the liberation struggle and the achievement of independence in 1980. The attainment of Uhuru through a protracted liberation struggle against settler colonialism marked the end of all struggles, and the triumph of ZANU(PF) was the last triumph. 1980 marked the victory of light over darkness, and in this line of thinking any other struggle in Zimbabwe would be tantamount to an attempt to bring back darkness. This thinking leads ZANU(PF) to brag that it delivered democracy and therefore there cannot be any other democratic struggle. In short, retaining power in ZANU(PF) is a historical imperative. In effect then, by posing a real challenge to take power from the anointed ruling party, the MDC was not only trying to 'reverse the gains of the revolution,' but was also challenging history by so doing. This is the context in which threats to 'go back to the bush' should be understood. For instance, two weeks before the run-off, Mugabe told youth members of his ZANU(PF) party that the war veterans from Zimbabwe's 1970s war of independence had told him they would launch a new bush war if the election was won by the opposition leader Tsvangirai.

> They came to my office after the [first round of] elections and asked me: 'Can we take up arms? They said this country was won by the barrel of the gun and should we let it go at the stroke of a pen? Should one just write an X and then the country goes just like that?'[46]

The old guard in ZANU(PF) and the military/security sector is locked into this 'end of history' paradigm and cannot accept let alone appreciate anything that is not explicable within the parameters of this paradigm. This is one of the tragedies of electoral democracy in Zimbabwe.

However one explains the motives behind the architects of Operation Makavhotera Papi, the bottom line is that they wanted to raise the cost of

45 'Zimbabwe is on a political precipice,' the *Los Angeles Times*, 24 May 2008.
46 BBC, 'Africa pressure grows on Mugabe', http://www.newsvote.bbc.co.uk (accessed 16/6/08).

participating in opposition politics and supporting the opposition MDC candidate in the run-off election. The organizers and implementers of the Operation constricted the space so much and lowered the bar so low that it became practically impossible for opposition politics to function. The strategy succeeded and the cost of opposition politics became so high that even the candidate himself was forced not only to withdraw from the race but to immediately seek refuge in the Dutch Embassy in fear for his life.

Tsvangirai's withdrawal and the one-candidate election

On 22 June, just five days before the run-off, the MDC-T candidate Morgan Tsvangirai held a press conference at which he announced his withdrawal from the run-off, citing eight reasons for pulling out; central to these was the intense and widespread violence and intimidation. 'We in the MDC cannot ask [voters] to cast their vote on the 27th when that vote would cost them their lives,' Tsvangirai said, and urged the United Nations and African Union to intervene to prevent 'genocide'.[47] He gave statistics of the victims of the violence as of that day: 86 deaths, 10,000 homes destroyed, 200,000 displaced, and 10,000 injured. He noted that:

> The victims have been MDC supporters. The violence has been clearly state-sponsored and carried out in most cases by members of the Zimbabwe National Army and ZANU(PF) militia. It is true that in some instances our supporters have fought back, in most cases in self-defence. Because of our inability to access the rural areas, the above statistics may be understated.[48]

Soon after the press conference, Tsvangirai sought refuge in the Dutch Embassy but the government and ZANU(PF) derided Tsvangirai's pull-out and his safety fears as groundless and a ploy to seek international attention and sympathy. The electoral body also refused to accept Tsvangirai's withdrawal and kept his name on the ballot paper. The ZEC chairman actually boasted that he was ready looking forward 'to a credible election'.[49] He also rejected other accusations levelled against ZEC:

- that the armed forces had been forced to vote for a particular candidate – he dismissed this as 'general allegations' and that he had been assured by the commanding officers that 'nothing of the sort had happened';
- that observers had been barred from witnessing the postal ballot process – Chiweshe said the law did not provide for the presence of observers but only a competent witness;
- that there had been a dramatic increase in the number of postal ballots (which allegedly increased from 8,000 to 64,000 postal applications) – the ZEC said this was because members of the army had also submitted returns unlike in

47 The *Zimbabwe Independent*, 27 June 2008.
48 Ibid.
49 'The MDC still to write pullout letter, says ZEC', *The Herald*, 24 June 2008.

March when only police officers applied for this facility; and

- that the public media was biased against the MDC – the ZEC said it had not received any formal complaint from MDC-T about equal access to public media coverage.

Oblivious of Tsvangirai's withdrawal and the inauspicious electoral environment, the ZEC went ahead with the run-off election with Robert Mugabe as the remaining candidate. There were 1,958 ward collation centres and 210 constituency collation centres and a national command centre was established in Harare.

The administrative and logistical arrangements for the election were adjudged by observers to have been satisfactory but there were many irregularities that compounded an already anomalous situation of having a one-race contest in an environment drenched in blood. These included demands by ZANU(PF) local leaders and activists that voters record the serial numbers on their ballots and hand this information over to ZANU(PF) 'wardens' together with their personal details. This was supposedly to enable the 'wardens' to check on who the voters had voted for. Another irregularity was forcing voters to first assemble at the headman's homestead where they would be given numbers after which they would proceed to the polling station led by their kraal heads. Yet another irregularity was that voters suspected of being opposition members or sympathisers were required by local ZANU(PF) leaders to feign illiteracy – no matter how well educated – so that they would be 'assisted' to vote. They would then proclaim their preference to vote 'paMasvingo' (the ZANU(PF) logo) meaning a preference for Robert Mugabe.

The strategic aim of the aggressive ZANU(PF) campaign was to ensure its candidate's victory. But an equally important aim was for Mugabe to win 'resoundingly' so as to shame the party's detractors, and to ensure high voter turn-out another 'operation' was mounted just before polling and this was dubbed 'Operation Red Finger': to avoid voting twice, each voter was required to dip a finger in red ink that is visible but indelible and the message spread by ZANU(PF) was that anyone who would not have voted (and therefore without a red finger) was going to be classified as an MDC person and subjected to the same 'disciplinary' action as meted out under Operation Makavhotera Papi. As a result, many people in the rural areas – but also in some urban areas – were compelled to go and vote just in order to secure the much valued red finger. This his how ZESN described voting day:

> The Polling Day was characterized by poor voter turnout in urban areas, an extraordinarily high number of spoilt ballots [39,975 in the March Election against 131,481 in the June Election] with a significant number reportedly carrying insulting messages, an unusually high number of assisted voters, and recording of serial numbers – incidents that point to a banal breach of voter rights and secrecy.

In most rural constituencies, voters were reportedly herded to polling stations by traditional leaders and allegedly instructed to vote for the ruling party candidate. They were also ordered to record their ballot papers' serial numbers and would after polling give them to the local leaders. Soldiers and police presence was reportedly heavy, in some cases their presence overshadowing that of voters.[50]

Table 1 shows the results of the 27 June run-off election and Table 2 compares the results of the March presidential election to those of the run-off election. It is clear from the results that Mugabe had won in the manner he and his party had intended, i.e. with a landslide. Compared to the March election, he had increased his votes by more than one million and spectacularly recovered from winning 43.2 per cent of the votes in March to 85.5 per cent, thus doubling his share. As already noted, Tsvangirai formally withdrew from the presidential race but ZEC decided to go ahead nonetheless. The results showed that Tsvangirai received nearly a quarter of a million votes and in some cases, notably in Bulawayo, he won more votes than Mugabe. Voter turnout in the run-off was almost exactly the same as that for March harmonized elections (42.37 per cent to 42.7 per cent).

Another visible feature of the run-off election was the unusually high number of spoilt ballots, more than treble those of the harmonized elections. There were even the bizarre cases – especially in Bulawayo – of the number of spoilt ballots at a polling station being higher than those of the winning candidate. It was also noteworthy that unlike in the March elections, when it took the electoral body over four weeks to announce the results, for the 27 June run-off ZEC only took two days to announce the final results, and within a few hours the winning candidate had been crowned the President of Zimbabwe.

How did observers assess the run-off election? There was near-unanimity that the elections were far from free and fair. Below is a sample of opinions expressed by the observers from the SADC, Pan-African Parliament and the African Union.

The pre-election phase was characterised by politically motivated violence, intimidation, and displacements.

The process leading up to the presidential run-off elections held on 27 June 2008 did not conform to SADC Principles and Guidelines Governing Democratic Elections. However, the Election Day was peaceful.

Based on the above mentioned observations, the Mission is of the view that the prevailing environment impinged on the credibility of the electoral process. *The elections did not represent the will of the people of Zimbabwe.*[51] (my emphasis)

50 ZESN 2008, p. 67.
51 SADC Election Observer Mission, Preliminary Statement presented by the Hon. Jose Marcos Barrica, Minister of Youth & Sports of the Republic of Angola and Head of the SOEM, on the Presidential Run-off and House of Assembly By-elections, Harare.
52 PAP Interim Statement, 29 June 2008.

Table 1: Run-off Presidential results by province

Province	Robert Mugabe	Morgan Tsvangirai	Rejected/ spoilt votes	Total votes
Bulawayo	21,127	13,291	9,166	43,584
Mash. West	25,699	18,459	10,821	285,979
Masvingo	321,404	12,804	7,940	343,948
Mat. North	84,185	40,099	9,907	134,191
Mat. South	92,654	21,687	7,353	121,694
Midlands	302,407	33,555	19,438	355,400
Manicaland	323,284	29,561	17,525	370,370
Harare	156,478	48,307	36,547	241,232
Mash. Central	276,912	4,066	3,409	284,337
Mash. East	315,119	11,171	7,675	333,965
TOTAL	2,150,269	233,000	129,781	2,514,750

Table 2: Results of Presidential Elections – March and June 2008

First Round	Robert Mugabe	Morgan Tsvangirai	Simba Makoni	Langton Towungana	Total valid
Popular vote	1,079,730	1,195,562	207,470	43,584	2,497,265
Percentage	43.2	47.9	8.3	0.6	100
Spoilt					39,975
Second Round					
Popular vote	2,150,269	233,000			2,383,269
Percentage	85.5	9.3			100
Spoilt					131,481

The prevailing political environment throughout the country was tense, hostile and volatile as it was characterised by an electoral campaign marred by high levels of intimidation, violence, displacement of people, abductions, and loss of life.

In view of the above *the Mission concludes that the current atmosphere prevailing in the country did not give rise to the conduct of free, fair and credible elections.*[52] (my emphasis)

The poll was peaceful and held in accordance with the electoral laws of Zimbabwe;

There was violence in the run down to the elections;

The fear of violence deterred popular participation in the electoral process;

There was no equitable access to the Public Media.

Against the backdrop of the foregoing factors, in the context of the AU Declaration on the Principles Governing Democratic Elections in Africa, *it is the considered view of the African Union Observer Mission that the Election process fell short of accepted AU standards.*[53] (my emphasis)

From whatever angle one looks at the 27 June presidential election, one thing reverberates: they were heavily militarized and the resultant ballot was more a barometer of people's fears than of people's choices. It was, in every sense, a choice-less election that failed to settle the question of who should legitimately lead the people of Zimbabwe. Rather than resolving the legitimacy question, the run-off election deepened it. This set the stage for the search for a non-electoral solution to the Zimbabwean crisis.

Conclusion

Elections to choose who will govern us are supposed to be political processes whose result is often indeterminate. This was the case with the 29 March harmonized elections in which politicians campaigned *politically* for the free expression of the people's choice. This element of free choice is precisely what the architects of Operation Makavhotera Papi wanted to eliminate and replace with a predetermined outcome. To this extent, the political process was overthrown and in its place came a militarized process in which the military elite came to the aid of their political counterparts in a toxic combination of ZANU(PF) and the military/security complex. In this political-military alliance, the military was the dominant player and this robbed the electoral process of its political character. In the process, the winds of democratic change were defied; a peaceful, election-centred process of transition away from authoritarianism and towards democracy was interrupted. Our conclusion is that the 27 June 2008 presidential run-off election was a militarized election without a choice.

53 AU Preliminary Statement of the African Union Observer Mission, 29 June 2008.

6

Illegality & Zimbabwe's 2008 Presidential Elections

Greg Linington

Introduction

In the end, Zimbabwe's presidential election turned into a complete fiasco. It was not simply a political and moral fiasco, but a legal one as well. The objective of this chapter is to look at how illegality undermined the democratic process in Zimbabwe's 2008 presidential election. There were many instances of illegality. It has only been possible to consider the more important of these in this chapter. Some space has also been devoted to discussing the structure of important electoral institutions such as the Zimbabwe Electoral Commission (ZEC) and the Electoral Court. In the case of the ZEC this is because its flawed structure facilitated illegality. The Electoral Court is mentioned because it seems inappropriate, in a chapter on electoral illegality, not to draw the reader's attention to the existence of the judicial institution responsible for 'resolving' electoral disputes.

Finally, a few words about the sources of Zimbabwe's electoral law. Of primary importance are those provisions contained in the Constitution, the supreme law of Zimbabwe. Most of the detailed electoral law is to be found in the Electoral Act and in the Electoral Regulations (subordinate legislation enacted under the authority of the Electoral Act). The Zimbabwe Electoral Commission Act is also important, although many of the ZEC's functions are in fact set out in the provisions contained in either the Constitution or the Electoral Act.

The Zimbabwe Electoral Commission

'When *I* use a word,' Humpty Dumpty said in a rather scornful tone, 'it means just what I choose it to mean – neither more nor less.'[1]

Ensuring that elections '... are conducted efficiently, freely, fairly, transparently and in accordance with the law' is a responsibility conferred upon ZEC by section 61 (4) (1) of the Constitution. Like Humpty Dumpty, ZEC decided that it was not going to be bound by the definitions of words contained in standard dictionaries. As will be seen later in the chapter, ZEC's interpretation of the words contained in section 61 (4) (a) was somewhat different from the meanings normally accorded to them.

That ZEC aspired to be another Humpty Dumpty is largely due to its structure which, to put it mildly, is not designed to facilitate fairness. Established as a result of a Constitutional Amendment in 2005,[2] it consists of a chairman and six other members (Section 61 (1) of the Constitution). The chairman must either be a judge or a person qualified for appointment as a judge (Section 61 (1) (a) of the Constitution). The appointment of the chairman is made by the President after consultation with the Judicial Service Commission (JSC) (ibid.). But the recommendation of the JSC is not binding on the President who must however inform the Senate if he appoints someone other than the person recommended by the JSC (Section 61 (1) (b) of the Constitution). The six other members – of whom at least three must be women – are also appointed by the President (ibid.). However, his discretion is limited – at least in a formal sense – by the requirement that he choose from a list of nine nominees submitted by the Parliamentary Committee on Standing Rules and Orders (ibid.).

Some comments on the appointment process are appropriate at this point. In the first place, the purely 'consultative' role played by the JSC is cause for concern. But even if the JSC had some 'teeth' in respect of appointing the ZEC's chairman, the significance of that would be diminished by the fact that the JSC is itself hardly an independent body. Its members are all appointed, either directly or indirectly, by the President (Section 90 of the Constitution). The JSC consists of the Chief Justice, the Chairperson of the Public Service Commission, the Attorney-General and up to three other members. The requirement that the Senate be informed should the President ignore a JSC recommendation is also of little significance. The Constitution does not authorize the Senate to do anything should such a situation arise. In any event, in the run-up to the 2008 elections, the Senate was dominated by ZANU(PF). The Parliamentary Committee on Standing Rules and Orders, responsible for compiling the list of 'nine nominees', was also under the control of ZANU(PF) at that time.

In view of all this it is not surprising that the ZEC did not act impartially when performing its functions. It is true that a number of provisions were

1 Carroll, Lewis (1871) *Through the Looking Glass, and What Alice Found There.*
2 See section 17 of Act 5 of 2005, Constitution of Zimbabwe Amendment (no. 17) Act, 2005, which came into force on 1 December 2005. This has been amended by section 12 of Act 11 of 2007, Constitution of Zimbabwe Amendment (no. 18) Act, 2007, which came into force on 30 October 2007.

inserted into the Zimbabwe Electoral Commission Act (ZECA) for the ostensible purpose of ensuring the 'independence, impartiality and professionalism of commissioners' (the language used in the heading to Section 8 of ZECA). For example, section 8 (2) (a) says that Commissioners '... shall exercise their functions in a manner that promotes ... free, fair and democratic elections.' In addition, they must maintain 'strict impartiality in the exercise of their functions' (Section 8 (2) (c) of ZECA). Provisions like this are all well and good of course. But the decisive role of the President in appointing the Commissioners, as well as ZEC's performance in practice, show that ZEC was never 'impartial' in any objective sense but only in a subjective, 'Humpty Dumpty' sense.

ZEC's structural partiality is also illustrated by section 6 (2) of the Electoral Act. In terms of that provision, ZEC must establish an 'Observer's Accreditation Committee' chaired by the chairperson of ZEC. Other members are: the vice chairperson of ZEC; one member of ZEC; one person nominated by the Office of the President and Cabinet; one person nominated by the Minister of Justice, and one by the Minister of Foreign Affairs (Section 6 (2) of the Electoral Act). The function of the Committee is to accredit observers. However, no one may be accredited if either the Minister of Justice or the Minister of Foreign Affairs objects (ibid.). A provision structured like that can hardly be said to facilitate free and fair elections. Indeed, the government used this provision to exclude observers from countries seen as hostile to its policies.

The Electoral Court

Section 161 (1) of the Electoral Act established an Electoral Court 'for the purpose of hearing and determining election petitions and other matters in terms of this Act.' According to Section 161 (2) of the Electoral Act, the court has no jurisdiction in criminal cases. Judges of the Electoral Court are in fact High Court judges appointed by the Chief Justice '...after consultation with the *Judicial Service Commission* and the Judge President of the High Court' (Section 1161 (1) of the Electoral Act; emphasis added). In the past the Electoral Act did not involve the Judicial Service Commission in the appointment process. This gave rise to concern that the appointment process was unconstitutional since it was not consistent with section 92 (1) of the Constitution. That provision says:

> 'The power to appoint persons to preside over a special court shall vest in the President, after consultation with Judicial Service Commission: provided that Parliament may provide that the Chief Justice may, after consulting the Judicial Service Commission, appoint a person holding the office of Judge of the High Court to preside over a special court for such a period as he may specify.'

Is the Electoral Court a 'special court'? According to section 92 (4) of the Constitution, there are three types of special courts. The Electoral Court does not fall within the scope of the types described in paragraphs (a) and (c) of section 92 (4). That leaves only those courts or other adjudicating authorities that qualify as special courts because there is no right of appeal from their decisions to the Supreme or High Courts (section 92 (4) (b)). Decisions of the Electoral Court on questions of fact are final (section 172 (1) of the Electoral Act), but questions of law may be appealed to the Supreme Court (section 172 (2)) and must be determined within six months (section 172 (3)). Because appeals on points of law are permissible, the question arose as to whether the Electoral Court qualifies as a 'special court'.

Answering this question in the affirmative, retired High Court Judge George Smith (writing extra judicially) said that the Electoral Court's main functions involve determining questions of *fact* such as '… whether or not a person has been guilty of corrupt or illegal practices [and] whether … an election was conducted in accordance with the principles laid down in the Electoral Act and [if] any mistake or non compliance affected the result of the election'.[3] Thus, in most cases, the right to appeal on a point of law will be no consolation to a petitioner, since electoral disputes normally turn on questions of fact.[4]

The issue was finally resolved by the Supreme Court in *Marimo and Another v Minister of Justice and Another*. The facts were that in 2005 the Chief Justice purported to appoint five judges of the High Court to sit in the Electoral Court. The Supreme Court ruled that the Electoral Court is a 'special court', and that the Chief Justice ought therefore to have consulted the Judicial Service Commission. Because this did not happen, the court said that the appointments were invalid. It was this decision which eventually led to the amendment of section 162 (1) of the Electoral Act so as to make that provision consistent with the Constitution.

The main task of the Electoral Court is to deal with election petitions which '… shall be presented within fourteen days after the end of the period to which the election relates' (section 168 (2)). Only candidates may present election petitions (section 167) which must be determined within six months of being presented (section 182).

The legal status within Zimbabwe of the SADC Principles & Guidelines Governing Democratic Elections

These Principles and Guidelines were adopted at the SADC summit in

3   Smith, G. (2006) 'An Opinion on Whether Electoral Courts are Special Courts.' Unpublished paper.
4   Ibid.

Mauritius in August 2004. Their purpose is to 'consolidate, defend and maintain democracy' in the SADC region (see Article 1 of the SADC Principles and Guidelines, which itself refers to article 5 of the SADC Treaty).[5] The Principles include: full participation of the citizens in the political process; freedom of association; political tolerance; regular intervals for elections; equal opportunity for all political parties to access the state media; equal opportunity to exercise the right to vote and be voted for; independence of the judiciary and impartiality of the electoral institutions; voter education and the right to challenge election results in court (Article 2). The Guidelines are contained in Article 4 and are designed to ensure that the elections are conducted in an environment that is free, fair and peaceful. There must be discrimination-free voter registration and the voters roll must be accessible and up-to-date. Polling stations must be in neutral places and the counting of votes must take place at those stations. SADC observers should be deployed at least two weeks before voting day.

In its preliminary statement on the presidential run-off and House of Assembly elections, the SADC Election Observer Mission (SEOM) said that the '… elections … did not conform to SADC Principles and Guidelines governing democratic elections'.[6] For this reason 'the elections did not represent the will of the people of Zimbabwe'.[7] The statement provides examples of violations of the Principles and Guidelines. It says: 'Few rallies were held by the opposition party, and SEOM observed with concern disruption of campaigning of the opposition party and the regrettable inaction of the law enforcement agencies, despite the court order authorising such rallies'.[8] Furthermore, there was '[t]he one-sided coverage in content and extent of one candidate on the part of the state media, print and electronic. In addition, no advertisements for the opposition party were carried'.[9] Widespread '… politically motivated violence led to the internal displacement of persons and impacted negatively on the full participation of citizens in the political process and freedom of association'.[10]

Since the Principles and Guidelines were violated, the question that arises is: are Zimbabwe's courts able to enforce them?

Section 111 B (1) (b) of the Constitution stipulates that a treaty 'shall not form part of the law of Zimbabwe unless it has been incorporated into the law by or under an Act of Parliament.' Since the SADC Principles and Guidelines were never incorporated, they are not *as such* part of Zimbabwe's law. However, in *Movement for Democratic Change v President of the Republic of Zimbabwe and Others* (2007), the applicant argued that it

5   The Guidelines may be found on <www.sadc.int/archives/read/news/167>
6   SADC Election Observer Mission: Preliminary Statement <www.aceproject.org/ero-en/regions/africa/ZW/zimbabwe-preliminary-statement-by-SADC-2008> p. 6.
7   Ibid.
8   Ibid. at p. 4.
9   Ibid.
10 Ibid.

had a legitimate expectation that the government would act, with respect to elections, in a way that accorded with its obligations under *international law* (i.e. the SADC Principles and Guidelines). In support of its argument the applicant referred to the Australian case of *Minister of State for Immigration and Ethnic Affairs v Teoh*. Australia had signed and ratified (but not yet incorporated) the United Nations Convention on the Rights of the Child. Article 3 (1) of the Convention says: 'In all actions concerning children ... undertaken by public ... institutions ... the best interest of the child shall be a primary consideration.'

Teoh was an alien who had been convicted of drug offences and was facing deportation. If the Immigration Department had to take into account article 3 (1) of the Convention, a decision other than deportation might be adopted. The court ruled that while the Convention was not part of Australian law, Teoh had a legitimate expectation that the Australian government's executive actions would conform with its international obligations under the Convention.

However, in *Movement for Democratic Change* (2007) Marakau J declined to follow this approach. In fact, it is quite clear that she did not understand the *Teoh* judgment. At page 7 of the cyclostyled judgment she says the Australian court '... reject[ed] the arguments advanced on behalf of Teoh.' Well, the correct position, as indicated above, is that the court *accepted* Teoh's argument! It was *for that very reason* that the court nullified the Immigration Department's decision to deport Teoh.

It is a pity that the MDC did not appeal against the High Court's decision. It is submitted that in terms of the legitimate expectations doctrine (which *is* part of Zimbabwe's law) executive actions performed by Zimbabwe's government in the context of elections *must* conform to the SADC Principles and Guidelines. Thus, the provisions of that treaty can, indirectly, be enforced by courts in Zimbabwe, even though it has not been incorporated.

The failure of the Nomination Court to accept the nomination papers of two prospective presidential candidates

An election can hardly be said to be free and fair if candidates are unlawfully deprived of the right to file their nomination papers. The Nomination Court for the presidential election sat on 15 February 2008. All persons wishing to contest the election had to file their nomination papers by 4.00 p.m. of that day. Daniel Shumba entered the Nomination Court with fifteen minutes to spare. Another prospective candidate, Bruce Chiota, was already inside and was filling in some forms. Mr Shumba was told to wait until Mr Chiota had been attended to. However, both of them were then told that the Nomination Court had closed, as a result of which their nomination papers would not be accepted.

The two men then brought an urgent chamber application before the High Court seeking an order compelling the ZEC to accept their nomination papers. However, Guvava J dismissed the application on the ground that it ought to have been brought before the Electoral Court.[11] When the application finally reached that court, Uchena J, in his capacity as an Electoral Court Judge, dismissed it saying that the matter had prescribed (section 46 (19) (c) of the Electoral Act says that a candidate has four days in which to appeal against the decision of the Nomination officer). Thereafter, Shumba and Chiota brought a constitutional application directly before the Supreme Court in terms of section 24 (1) of the Constitution. In this they argued that their freedom of association, as enshrined in section 21 (1) and (2) of the Constitution had been violated by the failure of the Nomination Court to accept their papers. They also stated that their right to the protection of law (section 18 (1) of the Constitution) had also been violated. The constitutional application did not seek an order compelling the acceptance of their nomination papers (the 'first' election was over when the case was argued before the Supreme Court on 22 May 2008). Instead, the applicants simply sought a declaratory order that their rights had been violated.

Handing down its judgment in *Shumba and Another v ZEC and Another* (not yet reported, judgment no. SC 11/08), the Supreme Court accepted the applicant's submission that the matter was '... more than a mere academic exercise' and that the applicants therefore had *locus standi* (at p. 1 of the judgment). This was because a judgment from the court would '... provide a useful guideline for the future conduct of election officials' (ibid.). In view of the rather strict approach adopted towards *locus standi* by the Supreme Court in recent years, the court's willingness to hear this matter is rather surprising. Since the applicants were only seeking a declaratory order, the matter was very close to being a 'purely academic matter' of the sort that has been rejected in the past. Normally applications will only be entertained if there is a real constitutional issue that requires a *real remedy*. Paradoxically, perhaps it was precisely because the applicants were not asking for a real remedy – such as an order nullifying the election – that a relieved court was prepared to hear the matter!

While on the subject of *locus standi*, it is worth noting that the Supreme Court decided – rightly – that the matter ought never to have gone before the Electoral Court and that the court of first instance – the High Court – had jurisdiction in the circumstances. This was because an appeal to the Electoral Court from the decision of the nomination officer will only lie if the latter has rejected the nomination papers on one of the grounds specified in section 46 (10) of the Electoral Act. In fact, the rejection was not based on any of the grounds specified in that provision. Rather, the

11 Reference was made by the judge to section 46 (19) of the Electoral Act.

evidence before the court pointed to the fact that the papers had been rejected because they were submitted – in the opinion of the nomination officer – too late. However, such a rejection was contrary to the proviso to section 46 (7) of the Act, which states that if a candidate is already *in the Nomination Court*, '... the nomination officer shall give him or her an opportunity to [submit a nomination paper].' The Electoral Act does not provide any right of appeal to the Electoral Court where section 46 (7) has been violated. The Supreme Court therefore rightly held that the ordinary *review* jurisdiction of the *High Court* would apply (at p. 6 of the judgment, per Chidyausiku CJ). Since both the High Court and the Electoral Court declined to entertain the Shumba/Chiota application, the Supreme Court held that a direct constitutional application to it in terms of Section 24 (1) of the Constitution was not prevented in the circumstances by section 24 (3) of the Constitution. (The latter provision says that once a constitutional point has arisen in proceedings in a lower court, a direct application to the Supreme Court is precluded. However, since the two lower courts concerned had declined to hear the matter, there had not been, strictly speaking, any proceedings in those courts.)

The Supreme Court concluded by finding in favour of the applicants. Chidyausiku CJ, writing for a unanimous bench, said: '... It is quite clear that the refusal to accept their nomination papers was not in accordance with the law' (at p. 12 of the judgment). He did not refer to any of the constitutional provisions cited by counsel for the applicants. However, his reference to 'the law' implies that the court found that the constitutional right to protection of law (section 18 (1)) had been violated.

The correctness of the court's decision cannot be disputed. However, it is perhaps surprising that the applicants restricted themselves to simply asking for a declaration that their right to be accepted as candidates had been violated. The case was argued after the 'first' presidential election, but before the 'second' one. It is interesting to speculate on what might have happened had the applicants sought an order invalidating the first election and compelling ZEC to hold an entirely fresh election. Section 24 (4) of the Constitution provides the Supreme Court with a wide range of measures to secure the enforcement of constitutional rights.[12] In *In Re Mlambo* (p. 355), Gubbay CJ said: 'It is difficult to imagine language which would give this court a wider and less fettered discretion.' So an order setting aside the first election would have been within the competence of the court.

The recounting of votes

The credibility of the presidential election was seriously undermined by the

---

12 Linington, G. (2001) *Constitutional Law of Zimbabwe*. Legal Resources Foundation, Harare, p. 243.

delay in announcing the results of the 29 March 'First Round' election. It seemed to many that something untoward was going on. (For more on this issue, see Chapter 8).

Because of ZEC's decision to delay the announcement of the result of the presidential election, the MDC brought an urgent chamber application before the High Court, seeking an order compelling ZEC to release the result. In his opposing affidavit, the Chairperson of ZEC, Justice Chiweshe, stated that ZEC 'had received several complaints in terms of section 67A of the Electoral Act.' The complainants were '... various ZANU PF candidates'.[13] Accordingly, he said that ZEC had to consider whether a recount would be necessary. He stated that even a single vote could affect the outcome. This was why the result had been withheld.

The issue of recounting votes is dealt with by section 67A of the Electoral Act. Section 112 of the Act makes it clear that section 67A applies to both parliamentary and presidential elections. In *Movement for Democratic Change and Another v Chairperson of the Zimbabwe Electoral Commission and Another* (2008), Uchena J ruled that ZEC had acted within the parameters of section 67A and he therefore dismissed the MDC's application. However, it is submitted that the court's decision was incorrect. Section 67A (1) states that a party or candidate may request ZEC to conduct a recount within 48 hours of the *declaration* of the result. (While parliamentary results need only be declared in the constituency concerned, the result of the presidential election must be declared by the Chief Election Officer; section 110 and paragraph 3 (1) of the Second Schedule of the Electoral Act.) As Alex Magaisa notes,[14] Uchena J correctly ruled (at p. 13-14 of the judgment) that section 67A (1) did not apply in the circumstances, because there had been no declaration of the result, a necessary prerequisite for the operation of that provision. However, the court then went on to rule that ZEC could proceed with a recount on the basis of subsection (4) of section 67A. That provision says:

> 'The Commission may on its own initiative order a recount of votes in any polling station if it considers there are reasonable grounds for believing that the votes were miscounted and that, if they were, the miscount would have affected the result of the election.'

Since ZEC was not itself claiming to be acting 'on its own initiative' but rather on the basis of 'complaints' received (the subsection (1) scenario), it is hard to see how Uchena J could properly invoke subsection (4).[15] The latter provision seems to envisage a situation where there has been no complaint or request for a recount from a party or candidate but ZEC, *for reasons of its own*, has decided to order a recount.

13 Matyszak, Derek (2008) 'How to lose an election and stay in power.' p. 7, http//:www. kubatana.net.
14 Magaisa, A. (2008) 'Zimbabwe's deflated wheels of justice.' *The Standard*, 19 April.
15 This point is also made by Magaisa.

Subsection (4) limits ZEC's discretion to order a recount. In the first place it may only do so '… if it considers there are *reasonable grounds* for believing that the votes were miscounted…' (emphasis added). This means that it is *not* sufficient that ZEC wants a recount. ZEC's subjective opinion, however sincerely held, must be based on *objectively* reasonable considerations. In *Forum party of Zimbabwe and Others v Minister of Local Government, Rural and Urban Development and Others*, the High Court accepted that the words 'when it appears to the President that a situation has arisen … which needs to be dealt with urgently …' in section 2 (1) of the Presidential Powers (Temporary) Measures Act indicate that the President has a subjective discretionary power to decide whether a situation is urgent. However, Adam J said, '… what appears to the President must surely accord with a true state of affairs ascertainable and not manifestly without reasonable foundation that a situation has arisen or is likely to arise which needs to be dealt with urgently. A situation cannot be said to have arisen if it is not so factually' (ibid. at p. 486; this case is discussed in Linington 2001:80). Similarly, ZEC cannot resort to the procedure set out in section 67A (4) unless objective facts exist which justify and make explicable a decision to recount votes. In the *Forum Party* case the court had to infer a reasonableness requirement, but section 67A (4) *expressly* stipulates that reasonableness is required.

Uchena J's decision in *Movement for Democratic Change* (2008) must therefore be wrong. There is nothing in the judgment that indicates the grounds upon which ZEC decided to act, let alone whether those grounds – if they exist at all – are reasonable. Moreover, section 61 (4) (a)[16] of the Constitution says that ZEC must '… ensure that … elections … are conducted efficiently, freely, fairly, transparently and in accordance with the law.' The effect of this language, like that used in section 67A (4) of the Electoral Act, is to limit the discretion of ZEC. By ordering a recount without good cause ZEC was not acting 'fairly'. Neither was it acting 'in accordance with the law', since, as has been said already, the 'reasonable grounds' requirement set out in section 67A (4) was not satisfied.

The recount ordered by ZEC applied to 23 constituencies. As Matyszak notes:[17] 'There were 1092 polling stations where a recount was to take place. With one ballot box for each of the four elections this makes at least 4368 ballot boxes to be opened and recounted.' Section 67A (4), understood properly, requires ZEC to have reasonable grounds for believing that a miscount occurred at a particular polling station. This means that ZEC had to reasonably believe that a miscount occurred at all 1092 polling stations in respect of all 4368 ballot boxes! As Matyszak says,[18] 'This is

16 Magaisa in his article refers to section 64 (1) of the Constitution. This is obviously a misprint (section 64 (1) no longer exists). It is clear that he means section 61 (4).
17 Matyszak, ibid. p. 11.
18 Ibid.

inherently implausible.' 'It will not suffice that there is a belief that a constituency total is incorrect.'[19]

Even if there are reasonable grounds for believing that a miscount occurred, according to section 67A (4) of the Electoral Act there must *also* be reasonable grounds for believing that '… the miscount would have affected the *result* of the election' (emphasis added). When one considers the huge margins in some constituencies, it is hard to believe that ZEC sincerely, let alone reasonably, thought that any of the alleged 'miscounts' would have affected the result. In fact, no significant discrepancies emerged as a result of the recount.[20]

In an effort to bolster his decision in *Movement for Democratic Change* (2008) to dismiss the MDC's application, Uchena J referred to section 67A (7) of the Electoral Act. That provision says: 'The Commission's decision on whether or not to order a recount and, if it orders one, the extent of the recount, shall not be subject to appeal.' He then said:

> 'The fact that [ZEC's] decision to recount and the extent thereof is not subject to an appeal means it was intended to act independently and that its decision would be final. The provision barring an appeal simply means [ZEC] has been given a very wide discretion as to whether or not to order a recount. The provision that [ZEC's] decision shall not be subjected to an appeal also means that this court cannot inquire into that decision. This should therefore be the end of the inquiry as [ZEC's] conduct can only be open to the jurisdiction of this court when it strays from the law.'

The judge added that since, in his opinion, ZEC had 'not strayed from the law,' the court was 'not entitled to intervene' (at p. 17 of the judgment).

Magaisa is right to question the constitutionality of section 67A (7). He does so on the grounds that prohibiting an appeal against a ZEC decision is inconsistent with the obligation cast upon ZEC by the Constitution (section 61 (4) (a)) to ensure that elections are conducted efficiently, freely, fairly, transparently and in accordance with the law. If ZEC decisions cannot be taken on appeal, how will it be possible to ensure that ZEC complies with these constitutional standards?

It is also probable that the appeal prohibition is inconsistent with section 18 (9) of the Constitution, which provides that every person is entitled to a fair hearing within a reasonable time before an independent and impartial court or other adjudicating authority. While section 79 (2) of the Constitution does permit an Act of Parliament to vest adjudicative functions in persons or authorities other than courts, such persons or authorities must still exercise their functions in a way that complies with the standards set out in section 18 (9). In view of everything that has happened in the course of the 2008 elections, serious questions about the impartiality and independence of ZEC have arisen.

19 Ibid.
20 Ibid. p. 12.

Even if the *appeal* prohibition is not itself unconstitutional, it would still be permissible to bring a constitutional *application* challenging ZEC's decision as a violation of sections 18 (9) and 61 (4) of the Constitution. In *Hambly v Chief Immigration Officer (1)* the court said that the right to bring a constitutional application under section 24 (1) of the Constitution is not affected by statutory provisions that deny persons the right of appeal in certain circumstances. This is because such applications are not appeals, but are a distinct form of legal redress, established by the Constitution itself.[21]

The requirement that ZEC must act fairly and reasonably is not in any way affected by section 61 (5) of the Constitution which states that ZEC '… shall not, in the exercise of its functions, be subject to the direction or control of any person or authority.' All this means is that, provided it acts within the parameters assigned to it by the Constitution, ZEC has a discretionary power, and cannot be subject to the dictation of any other person or authority when exercising that power. But an action by ZEC that is unfair, inefficient, non-transparent or unlawful, will fall *outside* the ambit of its proper discretion and may therefore be questioned by a competent court.

Was the second presidential election on 27 June lawful?

This is an important question because if the 'requirement' that there be a second or 'run off' election is unlawful, then Morgan Tsvangirai was lawfully elected President on 29 March, 2008.

None of the candidates in the presidential election held on 29 March managed to secure an absolute majority of the votes cast. The most popular candidate was Morgan Tsvangirai, who obtained 47.9 per cent of the votes cast. Section 110 (3) of the Electoral Act stipulates that if '… no candidate receives a majority of the total number of valid votes cast, a second election shall be held within twenty one days after the previous election in accordance with this Act.' According to section 110 (4) of the Act, '… only the two candidates who received the highest and next highest numbers of valid votes cast at the previous election shall be eligible to contest the election.' However, the same Act contains a provision that is not consistent with section 110. This is paragraph 3 (1) of the Second Schedule of the Electoral Act which bears the heading 'Determination, Declaration and Notification of Result of Presidential Poll.' It says:

'… The Chief Elections Officer shall forthwith declare the candidate who has received –

---

21 See Linington (2001:600). Magaisa refers to the possibility of review proceedings in his article, but does not mention constitutional applications. Reviews are, of course, distinct from appeals.

(a) where there are two candidates, the greatest number of votes;

(b) *where there are more than two candidates, the greatest number of votes*;

to be duly elected as President of the Republic of Zimbabwe with effect from the day of such declaration' (emphasis added).

How is this inconsistency to be resolved? Christo Botha[22] (2005:81) says that sections in the substantive part of an Act will prevail over conflicting provisions contained in a schedule to the Act, citing as authority *African and European Investment Co v Warren* (at 360). More recently this rule has been reiterated by the South African Constitutional Court in *Executive Council, Western Cape Legislature and Others v President of the Republic of South Africa and Others*. So on this basis it can be said that an absolute majority of votes is required in order to become President. Simply securing more votes than any of the other candidates will not suffice.

ZEC relied on section 110 when organizing the second (run-off) presidential election on 27 June 2008. But was that second election lawful? In fact, it is submitted that it was unconstitutional. There are a number of reasons for arriving at this conclusion. In the first place, it is necessary to consider section 28 (3) (a) of the Constitution. That provision says: 'An election to the office of President *shall* take place ... on the day or days fixed in a proclamation in terms of section 58 (1) as the day or days on which elections are to be held for the purpose of electing members of Parliament and members of the governing bodies of local authorities' (emphasis added).

Thus the Constitution states, in *imperative* language, that a presidential election *must* take place on the *same* day or days as parliamentary and local government elections. The election held on 29 March complied with this requirement, since all three types of election took place on the same day. The election on 27 June did not. Although three House of Assembly by-elections were held on that date, it would appear that what is required by section 28 (3) is a *general* parliamentary election. This interpretation of section 28 (3) is supported when the section is read together with section 29 (1) of the Constitution. The latter states:

'(1) The term of the office of the President shall be a period of five years concurrent with the life of Parliament ... or

(a) a lesser period where the President earlier dissolves Parliament ... or

(b) a longer period where the life of Parliament ... is extended ...;

in which event the term of office of the President shall terminate on the expiration of such lesser or longer period, as the case may be.'

From this it can be seen that the life of Parliament is closely linked to the term of office of the President. Moreover, the fact that section 28 (3) says that a presidential election must be held together with parliamentary *and*

22 Botha, Christo (2005) *Statutory Interpretation*. Juta, Cape Town. p. 81.

local government elections indicates that what the provision envisages is a general election and not merely parliamentary by-elections. Even if a parliamentary by-election is enough to satisfy the requirements of section 28 (3), the fact remains that no local government elections took place on 27 June. As already stated above, section 28 (3) does stipulate that a presidential election *must* take place on the same day or days as parliamentary *and* local government elections. Thus the second election did *not* comply with section 28 (3). Section 3 of the Constitution says: 'This Constitution is the supreme law of Zimbabwe and if any other law is inconsistent with this Constitution that other law shall, to the extent of the inconsistency, be void.' Thus sections 110 (3) and (4) of the Electoral Act, the provisions authorising the 'second' presidential election, must be invalid since they are inconsistent with section 28 (3) of the Constitution.

If sections 110 (3) and (4) are invalid, the issue of the clash between those provisions and paragraph 3 (1) of the Second Schedule of the Electoral Act automatically falls away. This means that paragraph 3 (1) is the only valid provision in the Electoral Act dealing with who becomes President where no candidate secures an absolute majority of votes. Since it states that a candidate need only secure 'the greatest number of votes,' and since Tsvangirai did just that on 29 March, it would appear that he was lawfully elected President on that date.

Could ZEC argue that the second or 'run-off' election was '... a continuation of the constitutionally set polling day ... in the same way that a reconvened company board meeting may legally be a continuation of one adjourned'?[23] If so, this would mean that sections 110 (3) and (4) are not unconstitutional. However, the argument is not sustainable. As Matyszak notes,[24] '[t]he word "election" in [section 28 (3) of the Constitution] clearly refers to polling day.' The election that took place on 29 March ended on that date. Moreover, by making reference to the 'second election' and 'the previous election' section 110 (3) of the Electoral Act is also making it clear that an 'election' is a thing that begins and ends on polling day. This understanding of the word 'election' is not undermined by the definition of 'election period' in section 4 of the Electoral Act. There we read that an 'electoral period' is 'in the case of a presidential election, the period between the calling of the election and the declaration of the result of the poll in terms of paragraph 3 (1) of the Second Schedule.' As Matyszak observes,[25] '"election" here undoubtedly refers to the day of the poll.' The declaration of the *result* of the election is thus a thing distinct from the election itself.

A somewhat different approach to the section 110/Second Schedule clash has been advanced by South African advocate David Unterhalter. He sees paragraph 3 (1) of the Second Schedule as having the status of a kind

23   Matyszak (2008) ibid, p. 15.
24   Ibid.
25   Ibid. p. 14.

of 'residual principle' that 'kicks in' when the second election required by section 110 does not take place lawfully within the stipulated 21 day period.[26] Since the stance adopted in this chapter is that sections 110 (3) and (4) are *ultra vires* the Constitution, and therefore invalid, it follows that Unterhalter's argument must be rejected. Paragraph 3 (1) is *not* a residual principle. As stated above, it is the *only* valid provision dealing with the question of who becomes President when no candidate has managed to secure an absolute majority of the votes cast. It is worth noting however that in view of the fact that the 21-day period expired long before the 27 June 'election', his ultimate conclusion – that the decisive provision is paragraph 3 (1) of the Second Schedule – is correct.

Even if one were to regard sections 110 (3) and (4) as constitutionally valid, the 27 June election would still be invalid. This is because ZEC unlawfully purported to extend the 21 days by 'amending' the Act and substituting '90 days' for '21 days'. In doing this ZEC relied on section 192 of the Electoral Act which states that ZEC can amend the time limits contained in the Act.

However, a careful reading of the Constitution reveals that section 192 of the Electoral Act is in fact unconstitutional and therefore invalid. Accordingly, any purported changes to the Electoral Act effected by ZEC in terms of section 192 are obviously also unconstitutional and invalid. Section 28 (4) of the Constitution stipulates that 'the procedure for ... the election of the President shall be as prescribed in the Electoral Law.' Section 113 (1) of the Constitution defines 'Electoral Law' as 'the Act of Parliament having effect for the purposes of section 58 (4) of the Constitution which is for the time being in force.' Section 58 (4) of the Constitution is concerned with parliamentary elections and says: 'An Act of Parliament shall make provision for the election of Members of Parliament.' As can be seen, these three constitutional provisions are closely linked and must therefore be read together. The requirement that *only Parliament* can enact the law governing parliamentary elections (contained in section 58 (4)) applies equally to *presidential* elections through the operation of sections 28 (4) and 113 (1). As Sandura JA said in *Tsvangirai v Registrar General and Others* '[w]hat all this means is that the legislation which comprises the electoral law *must be an Act of Parliament*' (emphasis added). He noted that '[t]hat Act of Parliament is the Electoral Act.' Since the Constitution stipulates that only Parliament can make electoral law, Parliament cannot abrogate its duty in that regard by purporting to give other persons and bodies the authority to make electoral law. Because section 192 of the Electoral Act is clearly inconsistent with the constitutional duty imposed on Parliament to enact electoral law, it must be void.

26 Unterhalter, David (2008) 'In RE: The procedures governing the determination and declaration of the President in the event of an unlawful run off,' p. 5. Prepared for the Southern Africa Litigation Centre.

The case of *Tsvangirai v Registrar General*, referred to above, was a 2002 Supreme Court decision in which the constitutionality of section 158 of the old Electoral Act (a provision similar to section 192 of the current Act) was challenged. Although Sandura JA's judgment was a dissenting judgment, the majority of the court dismissed the application on the (incredible) ground that the applicant lacked *locus standi*. The majority judgment (unlike that of Sandura JA) did not therefore address the substantive merits of the application. Sandura JA's view that Parliament alone must make electoral law has thus not been contradicted by the Supreme Court in any case, and must therefore be regarded as accurately stating the law.

Prior to the election, the President purported to amend a number of provisions in the Electoral Act by utilizing the Presidential Powers (Temporary) Measures Act. For example, changes were made to sections 55, 59 and 60 of the Electoral Act in order to facilitate a police presence within polling stations, supposedly in order to 'assist' illiterate voters.[27] These 'amendments' were in fact void for the same reason that the 'amendment' made by ZEC was void: only Parliament can create electoral law. So neither ZEC nor the President is constitutionally empowered to remove or change provisions in the Electoral Act.

Even if the Constitution did not expressly state that electoral law must be made by Parliament, the exclusive power of Parliament in this regard may still be inferred from the structure of the Constitution. In *Executive Council of the Western Cape Legislature and Others v President of the Republic of South Africa and Others* the Constitutional Court of South Africa held that the South African legislature may only confer *subordinate* law making powers upon the South African President.[28] Chaskalson P (*Executive Council*, at 1311-131, paragraph 51) said:

> 'The legislative authority vested in [the South African] Parliament under section 37 of the Constitution is expressed in wide terms – "to make laws for the Republic in accordance with this Constitution." In a modern state detailed provisions are often required for the purpose of implementing and regulating laws, and Parliament cannot be expected to deal with all such matters itself. There is nothing in the Constitution which prohibits Parliament from delegating subordinate regulatory authority to other bodies. The power to do so is necessary for effective lawmaking. It is implicit in the power to make laws for the country and I have no doubt that under our Constitution Parliament can pass legislation delegating such legislative functions to other bodies. There is, however, a difference between delegating authority to make subordinate legislation within the framework of a statute under which the delegation is made, and assigning plenary legislative power to another body, including ... the power to amend the Act under which the assignment is made.'

The court in this case was applying what is known as the delegation doc-

---

27 See SI 43/2008 – Presidential Powers (Temporary Measures) (Amendment of Electoral Act) (no. 2) Regulations 2008.
28 See Linington (2001) ibid. p. 556.

trine. The doctrine has its origins in the separation of powers theory, and has been developed and applied in a number of countries including the United States. The essence of the doctrine is that law-making is a function properly left to the legislature. Accordingly, excessive legislative powers should not be delegated to the executive.[29] The court noted that in South Africa Parliament '... is subject in all respects to the provisions of the Constitution and has only the powers vested in it by the Constitution expressly or by necessary implication' (*Executive Council*, 1317, paragraph 62). Thus, delegating the power to make primary legislation to the executive or any other person or body would amount to subverting the Constitution.[30]

The approach adopted by the South African Constitutional Court in the *Western Cape* case applies equally to the Zimbabwean Constitution. Section 32 (1) of the Constitution states that '[t]he legislative authority of Zimbabwe shall vest in the legislature'. It is true that section 32 (2) permits Parliament to confer legislative functions on 'any person or authority'. However, it is submitted that this refers to Parliament's power to confer *subordinate* legislative powers, *not* primary law-making powers. Even if this were not the case, the fact remains that the Constitution stipulates that electoral law must be made by Parliament.

As has been indicated above, the stance adopted in this chapter is that sections 110 (3) and (4) of the Electoral Act are unconstitutional and therefore invalid. However, it is worth mentioning here an ingenious argument advanced by Sheila Jarvis.[31] She states – in effect – that section 110 and paragraph 3 (1) of the Second Schedule of the Electoral Act can be interpreted in a way that removes any inconsistency between the two provisions. Her conclusion is that Morgan Tsvangirai was entitled to become president following the 29 March election.

According to Jarvis – relying on paragraph 3 (1) – the candidate who got the 'greatest number of votes' in the 29 March election was entitled to be declared President. That candidate was Tsvangirai. However, since he did not get more than 50 per cent of the votes cast, a second election had to be held, as required by section 110. But between the first and second elections Tsvangirai, not Mugabe, was entitled to be President.[32]

David Coltart has been highly critical of the approach adopted by Jarvis and says that she does '... not refer to section 110 in her article'.[33] It is true that she does not refer to the provision by its section number. But when she

---

29 See Linington, ibid. p. 557 and Chaskalson, A. *et al* (1996) *Constitutional Law of South Africa*. (Revision Service 5, 1999 update). Juta, Kenwyn pp. 3-4.

30 See too the opinion by Wim Trengrove and Max du Plessis (2008) 'Lawfulness of Zimbabwe Presidential Run-off', South African Litigation Centre.

31 Jarvis, S. (2008) 'Rebutting Ncube: the agreed rules gave Tsvangirai the presidency, & Mugabe a run-off. http://www.nehandaradio.com/zimbabwe/opinionwriters/jarvis/welshmannotes020908.html

32 Ibid.

33 Coltart, D. (2008) 'A perspective on the Zimbabwean talks and the election of the speaker'. list@davidcoltart.com.

says that '[t]he run-off requirement is a separate rule in the electoral law ...', she obviously means section 110.[34] In fact, it is clear that Coltart has not understood her argument. As far as the present writer is concerned, the problem with the 'Jarvis argument' is that it does not take account of the Constitutional requirement, referred to earlier, that presidential, parliamentary and local government elections must all take place on the same day. This precludes a 'run-off' presidential election. However, it is submitted that if this constitutional argument were to be rejected by the courts, they would have no option but to accept and apply the interpretation enunciated by Jarvis.

Thus, for all of the reasons advanced above, it is submitted that the 'second' presidential election was unlawful, and that Morgan Tsvangirai was lawfully elected President in the 'first' election. He ought therefore to have been declared President.

When does a new President assume office?

According to section 28 (5) of the Constitution, '[a] person elected as President shall, on the day upon which he is declared to be elected or no later than forty-eight hours thereafter, enter office by taking and subscribing before the Chief Justice or other judge of the Supreme Court or the High Court the oaths of loyalty and office in the forms set out in Schedule 1.' Thus, the new President must assume office, *at the latest*, 48 hours after having been declared elected. Some confusion arose because of the wording used in section 110 (7) of the Electoral Act. That provision says:

> 'Notwithstanding subsection (5) of section 23 of the Constitution, a person elected as President in terms of subsection (5) [of section 110 of the Electoral Act] shall assume office on the day upon which he or she is declared so elected by the Chief Elections Officer.'

First of all, section 23 (5) of the Constitution has nothing to do with elections. In fact, section 23 is the protection from discrimination provision. There is obviously a mistake in section 110 (7) of the Electoral Act: the reference ought to be to section 28 (5) of the Constitution. Secondly, the application of a constitutional provision cannot be limited by an inferior law, which of course is what section 110 (7) of the Electoral is. The exact purpose of the latter provision is unclear. It makes reference to section 110 (5) of the Electoral Act. That provision is designed to deal with a very unlikely scenario: a situation where both candidates in a 'second' presidential election secure an equal number of votes. It says that if this occurs, '... Parliament shall, as soon as practicable after the declaration of the result of that election, meet as an electoral college and elect one of the two can-

---

34   http:www.nehandaradio.com

didates as President by secret ballot and without prior debate.' It may be that the draftsperson responsible for producing the text of the Electoral Act read section 28 (5) of the Constitution as imposing a time limit of 48 hours within which a candidate has to become President after the 'second' election. In order to secure extra time he sought to limit the application of the constitutional provision through the use of the word 'notwithstanding' in section 110 (7) of the Act. However, as indicated above, the supreme law cannot be limited by provisions contained in an ordinary Act of Parliament. If the draftsperson was in fact concerned in some way – rightly or wrongly – about the possible limiting effect of a constitutional provision, he ought to have sought the amendment of the constitutional provision concerned.

This chapter has already argued that Morgan Tsvangirai ought to have been declared President after the 'first' presidential election. But this was not done. What is the legal effect of such a declaration, or of a failure to make such a declaration? If the Chief Elections Officer fails to declare the result of the presidential election, does this mean that the incumbent President can simply remain in office indefinitely? In other words, is a declaration an absolutely necessary prerequisite in law to the advent of a new President? The answer must be no. Any other view would amount to saying that the Chief Elections Officer has the power to derail the whole democratic process. Accordingly, it is submitted that a declaration has no *ultimate legal significance*: it is simply a statement about an existing factual situation – that one of the candidates has won the election.

Section 114 (1) of the Constitution says: '[a]ny power, jurisdiction or *right* conferred by this Constitution may be exercised and any duty imposed by this Constitution shall be performed from time to time as occasion requires' (emphasis added). Subsection (1a) of the same provision says: 'Where any power, jurisdiction or *right* is conferred by this Constitution, any other powers that are reasonably necessary or incidental to its exercise shall be deemed also to have been conferred' (emphasis added). When a person is *elected* President, he acquires the right to *become* President. This right is protected by section 18 (2) of the Constitution which says: 'Subject to the provisions of this Constitution, every person is entitled to the protection of law.' Thus, the decisive consideration is that someone has been *elected*, *not* the declaration of the result. This also accords with common sense.

It is also quite obvious that the Chief Elections Officer has no discretion with regard to whether or not to issue a declaration. This chapter has adopted the stance that Mr Tsvangirai won the presidency in the 'first' election, and that the 'second' election procedure set out in section 110 (3) is unconstitutional. Therefore, the relevant 'declaration' provision is the one contained in paragraph 3 (1) of the Second Schedule of the Electoral Act. This says: '... The Chief Elections Officer *shall forthwith declare* the candidate who has received ... the greatest number of votes, to be duly elected as President' (emphasis added). The effect of the emphasised words is to impose a mandatory obligation on the Chief Elections Officer. First, he *must* declare the winning candidate to be duly elected as President. He has no discretion in the matter. Secondly, he must do this 'forthwith'. The meaning of 'forthwith' was considered by the High Court in *Hickman and Another v Minister of Home Affairs* (at 185) where it was held to mean 'as soon as reasonably possible in the circumstances.' Implicit in this definition is the idea that the action concerned must proceed unless reasonable grounds exist justifying and making explicable any delay.

For the reasons set out above, Tsvangirai ought to have been declared the winner of the presidential election. But the fact that no such declaration was made does not change the fact that, legally, he was entitled to become President after the 'first' election.

Conclusion

Unless and until all those participating in elections in Zimbabwe are properly afforded the protection of law, the prospects for genuinely democratic elections will remain slim. The requirement of legality and the rule of law cannot be satisfied merely by setting out fine words on a piece of paper. It is essential that those concepts are upheld by those administering the election concerned. Sadly, there is little sign of that happening in Zimbabwe at the moment.

The Presidential Election was a fiasco because of one man: Robert Mugabe. His vast executive and legislative powers enabled him to undermine, both directly and indirectly, the democratic process. He appointed the members of the country's electoral institutions. The violence and intimidation perpetrated by members of ZANU(PF) made it impossible for Tsvangirai to participate in the 27 June 'run-off' election. Like Shakespeare's Richard III Mugabe was '... determined to prove a villain'.[35] Sadly, he succeeded. Illegality blocked the winds of change.

35 Shakespeare, William, *Richard III*. Act 1, scene 1, verse 30.

References

Judgments

African and European Investment Co v Warren, 1924 AD 308.

Executive Council, Western Cape Legislature and Others v President of the Republic of South Africa and Others, 1995 (10) BCLR (CC).

Forum party of Zimbabwe and Others v Minister of Local Government, Rural and Urban Development and Others, 1996 (1) ZLR 461 (H).

Hambly v Chief Immigration Officer (1), 1995 (2) ZLR 264 (H).

Hickman and Another v Minister of Home Affairs, 1983 (1) ZLR 180 (H).

In Re Mlambo 1991 (2) ZLR 339 (S).
Marimo and Another v Minister of Justice and Another, not yet reported, judgment no. S-25-06.
Minister of State for Immigraiton and Ethnic Affairs v Teoh (1995) 128 ALR 353.
Movement for Democratic Change and Another v Chairperson of the Zimbabwe Electoral Commission and Another, not yet reported, judgment no HH E/P 24/08.
Movement for Democratic Change v President of the Republic of Zimbabwe and Others, not yet reported, judgment no HH 28-2007.
Shumba and Another v ZEC and Another, not yet reported, judgment no. SC 11/08.
Tsvangirai v Registrar General and Others, 2002 (1) ZLR 268 (S).

Legislation

Constitution of Zimbabwe
Electoral Act
The Zimbabwe Electoral Commission Act (ZECA)
Presidential Powers (Temporary) Measures Act

7

Theft by Numbers
ZEC's Role in the 2008 Elections
John Makumbe

Introduction

Prior to the setting up of the Zimbabwe Electoral Commission (ZEC), most of the work of refining the voters roll and monitoring elections was undertaken by the now defunct Electoral Supervisory Commission (ESC). The five members of the ESC were all appointed by the President, which clearly affected its objectivity. In a critical study of the 1995 Parliamentary Elections in Zimbabwe, John Makumbe and Daniel Compagnon[1] identify the following as some of the major weaknesses of the ESC:

- The appointment of all the commissioners by the President, who is himself a member of one of the contesting political parties in an election, effectively erodes the ESC's impartiality in the management of the electoral process;[2]
- Dismissal of commissioners from the ESC was vested only in the President;[3]
- The Constitution of Zimbabwe did not extend any executive powers to the ESC, and this effectively made it impotent, and it became '...a mere consultative and weak body';[4]
- For the most part, virtually all members of the ESC were prominent ZANU(PF) members.

Demands by opposition political parties and civil society organizations for the reform of the electoral law, and the government's purported attempt to comply with the SADC Principles and Guidelines Governing Democratic Elections, eventually resulted in the creation of the ZEC as a parallel elec-

---

1   Makumbe, John and Daniel Compagnon (2000) *Behind the Smokescreen: The 1995 General Elections in Zimbabwe*. University of Zimbabwe Publications, Harare, p. 340.
2   As Section 61 of the Constitution then provided.
3   As Section 9 of the Electoral Act Chapter 2:13 then provided.
4   Makumbe and Compagnon, p. 13.

toral body in 2005.[5] The purpose of this chapter is to critically examine the role that the ZEC played in the harmonised elections of 2008. We proceed from the basic premise that the ZEC is not an effective and autonomous electoral body. Institutionally weak and politically partisan, it effectively seeks to promote and protect the interests of ZANU(PF). The ZEC's role in the so-called harmonized elections of 2008 essentially amounted to theft by numbers as the institution sought to defy the winds of democratic change that were blowing throughout Zimbabwe.

Methodological note

This chapter is largely reflective in its approach. Media reports, interviews with key informants and direct access to a few members of the ZEC – who agreed to participate on condition of anonymity[6] – have informed our analysis and conclusions.

Institutional characteristics of the ZEC

According to the ZEC website, the commission was established by Section 61 of the Constitution of Zimbabwe through the promulgation of Constitutional Amendment Act No 17, (Act 5 of 2005), which defines its membership, the appointment of members, and its functions. The ZEC is constituted of seven members appointed by the President, three of whom must be women.[7] The tenure of office for the commissioners is five years.[8] (This is significant in that if, for example, the next elections are held within two or three years, they will be presided over by the same commissioners who oversaw the 2008 polls.) The chairperson is appointed after consultation with the Judicial Service Commission, while the other six commissioners are appointed from a list of nominees submitted by the Parliamentary Committee on Standing Rules and Orders. The day-to-day operations of the ZEC fall under the direction of the Chief Elections Officer, who is constitutionally the head of the secretariat,[9] a very small,

---

5   The Zimbabwe Electoral Commission Act, Act 22 of 2004, Chapter 2:12. Since the Electoral Supervisory Commission was established by virtue of the constitution, a constitutional amendment was thus required (see immediately below) to avoid the duplication of electoral administrative bodies and replace the ESC. There was thus considerable confusion over the functions of each for purposes of the 2005 election.

6   It is well known that ZANU(PF) does not take kindly to negative exposure of its political activities by persons who are otherwise considered to be beneficiaries of the regime's benevolence, however defined.

7   Section 61(10(a) and (b) of the Constitution.

8   Schedule One paragraph 1(1) of the Amended Zimbabwe Electoral Commission Act, Chapter 2:12.

9   Section 11 of the Act.

limited entity when compared to the scale of ZEC's task. Such an inadequate administrative structure has resulted in serious inadequacies on the part of the ZEC. These have attracted strong criticism, primarily from opposition political parties.

Functions

The Constitution of Zimbabwe (61(4)) outlines the following as the main functions of the ZEC:

- To prepare for, conduct and supervise all elections and referenda.
- To ensure that those elections and referenda are conducted efficiently, freely, fairly, transparently and in accordance with the law.
- To direct and control the registration of voters by the authority charged with that responsibility under the Act of Parliament.
- To compile voters rolls and registers.
- To ensure the proper custody and maintenance of voters rolls and registers.
- To design, print and distribute ballot papers, approve the form of and procure ballot boxes, and establish and operate polling centres.
- To accredit observers and journalists for elections and referendums in accordance with an Act of Parliament.
- To conduct voter education.
- To supervise the registration of voters by the authority charged with that responsibility under the Electoral Law.
- To give instructions to the Registrar General of Voters in regard to the exercise of his functions under the Electoral Law or any other law.
- To demarcate electoral boundaries.
- To give instructions to any other persons in the employment of the state or of a local authority for the purpose of ensuring the efficient, proper, free and fair conduct of elections or referenda.
- To keep the public informed on the delimitation of constituencies and other electoral boundaries; the location of polling stations and when they open for inspection; political parties and candidates contesting every election or supporting or opposing any question put to a referendum.
- To exercise any other functions that may be conferred or imposed on the commission by the Electoral Act or any other enactment.

The numerous problems encountered by opposition political parties and their candidates during the 2008 harmonised elections reveal that the ZEC did not execute its duties to the standards required. We shall now briefly discuss some of the findings of this study in relation to selected functions of the ZEC.

Operational ineptitude of the ZEC

In terms of resources and capacity, the ZEC is institutionally incapable of performing such an enormous task as the preparation of the voting register.[10] During the run-up to the 2008 harmonized elections, there were numerous complaints from political parties regarding the accuracy of the register. Indeed, the ZEC itself admitted that the voters roll used in the 29 March, 2008 poll was '...in shambles'. This confirmed opposition parties' accusations that the roll was 'a mess', according to media reports. Although the chairman of the ZEC admitted to the deplorable nature of the voters roll, he nonetheless argued that it was still one of the most credible in the world. In fact, the voter register was actually prepared by the Registrar-General – purportedly under the supervision of the ZEC. Some opposition political parties claimed to have unearthed around 8,000 'ghost voters' listed on the roll in just one undeveloped stand near Hatcliffe. Indeed, an interesting feature of the register is the claim by the ZEC that 5,934,768 people had registered to vote in the harmonised elections.[11] With an estimated population of 13 million, this would represent 45 per cent of the total, approximately 50 per cent of whom would be children or under voting age. This must also be read in the context of the HIV/AIDS pandemic, and the fact that some three million Zimbabweans are estimated to have left the country in the past ten years. It soon became clear that the ZEC had actively inflated the number of registered voters, particularly in rural areas, the alleged stronghold of ZANU(PF). Indeed, the figures that later obtained at the polls were a far cry from the purported 5,9 million voters. The ZEC's own website indicates that a total of 2,49 million valid votes were cast during the harmonised elections.[12] It is obvious that during the run-up to the polls the ZEC was playing a numbers' game aimed at ensuring Mugabe's and ZANU(PF)'s victory. This theft by numbers was, however, thwarted or overwhelmed by the level of support received by Morgan Tsvangirai and his MDC; the rigging that the ZEC may have engaged in was not successful in giving Mugabe and ZANU(PF) an electoral victory.

The ZEC was further accused of failing to ensure that all political parties and registered candidates would be accorded adequate and equitable coverage by the public media.[13] State-owned and -controlled media are

10 Since its formation, the ESC had never been able to maintain a valid voter register. There are numerous complaints about deceased people and people who have long since migrated from Zimbabwe appearing on the register.
11 *The Herald*, 13 March 2008.
12 Zimbabwe Electoral Commission. Harare, 2008. http://www.zimbabweelectoralcommission.org/
13 *The Herald*, 4 March 2008.

notorious for shunning opposition political parties and their activities, while providing ZANU(PF) with ample coverage during elections.[14] In its self-defence, the ZEC accused political parties of manhandling media personnel when they tried to cover certain rallies.[15] In practice, the ZEC simply does not have the power to enforce its own regulations regarding fair media coverage in an election or referendum, a fact that emphasizes its lack of institutional autonomy. State-owned media houses will always comply with the political preferences of ZANU(PF) rather than with issues of fairness. The ZEC cannot ensure a level playing field; even had they the will to do so, they do not have the capacity. In conclusion, the ZEC was not able to ensure that the harmonised elections were conducted '...efficiently, freely, fairly, transparently and in accordance with the law'.

With regard to conducting voter education, the Zimbabwe Electoral Commission Act (section 15(1)) empowers the ZEC to license civic organizations wishing to participate in this exercise.[16] The ZEC is itself far too small and under-resourced to undertake any meaningful voter education. During the 2008 elections, it placed several advertisements in the media as a way of fulfilling this responsibility; they were seriously limited in terms of their content and outreach, since only a fraction of the population has access to mainstream media facilities. Some advertisements urged people to inspect the voter register but without indicating where this could be done. Others urged people to register to vote, long after the deadline for doing so had passed. Furthermore, some advertisements incorrectly stated what documentation had to be produced before voting (see Chapter 3). Meantime, the ZEC insisted that any civic groups undertaking voter education without its approval would be deemed to have breached the law.[17] (This provision of the ZEC Act may actually be unconstitutional since it is not consistent with clause 20 of the Constitution of Zimbabwe, which provides for freedom of expression.)

The Zimbabwe Election Support Network (ZESN), for example, was barred from conducting voter education by the ZEC, which alleged that it had not been licensed to do so.[18] The Mugabe regime has never been comfortable with progressive civil society organizations when it comes to voter education. Civic groups have generally been accused of aiding opposition political parties while negating ZANU(PF)'s achievements in liberating the country from colonialism. The civic education provision of the ZEC Act was designed to ensure that the content of programmes would not challenge whatever the ruling ZANU(PF) party preferred or even desired.

Because of its limited capacity, the ZEC needed to recruit election offic-

---

14 Makumbe, John, 'Zimbabwe's Hijacked Election', *Journal of Democracy*, Vol. 13, No. 4, October 2002, pp. 87-101.
15 *The Herald*, 4 March 2008.
16 *The Chronicle*, 28 February 2008.
17 Under Section 15 of the Act.
18 *The Standard*, 17 February 2008.

ials from public institutions. Whereas previously teachers were recruited as electoral officers, the catchment was considerably expanded during the 2008 harmonized elections to include public servants from parastatals, statutory bodies and local authorities.[19] Although more electoral officers were needed, there was obvious fear in the ruling party that some would sabotage ZANU(PF)'s performance in the contest, while favouring the MDC. Indeed, many schoolteachers had been victimized ahead of the presidential election run-off on 27 June by militia and war veterans for this supposed reason.[20] Ironically, following the publication of the parliamentary and senatorial election results, several ZEC officials were arrested for alleged electoral fraud, and were said to have prejudiced Robert Mugabe, the ZANU(PF) presidential candidate.[21] The majority of the arrested ZEC officials were not teachers. Charges levelled against them, however, included:

- Tampering with election results and prejudicing ZANU(PF) presidential candidate of 4,993 votes.
- Fraud or criminal abuse of duty as public officers.
- Prejudicing Mugabe of 1,392 votes, and a further 773 votes.
- Manipulation of votes to prejudice Mugabe of 1,000 and 1,828 votes.
- Accepting bribes to 'doctor' election results during the counting of votes to prejudice ZANU(PF).
- Conniving with the opposition to manipulate election results in favour of the MDC.
- Influencing voters to vote for the opposition.[22]

Needless to say, most of the arrested officials were acquitted since the state found it difficult to prove that they had deliberately committed these offences. Only four were convicted and fined.[23] What is of interest is that in the past, when Mugabe and his ZANU(PF) were winning elections, no ZEC or ESC officials were ever suspected of electoral fraud or arrested. The ruling party's defeat in the parliamentary and presidential elections struck a raw nerve, and ZEC officials were made scapegoats. Indeed, ZANU(PF) turned upon anyone who could be held responsible; ZEC officials were soft targets against whom the former ruling party could vent its political fury. ZANU(PF) could not accept that the MDC was as popular with the voters as the election results indicated. The ZEC did nothing to assist its own hapless electoral officials.

Perhaps the most disturbing story in this respect concerns the late Ignatius Mushangwe, a senior ZEC official who went missing during the run-up

19 *The Herald*, 23 February 2008.
20 Human Rights NGO Forum, June 2008.
21 *The Herald,* 8 April 2008.
22 Ibid., and 24 April 2008.
23 *The Herald*, 11 April 2008.

to the violent presidential run-off.[24] Mushangwe had apparently attended a heated meeting of the multi-party liaison committee[25] in Harare on 10 June 2008:

> ...a source who attended the... meeting said... Mushangwe had clashed with senior security officers after he told the meeting that ZEC would only issue out postal ballots to [police] officers who would be on duty. The following week when the committee met, Mushangwe was not present. Other members asked about his whereabouts but one official told the meeting ... 'You won't see him again.'[26]

Some five months later, his body was found in a mortuary in Norton. It is widely believed that he had been murdered by state security officials for insisting that the regulations for running the harmonized elections and postal ballots be scrupulously followed.[27] The ZEC failed to condemn this brutal act. By pretending that nothing untoward had happened when its own official was assassinated for simply following electoral laws and procedures, it wantonly undermined its own credibility.

Further, the allegations levelled against ZEC officials, whether imagined or real, indicate that it is institutionally incapable of instilling in its officials any sense of ethical conduct in the execution of their duties. The electoral management process designed and followed by the ZEC gives excessive discretion to electoral officials, thereby creating a working environment highly conducive to the commission of electoral fraud and other criminal offences. The fact that most of the ZEC electoral officials were merely hired hands meant that their commitment to the organization and its reputation was questionable. Their recruitment and training did not adequately equip them to resist temptation to act in an unethical manner. More important, is the fact that ZANU(PF) has, over the years, created an electoral culture that thrives on fraud and corruption. Every electoral official is therefore suspected of manipulating the process in favour of whichever political party or candidate they may support. Perhaps the fact that the majority of Zimbabweans were desperate for change and for the defeat of ZANU(PF) also contributed to the alleged proliferation of cases of electoral fraud during the harmonized elections of 2008 in Zimbabwe.[28]

One of the key functions of the ZEC is that of accrediting election observers and journalists. In order to get accredited, foreign journalists were required to pay in foreign currency. Those from media houses within Africa were asked to pay US$100 each while those who worked

---

24   *The Standard*, 19-25 October 2008.
25   A committee set up by the ZEC during the campaign period to discuss issues raised by political parties and contestants with regard to the electoral process.
26   *The Standard*, 19-25 October 2008.
27   Ibid.
28   The MDC filed a total of 35 petitions, while ZANU(PF) filed 38 cases where they sought the intervention and investigation of the Electoral Court in order to determine the accuracy of the published results.

for non-African media houses were asked to pay US$300.[29] Further, foreign observers and journalists were required to bring with them a letter of invitation from the Ministry of Foreign Affairs. In addition, the journalists had to be accredited with the Media and Information Commission (MIC). These controls provided both a way for the government to make money and a means of controlling, if not manipulating, foreign opinion on the electoral process. In other words, the regime was determined to ensure that observers and journalists from countries considered hostile to the ZANU(PF) government would not be accredited.

During the presidential run-off election on 27 June, the ZEC claimed that there was a high turnout of voters throughout the country, especially in rural areas. This claim was manifestly false, as observers pointed out that most polling stations were practically empty throughout polling day.[30] Here again, the ZEC was attempting to play a fraudulent numbers' game, i.e. suggesting that Mugabe had suddenly become very popular with the voters at the expense of Tsvangirai. Few voters were foolish enough to believe the ZEC's stories and figures and the official results of the presidential run-off election were dismissed both in Zimbabwe and throughout the southern African region.

Political violence

One of the key functions of the ZEC is, 'To give instructions to any other persons in the employment of the State or of a local authority for the purpose of ensuring the efficient, proper, free and fair conduct of elections or referendum.'[31] It is our submission that given the widespread violence that engulfed the nation before the presidential election run-off (see Chapter 5), the ZEC failed to perform this critical function. Not once did it issue a statement or release an advertisement condemning political violence or decrying the likely impact of violence on the conduct of free and fair elections. The reason for this is not at all difficult to ascertain. As has already been stated, the composition of the ZEC and the appointment of its members by President Mugabe are partisan. For the ZEC to condemn political violence would be to criticize the political party on whom it depends for its existence. There is ample evidence that most incidents of violence were committed by elements within ZANU(PF). As the Zimbabwe Human Rights NGO Forum noted:

> The information and evidence that is in possession of the Human Rights Forum points to a situation of an organized and well-orchestrated plan of action to

---

29 *The Herald*, 3 March 2008.
30 Tsvangirai's withdrawal acted as a major disincentive for people to go and vote, both in urban and rural areas.
31 Government of Zimbabwe, 1980.

annihilate the MDC party structures countrywide and to instil fear in the electorate before the 27 June Run-off.

These characteristics were noted in an alert produced by the Human Rights Forum soon after the 29 March elections when the violence escalated. The Human Rights Forum maintains that after aareful analysis of the reports to the end of the month of April, the situation remains unchanged. The characteristics of the violence remain as follows:

- All reports show that the violence has been disproportionately one-sided, and against the MDC and other groups not supporting ZANU PF;
- All reports show that the violence attributed to ZANU PF is different from the violence attributed the other groups, both in the scale and in the nature;
- The violence attributed to ZANU PF shows evidence of systematic torture, abductions, disappearance, summary executions and extra-judicial killings, and this is very rarely the case with violence attributed to other groups such as the MDC;
- The systematic torture shows a strong associations with officials of the State – members of parliament, the police, the CIO, and other officials – as well as an association with groups closely affiliated to the ZANU PF political party – 'war veterans', youth militia, ZANU PF youth, ZANU PF supporters, ZANU PF party officials, etc;
- The evidence shows there are plausible allegations of the involvement of senior party and government leaders, and there are many statements from victims implicating such persons;
- There is no, or very little, evidence of any attempt by the executive or organs of the State to pro-actively deal with the violence;
- The evidence suggests, to the contrary, that there are an enormous number of examples of hate speech, and encouragement to violence and lawlessness by virtually all members of the executive, the parliament, the party, and the supporters of the ZANU PF party.[32]

The ZEC's failure to condemn political violence constitutes a serious dereliction of duty. Instead of condemning violence as not conducive to free and fair elections, the Commission rejected Morgan Tsvangirai's withdrawal from the June run-off arguing that his notification had come too late.[33] This view was consistent with what Mugabe and ZANU(PF) wanted, since the President faced a rather embarrassing situation of participating in a one-horse race as a result of his opponent's withdrawal.[34] ZEC's autonomy was severely undermined by its own inaction regarding the widespread violence during the run-up to the run-off presidential election, and its standing was undermined by a bias that was transparent for all to see.

---

32 Zimbabwe Human Rights NGO Forum, June 2008, p. 4.
33 The Electoral Act is silent on when a withdrawal from a run-off election is permissible.
34 This was disclosed by a state agent whose identity cannot be divulged for personal safety reasons.

Delayed results

Legislation provides for the release of election results by the ZEC officials as soon as they become available. However, it carefully stage-managed the announcement of parliamentary and senatorial results for the 29 March poll. Both senatorial and parliamentary results were announced in such a way that the MDC and ZANU(PF) were always at par in terms of the seats that each had won. This went on for some 24 hours and only ended when they could no longer hide the fact that the MDC had defeated ZANU(PF) at the parliamentary level. To this day it is not clear why the ZEC engaged in such a futile exercise. It may be true that it was an attempt to manage possible outbreaks of violence; or they may simply have wanted keep the nation guessing for as long as possible while they waited for further instructions on how to proceed. It is also possible that the process, prolonged over two days, enabled the ZEC to buy more time to manipulate the numbers pertaining to those seats where ZANU(PF) had lost to MDC candidates.

Perhaps the most glaring example of the ZEC's ineptitude was demonstrated when the commission failed to release the results of the presidential election for five weeks after polling day. The *Zimbabwe Independent* reported that the results were withheld on the instructions of Mugabe:

> Staring defeat in the face after week-end polls, President Robert Mugabe has gone on the offensive, directing the Zimbabwe Electoral Commission (ZEC) to delay the result in order to manage a political crisis triggered by his defeat. Sources said the delay was part of government's crisis management plan following clear indications that Mugabe had lost the election to Morgan Tsvangirai of the Movement for Democratic Change (MDC)... Mugabe is said to have ordered the withholding of the results to buy time to manage his defeat and allow the three weeks for the run-off to elapse, creating new circumstances for him to try to survive.[35]

That the ZEC complied with such blatant manipulation of the electoral process is adequate testimony that it was at the beck and call of the President. A ZEC official is reported to have admitted that they had been told to hold onto the numbers as Mugabe was attempting '...to manage a potentially volatile situation'.[36] As it was, it provided just another instance of the Commission's credibility being undermined by its own actions. It was clear to most analysts that Mugabe was deliberately extending his term of office by taking advantage of selected provisions of the Constitution of Zimbabwe or other pieces of legislation. Derek Matyszak writes:

> The first mechanism by which Mugabe extended his term of office was by a protracted delay in announcing the results. A president remains in office after

35 *Zimbabwe Independent*, 4 April 2008.
36 Ibid.

an election until the entry into office of the next elected president. The person is duly elected on the day a winner of the poll is declared, and after taking the oath of office, and must assume office within 48 hours of being declared duly elected. A delay in announcing the result effectively suspends these provisions. In the event, it delayed the run-off. [37]

Two tactics were deployed to this end. The ZEC disingenuously announced that with over 9,000 polling stations, the task of collating the figures was a difficult and time-consuming exercise and that results were still awaited. This explanation was inherently implausible. The procedure for the counting of the vote, the announcement of the results and the time-frame for the process is reasonably straightforward and is set out in the Second Schedule and sections 61 to 67 and 112 of the Electoral Act.

Further, the ZEC did not comply with its own procedures for handling election results, and for their conveyance from ward level to the so-called National Command Centre. For example, unlike in previous elections, the ballot papers for all candidates were counted at the polling stations and the results posted outside for all to see. Indeed, it was this practice that enabled the MDC to total the results and claim victory for Tsvangirai well ahead of the publication of the official results. Subsequently, however, the violation of procedures by the ZEC indicated a desperate attempt to safeguard a possible defeat of Mugabe and ZANU(PF). In a detailed analysis of the delay in announcing the presidential results, Matyszak makes the following specific observations:

> ZEC did not comply with the procedures it had itself spelt out. Firstly, ZEC arrogated to itself the right to announce the results for the Houses of Parliament, despite the fact that the Constituency Elections Officers had announced the results forthwith as required at constituency level many days before the results were announced by the National Command Centre and all that was required was for these results to be made more widely known. When ZEC was challenged on this point in the MDC's court application, the Chairperson of ZEC conceded that the results are announced at constituency level and that ZEC was merely assisting the nation by revealing the results nationally. The results were released painfully slowly and initially for the House of Assembly only, at the rate of about 40 a day. Furthermore, the manner in which they were released was both curious and revealing. The results were released as if ZEC were dealing a pack of cards to the two parties, adopting a one each approach. Hence, at the end of each broadcast there was a rough parity of seats won between the two parties. In order to accomplish this, ZEC must have had the results of all constituencies to know that the process could be continued until all results had been disclosed. Yet ZEC sought to explain the delay by maintaining that results were still awaited from far flung polling stations. In view of the 'one each' approach this explanation was already implausible, but rendered more so by the fact that the results released bore no relation to their distance from the command centre. Results from outlying rural areas were given well in advance of results for

37 Matyszak, Derek, *An Inconvenient Truth Parts I and II*, Research and Advocacy Unit, Harare, 2008.

constituencies in Harare. Given that the National Command Centre must have had all the House of Assembly results in order to release them in this manner, the presidential returns must also have been received and the Chief Elections Officer was obliged to proceed as described above. He did not.[38]

A week after the polls, lawyers representing the MDC filed a High Court application seeking to compel the ZEC to announce the presidential election results.[39] The lawyers pointed out that the Commission must have received the results of the presidential race at the same time that it had received the results of the House of Assembly and senatorial elections.

Therefore, the ZEC's failure to release the presidential results was deliberate and aimed at appeasing certain specific quarters in the political arena. The same sentiments were echoed by a group of eighteen civil society organizations, which appealed to both the Southern African Development Community (SADC) and the African Union (AU) to intervene.[40] But the ZEC was not disconcerted by any of these moves, and the presidential election results were held in abeyance for five weeks, to the amazement of both regional and international election observers. In fact, the Commission challenged the urgency of the MDC application, but the High Court ruled in favour of the latter.[41] The lawyer handling the opposition political party's case argued that because the ZEC had deliberately failed to act reasonably '...it must be ordered to act. The applicants have the legitimate expectation to have results announced expeditiously.'[42]

Rather than announce the presidential election results, the ZEC proceeded to make use of the MDC's application as an excuse for refusing to comment on their status. They argued that the announcement of these results was now a legal matter before the courts, and that they therefore could not divulge any information until the court had reached a verdict.[43] This arrangement suited ZANU(PF), which was desperately trying to buy time in order to devise ways of salvaging whatever 'political dignity' it could, after it became clear that both the party and Mugabe had been defeated by the MDC in the 29 March polls. In other words, the ZEC was once again working in concert with ZANU(PF) to thwart the people's democratic choice. Given all the above it is ridiculous for the ZEC to claim to be a neutral or non-partisan electoral management body.

When the results of the presidential contest were finally announced, they reflected that the MDC's Morgan Tsvangirai had won 1,195,562 votes (47.9%) while Robert Mugabe of ZANU(PF) had received 1,079,730 votes (43.2%).[44] Since neither of the candidates had apparently won the requisite

---

38 Ibid.
39 *Zimbabwe Independent*, 4 April 2008.
40 Ibid.
41 *The Herald*, 9 April 2008.
42 Ibid.
43 Ibid. 11 April 2008.
44 Ibid. 3 May 2008.

50 per cent of votes plus one or more, it became necessary to conduct a run-off election (see, however, the views expressed by Greg Linington on this point in Chapter 6). ZANU(PF) readily accepted the results, clearly indicating that a way had been found to give Mugabe a second chance.[45] There is, however, considerable suspicion that the ZEC had deliberately participated in the manipulation of the results – probably by reducing Tsvangirai's winning margin to a level below 50 per cent of the valid votes, in order to justify a second round of voting. Indeed, while accepting the announced results on behalf of Mugabe, Emmerson Mnangagwa, a senior member of ZANU(PF), indicated that his party did not believe the results represented the genuine expression of the will of the Zimbabwean people. He also elaborately spelt out what can only be argued to be some of the major weaknesses of the Commission in its management of the electoral process. Mnangagwa stated:

> Given the many anomalies, malpractices, deflation of figures of ZANU(PF) candidates as information was transmitted upwards, inflation of figures relating to opposition candidates as information was transmitted to higher command levels, multiple voting and people who are not on the voters roll being allowed to vote, persons on the voters roll being turned away and not allowed to vote, and irregularities in the manner that handicapped persons were assisted to vote.[46]

Of course, some of these are baseless allegations since none of them were ever proved to have been committed in order to ensure Tsvangirai's victory over Mugabe, though they are tactics surely used by ZANU(PF). So it is an irony that this was the first time that ZANU(PF) had ever raised a complaint against the ZEC or its predecessor, the ESC. It is our contention that it was a case of sour grapes. Mugabe had lost the election to Tsvangirai and attempted to prepare a plausible explanation for what would appear to be a sudden shift in voter preference for the run-off. Indeed, in previous elections, numerous complaints had been levelled against the ZEC and the ESC in relation to virtually all of the alleged anomalies listed above. It is our submission that as currently structured and constituted, the Commission is a long way from eliminating this type of fraud, nor do they want to do so if it will advantage ZANU(PF). Moreover, the speed – two days – with which the ZEC was able to release the results of the presidential run-off election that Mugabe 'won', compared to the five weeks of the 29 March poll, gave away its deliberate collaboration in theft by numbers with Mugabe and his losing political party.

Finally, legislation requires that a recount of the ballots be conducted within 48 hours of the announcement of the results, providing that a petition to this effect has been submitted by one of the contestants. The various re-counts that the ZEC undertook were carried out long after the stipulated period. Matyszak puts it more succinctly:

45   Ibid.
46   Ibid.

The ZEC initiated recount was thus clearly unlawful. Combined with the judgment of Uchena J., the effect was to delay the release of the result of the presidential election until 2nd May, 2008, and effectively to extend Mugabe's term of office.[47]

The recounts, however, failed to result in any changes to the initial results of the presidential election. It was clearly a futile exercise carried out at ZANU(PF)'s request – or orders – in a desperate attempt to forge a Mugabe win, or minimize the margin by which Tsvangirai had defeated him. This theft by numbers had reached a level that was clearly embarrassing for both Mugabe himself and for the ZEC. The manner in which the ZEC was used as a blunt instrument to defy the winds of democratic change in Zimbabwe is remarkable.

Conclusion

The creation of the ZEC was controversial from the outset since the MDC had vehemently disagreed with the procedures for the appointment of the commissioners. The fact that President Mugabe appointed all the commissioners from the list submitted by the parliamentary committee, albeit some of them after consulting with the Judiciary Services Commission, essentially meant that the electoral commission was inclined to function in a manner partisan to ZANU(PF). The ZEC's handling of the 2008 harmonised elections provides ample evidence of this thesis. Indeed, the commission went so far as to violate laid-down laws, as well as its own procedures, in order to comply with the dictates of a defeated presidential candidate, Robert Mugabe. This chapter has outlined the various ways in which the ZEC engaged in a partisan manner in a futile attempt to thwart the people's choice of a democratically elected leader. There is ample evidence that ZANU(PF) desperately needed the co-operation of the ZEC in order to win the seats it 'won'. The ZEC was apparently willing to be so used, and thus became the key instrument in defying the winds of change in Zimbabwe. We submit here that as presently structured and staffed, the ZEC cannot effectively claim to be a credible and autonomous electoral supervisory and management body. Serious revisions need to be made to existing legislation if the ZEC is to manage free and fair elections in the future.

47 Matyszak, ibid.

8

Civil Society & the Long Election
Derek Matyszak

Introduction

1991 was a watershed year for the Zimbabwean polity. It saw the lifting of a national State of Emergency, imposed by the pre-independence government and renewed six-monthly by the post-independence government of Robert Mugabe and his ruling Zimbabwe African National Union (Patriotic Front) (ZANU(PF)) party. It also saw the accession by Zimbabwe to the International Covenant on Civil and Political Rights, the government's motivation for which was probably to gain access to badly needed International Monetary Fund (IMF) balance of payments support. The result, however, gave the impression that Zimbabwe had entered a 'glasnost'-like period. The removal of the State of Emergency meant that the Declaration of Rights provided for in Zimbabwe's Constitution became fully operational. There was no longer a possibility of people being legally detained indefinitely and without trial.

Despite the fact that in this period independent publications clearly felt more freely able to level criticism at the government, such criticism was restrained and somewhat muted. Notwithstanding the massacres of civilians which had taken place in Matabeleland in the early years of independence under 'Operation Gukurahundi' – which the Shona-dominated government claimed was aimed at dealing with violent 'dissidents' of the minority Ndebele ethnic group – Mugabe enjoyed extensive immunity from criticism. As an iconic leader of the party which had rescued Zimbabwe from white minority rule, any of his critics faced the risk of being portrayed as motivated by white reactionary racism. Criticism from the left was minimal and was regarded as the impractical and ineffectual sentiments of quixotic ideologues.

This situation changed dramatically in 1996 when a small non-governmental organization (NGO) of gay and lesbian activists, the Gays and Lesbians of Zimbabwe (GALZ), decided to utilise the democratic space which had opened for civil society. The government very publicly but illegally declared that it would prevent GALZ from participating in the annual Zimbabwe International Book Fair in Harare. The ban had been preceded by a series of vitriolic and derogatory attacks by Mugabe on gays and lesbians in Zimbabwe and generally. Mugabe saw his public homophobic pronouncements as a populist opportunity to garner support from an increasingly disenchanted electorate which was feeling an economic pinch that the IMF structural adjustment programme had exacerbated rather than ameliorated. GALZ successfully challenged the government's ban through the courts, relying on constitutional provisions relating to freedom of speech and assembly. For the first time, Mugabe's government had been successfully and very publicly defied. The affair opened the door for constitutionalism and the courts to be used successfully against governmental oppression. But, more importantly, Mugabe's strident homophobia burst the enveloping bubble of political correctness which had shielded him and his government from criticism.

The result was increased confidence and activism amongst the few extant civil and human rights NGOs, such as ZimRights, and the growth of new NGOs with a human rights mandate. At this time, a series of policy blunders by the government led to a worsening of socio-economic conditions. In 1997, Mugabe unilaterally ordered a large and unbudgeted pay-out and pension increase for restless liberation war veterans, many of whom were unemployed and felt the economic downturn more acutely than others. The result was a dramatic, overnight fall in the value of the Zimbabwe dollar. Mugabe then sought to rescue the economy from further decline by (again unilaterally) deciding to enter into a disastrous military adventure. Mugabe hoped that Zimbabwe would reap financial rewards for defending the Kabila government in the mineral-rich Democratic Republic of the Congo (DRC). The opposite occurred. The war was an immediate and substantial imposition on Zimbabwe's fiscus which required urgent support rather than having demands placed upon it against hypothetical and deferred benefits. Furthermore, the IMF resolved to withhold balance of payments support until Zimbabwe withdrew its troops from the DRC. Inflation reached an unprecedented 50 per cent per annum. With subsidies removed from staple foodstuffs in accordance with IMF policies, food prices soared. The result was rioting over the price of bread in January, 1998. In targeting government property, such as police vehicles, rather than retailers, rioters clearly showed who they blamed for the price increases.

The response of the government informed the subsequent policies of civil society, opposition activist groups and supporters, and is important for an understanding of their *modus operandi* thereafter. The government mobilized both the police and the army. Rather than simply try to quell the disturbances, the mandate of the army and police was clearly to 'teach the urban populace a lesson'. Indiscriminate and brutal violence was unleashed. Innocent motorists, passers-by and almost anyone the army or police happened to encounter were liable to receive a rifle butt in the face, or some other form of beating. The army and police fired live ammunition randomly at large groups of people, regardless of any threat they presented. By the end of the operation, eight people had been shot dead, hundreds more severely injured, and thousands unlawfully arrested and detained for extended periods.

The police and army periodically revise the lesson of the food riots by using live ammunition with lethal effect against those who still have the courage to demonstrate against the government. This fact is often overlooked by those who question why an 'orange' or 'popular' revolution has not taken place in Zimbabwe. The storming of the Bastille, which heralded the end to the despotism of Louis XVI, would not have been possible but for the fact that the French Guard decided to align itself with the people of Paris. In recent times, 'orange' revolutions have only succeeded where it has been correctly anticipated that the military will remain passive. Calls for mass demonstrations in Zimbabwe rarely bring more than a few hundred people out onto the streets. Demonstrations have thus been discredited as a means of exerting any effective pressure on the Mugabe government; they result simply in arrests and extended periods of incarceration for the participants.

The current role of civil society

Human and civil rights organizations in Zimbabwe thus have largely confined their activities to monitoring, documenting and exposing violations and providing assistance to victims. This has taken the form of measuring the extent of freedom of assembly, association and expression, and freedom from arbitrary and wrongful arrest; examining the nature, extent and effect of undemocratic legislation; documenting and providing legal and medical assistance to victims of political violence; and assessing the framework, context and conduct of elections in Zimbabwe against democratic norms.

Following the food riots of early 1998, seventeen NGOs came together to form the Zimbabwe Human Rights NGO Forum ('the Forum') with the objective of providing co-ordinated assistance to detainees, victims of political violence and persons complaining of rights violations. This alliance remains a focal point for human rights monitoring today and is one of the few bodies reflecting an effective collaborative response from Zimbabwe's notoriously fractured civil society. It allows for extremely effective monitoring of the human and civil rights terrain. When victims of rights violations and political violence approach member organizations, such as the Counselling Services Unit, or Zimbabwe Lawyers for Human Rights, for assistance and redress, qualitative and quantitative data are compiled and forwarded to the Forum for collation. The Forum then produces 'Monthly Political Violence Reports', which constitute an effective barometer of democratic freedoms, political tolerance and political violence. In addition, the Forum draws on the jurisprudential and human rights activist experience of its members to examine the legislative and human rights framework within which elections are held in Zimbabwe. All elections since 2000 have thus been the subject of pre- and post-election reports; these have played a crucial role in exposing dishonest attempts by the government to present deeply flawed elections as being free and fair. Furthermore, it should be borne in mind that the government maintains strict control over the presence of international election observers, and since 2002 has ensured that only observers deemed sympathetic to the ruling party have been allowed into the country.

Civil society election reports have embarrassed sympathetic regional observers into moderating statements about the Zimbabwean electoral process that have tended to suggest a legitimate outcome in the face of considerable evidence to the contrary. For example, the South African government's observer mission's initial report pronounced the 2000 parliamentary elections 'free and fair' because the two days of voting had been marked by 'tranquillity', ignoring the numerous violations of human rights and extensive violence and intimidation in the months that had preceded the voting. On return to South Africa, and in the face of substantive evidence from NGO electoral reports to the contrary, the report was amended, and 'free and fair' was replaced with 'credible'. The electoral reports gave the South African opposition ample basis to challenge even this moderated finding.

Similarly, given the information supplied by civil society, the South African government's observer group dared to do no more than announce the 2002 presidential election as 'legitimate', rather than free and fair. The electoral reports again ensured that this disingenuous finding by the South African group was not without political cost when presented to the South African parliament.

Apart from the electoral reports produced by the Forum and other NGOs, reports by the Zimbabwe Peace Project (ZPP) are of particular significance.[1] These reveal that in 2007, the organization established a national and rural-focused monitoring system to assess levels of violence in the impending elections. The system is a three-tier network comprising trained Monitors, Provincial Co-ordinators, and Investigators, which allows for rapid verification of evidence in terms of source, circumstances,

1   See, for example, ZPP July 2008: *Run Up to 27th June 2008 Presidential Run Off Election.*

136

perpetrators and victims. Because the network is country-wide and based in the rural areas, the reports are a powerful and extremely credible resource for determining the extent of electoral malpractice and intimidation, and they provide independent and corroborative evidence for the publications produced by the Forum and others.

During electoral periods the Zimbabwe Election Support Network (ZESN), a conglomeration of 38 NGOs, plays a crucial and central role. ZESN's objective is 'promoting democratic elections' in Zimbabwe. Accordingly, it is inevitable in considering civil society and the 2008 harmonized elections that the spotlight will fall on ZESN more than on any other NGO.

To accomplish its objectives, ZESN employs Long Term Observers who monitor electoral conditions nationally prior to elections, Short Term Observers who monitor the actual voting, and Community Educators who carry out voter education. Its reports on the actual voting thus provide an important and impartial assessment of the voting process. In this regard the Media Monitoring Project of Zimbabwe (MMPZ) plays a useful auxiliary role. The MMPZ monitors all electronic and print media in Zimbabwe, calculating the air time given to ZANU(PF) and MDC 'voices' in the electoral period, and exposing any bias and violation of electoral regulations.

The harmonized elections of 29 March 2008

Before considering the role of civil society during these elections it is worth taking note of the stance adopted by the National Constitutional Assembly (NCA). The NCA comprises a diverse and large grouping of NGOs, individual members and even political parties, and is a single-issue organization, which has as its objective the introduction of a people-driven constitution for Zimbabwe. The NCA's central premise is that, given the inordinate powers held by Mugabe and the inadequate protection afforded to civil and human rights under the current constitution, no political change will or can be effected until a new constitution is in place. The NCA is sceptical of change through the elections due to the power Mugabe has over the electoral process and his control of the police and security forces. Consistent with this stance, the NCA expressed doubt that the harmonized elections would yield anything positive for the Zimbabwean electorate, and that, even if the opposition won the elections, doubted whether the result would be respected by the Mugabe regime. Nonetheless, departing from the non-partisan position formally adopted by NGOs, the head of the NCA, Lovemore Madhuku, encouraged the organization's constituents to vote for the MDC in the elections.

As outlined above, and as is usual, many human rights NGOs published reports on the pre-election conditions and on the conduct of the poll. All reported that the elections held on 29 March 2008 conformed more closely with democratic requirements for free and fair elections than any other in Zimbabwe's history. They were certainly the most free in that, for the first time, opposition parties were able to campaign in rural areas – including places which had in the past been regarded as ZANU(PF) strongholds and had been turned into no-go areas for opposition party supporters during election periods. Furthermore, for the first time, the MDC was able to flight party political campaign material in the state-controlled media well before polling day. This was highly significant in that not only was the opposition party able to disseminate its message nationally, but the very fact of being able to do so was highly symbolic and conveyed a message that would not have been lost on the electorate. This message was that ZANU(PF) no longer enjoyed monolithic and all-pervasive control over every aspect of Zimbabwean society. The pre-electoral period was not characterized by the endemic violence that had been the hallmark of previous elections. It is quite likely that the opening of democratic space for the harmonized elections was a result of the South African-brokered negotiations between ZANU(PF) and the MDC. South Africa's then president, Thabo Mbeki, had probably persuaded Mugabe that the means to the resolution of the crisis in Zimbabwe was for the poll to be seen and accepted as free and fair both regionally and internationally (an issue discussed elsewhere in this volume).

As NGOs pointed out, however, the 'freeness' of the election was not without blemish. As they had done in the past, service chiefs warned that they would not tolerate an opposition victory, and Mugabe also stated that he would never allow the MDC to assume power. De-campaigning electoral rhetoric by ZANU(PF), monitored by MMPZ, lapsed into hate speech well beyond democratic norms, with the MDC being portrayed as an enemy of the country rather than a legitimate opposition party. Several opposition party rallies and meetings were banned by the police or prevented from taking place by ZANU(PF) militants. Traditional leaders threatened villagers with expulsion if they were seen to be supporting the MDC.

Several other factors impaired the 'fairness' of the election. Although the MDC was able to broadcast its advertisements, the MMPZ exposed the state media as remaining heavily biased in favour of the ruling party. Throughout the electoral period, ZTV's nightly 'News Hour' was neither news nor an hour, but rather a two-hour ZANU(PF) party political broadcast during prime-time viewing.

This use of public resources for party political purposes extended to numerous other areas. ZPP reports exposed ZANU(PF)'s retention of close control over vital governmental food distribution programmes, skewed with the objective of ensuring that ruling party supporters received favourable treatment and MDC supporters were excluded. Government vehicles, fuel and other resources were used by ZANU(PF) for campaigning, and farming inputs purchased with government funds were distributed by the party's agents to its supporters.

ZANU(PF) government officials carefully controlled the accreditation of international observers in an attempt (undermined by NGOs) to ensure that this 'unfairness' was not given any public prominence.

There were also several procedural failures and points of contention. The MDC believed that a *quid pro quo* for concessions it had made during the negotiations with ZANU(PF), reinstituted in March 2007, was that (in line with the demands of the NCA) a new constitution for Zimbabwe would be introduced before the elections. Without the introduction of a new constitution, and without reference to the MDC, Mugabe set an early election date.

As NGO legal analysts observed, the precipitate calling of the election led to other procedural irregularities. Many of these were the responsibility of officials of the Zimbabwe Electoral Commission (ZEC). Although legislation introduced in December 2007 changed the Electoral Act and the manner in which ZEC was to be composed, incumbent Commissioners, all appointed by Mugabe, remained in office until their terms expired. As several NGO reports noted, ZEC carried out its duties in a highly partisan and sometimes irregular fashion.[2] Changes to the constitution increased parliamentary constituencies from 120 to 210 for the House of Assembly, and elected seats from 50 to 60 in the Senate, which was to have a further 33 seats occupied *ex-officio* and via presidential appointment. The subsequent delimitation exercise to effect these changes, lacked transparency and failed to follow legislated requirements. Furthermore, the number and location of polling stations established in the newly demarcated wards and constituencies, and eventually publicized by ZEC, contained several inaccuracies.

Similarly, responsibility for the voters roll, a perennial point of contention, fell under ZEC in terms of the new legislation. Compiled by a self-proclaimed ZANU(PF)-supporting Registrar-General, the roll is stuffed with ghost voters and the registration process is biased towards that party's supporters. Previously, the Registrar-General has made examination of the roll as difficult as possible and has refused to supply the MDC with an electronic copy. Changes to the Electoral Act for the harmonized elections required that electronic copies be supplied to all political parties. It was now the duty of ZEC to comply with these changes. In fact, the Commission left the compilation of the voters roll entirely to the Registrar-General, and a prohibitive price was set for electronic copies, requests for which were later turned down by ZEC on the grounds that it did not have the resources to supply the discs. A few requests were met, but only after 210 discs had been supplied. Such a large number of discs was needed because rather than supplying electronic copies as required, the ZEC (or

2   Matyszak, Derek (April 2008)(a). *An Inconvenient Truth Parts I and II*. Research and Advocacy Unit, Harare. Also available on www.kubatana.net.

more correctly the Registrar-General) supplied the roll in JPEG or a similar format; this provides a digital photograph of the roll, rather than an electronic copy, and does not enable electronic audit of the roll. A spreadsheet format would have required a single disc rather than the 210 that were used. Nonetheless, NGOs managed to convert the files and an initial audit exposed the registration of 8,000 voters at a single address.

The increased number of constituencies, consequent revised delimitation, the unprecedented harmonization of all elections and the possibility for the first time of a run-off in the presidential election if none of the four candidates achieved the necessary 50 per cent plus one of votes, heightened the need for voter education. ZEC's own voter education programme began late, was inadequate and was in some instances inaccurate. ZESN was well placed to fill the gaps left by ZEC and, unlike the Commission, it had the resources to do so. However, in mid-February, ZESN received an instruction from ZEC to discontinue all voter education and to withdraw its voter education material from the media. The Commission pointed out that Electoral Regulations required all voter education material to be approved by it. ZESN's subsequent application to ZEC in this regard received no response, and so it was unable to continue with this important activity.

However, together with Radio Dialogue, the Catholic Commission for Justice and Peace, ZimRights, CIVNET (the Civil Education Network Trust), Global Arts Trust, Crisis Coalition, and Women's Trust, ZESN was able to continue with programmes aimed at encouraging people to register and to vote, using workshops, plays and even a music concert to spread their message. But even these – including programmes run by the National Association for the Care of the Handicapped (NASCOH) and the Irish NGO, GOAL – were impeded and their advertisements stopped by ZEC.

In addition to its pre-election reports, analysis of the electoral legislative framework, and voter and civic education, ZESN managed to have 8,667 election observers accredited in the over 9,000 polling stations established by ZEC. Subsequent events were to prove that comprehensive and efficient implementation of the tasks assigned to these observers was vital.

The March election and its aftermath

The March elections proved what had long been claimed by the opposition and human rights NGOs: ZANU(PF) could not win an election in Zimbabwe where there was even anaemic compliance with democratic norms for the conduct of an election. The combined MDC formations overturned the majority that ZANU(PF) had held in the House of Assembly since independence. As detailed elsewhere in this volume, the announcement of the result of the presidential poll was delayed by ZEC, under various pretexts.[3]

3   See also ibid.

Given the method of vote tabulation, these explanations were inherently implausible. The Electoral Act provides that votes must be counted at polling stations and the results immediately posted outside the polling station. ZESN suggests in its Electoral Report[4] that this salutary requirement was introduced by recent amendments to the Electoral Act, and the MDC points to it as one of the victories achieved in the negotiation process. In fact, the requirements had long existed in the Electoral Act, but had never been followed. The amendment did, however, remove an ambiguity relating to the moment in the electoral process when the results had to be posted.

Monitoring the results

In accordance with the Act and as publicized by ZEC, the result of the vote count at each polling station was entered into prescribed forms and forwarded to the ward centres. The forms required the entry of the results for each of the four simultaneous elections: the presidency, two houses of parliament and local government. The returns were added up at ward level, the winner of the local government election for the ward level announced and the totals forwarded to constituency centres. From the constituency, the totals were forwarded to the provincial centres for determination of the Senate results. At each step in the process, the parties' polling agents and candidates could verify and sign the returns. With 60 elected seats in the Senate, by the time returns were presented at provincial level the summation of 60 figures for each of the four presidential candidates would have determined the result of the presidential election. However, the Electoral Act, anomalously, requires that the constituency and not provincial returns are forwarded to the Chief Elections Officer for the determination of the result of the presidential poll. This required adding up 210 figures for each of the four candidates – hardly an onerous task, and one which could have been completed within minutes of the receipt of all constituency returns. The presidential result would thus have been known shortly after the results of the House of Assembly poll, i.e. within about 36 hours of the end of polling.

In fact, ZEC only announced the results of the presidential poll on 2 May 2008. Their figures showed the two front runners, Tsvangirai and Mugabe, to have garnered 47.9 per cent and 43.2 per cent of the vote respectively. It is apparent that ZEC acted on the instructions of ZANU(PF) in withholding the result. The motivation for so doing is less obvious and speculation in this regard is rife.

While the results had caused panic within the Mugabe camp, credible information received by NGOs indicated that, within days of the result being known to the Mugabe administration, a determination had been made

4   ZESN, (October 2008) *Post Election Update*. Harare.

to proceed with a run-off election and to create conditions which would render a Tsvangirai victory impossible. A list of 200 army and police officers chosen to establish nationwide militia bases and co-ordinate a bloody and brutal campaign of intimidation was leaked to the NGO community.

It was thus suggested that the delay in releasing the results was to allow this intimidatory operation to be implemented. In fact, ZEC subsequently claimed that the Electoral Act gave it the power to extend the 21-day maximum period for holding the run-off poll and set the date for 27 June 2008.[5] Accordingly, the date could have been set in this way without the subterfuge of delaying the announcement of the result of the poll. The delay in releasing the result could also simply have been a ploy to temper the euphoria in the opposition ranks arising from their victory in the House of Assembly and to stem the gathering of a possibly unstoppable momentum in favour of Tsvangirai. It may also have been simply a show of strength and reflexive exercise of control by the ZANU(PF) government.

The most commonly presented explanation, however, was that the results were delayed to facilitate a manipulation of the figures in favour of Mugabe; that Tsvangirai had in fact won more than 50 per cent of the vote, and ZANU(PF) needed to 'massage' his tally downwards to allow the possibility of a run-off.

For the purposes of this chapter, what is important is that this speculation regarding the delay, and the delay itself, ought not to have been possible and ought to have been scuppered by ZESN. The method of tabulation and the public posting of results at each level of the polling process meant that the results of all polls were in the public domain within a day of the poll. With over 8,000 ZESN monitors deployed countrywide one would have thought that ZESN, MDC and other local and international monitors between them could have noted the 210 returns at constituency level, added the four columns of 210 figures and had clear and indisputable figures relating to the presidential result, leaving little room for manoeuvre by the Mugabe regime and ZEC.

Remarkably, and incomprehensibly, this did not happen.

In the days immediately following the poll the MDC convened press conferences at which it hinted that its figures showed that Tsvangirai had won enough votes to obviate the need for a run-off. Significantly, it failed to present its figures, claiming initially that they were still being double-checked, and later that it feared reprisals from the government if it released them because – despite the figures being theoretically in the public domain – the ZEC and the Chief Election Officer had claimed the sole legal authority to announce the result and that an announcement by any other person would be a criminal offence. Whispered figures suggested variously that Tsvangirai had obtained anything between 50.3 per cent and 67 per cent of the poll. The MDC Secretary-General, Tendai Biti, eventually announced

5   See Chapter 6 in the volume by Greg Linnington and Matyszak 2008a.

that Tsvangirai had obtained 51.7 per cent of the vote, but did not provide anything to show how these figures had been arrived at.

ZESN ought to have presented its figures and calmed the febrile atmosphere that prevailed in the first few days after the poll. It did not, arguing at first that it was still awaiting results from around the country, and later that to do so would render it liable to prosecution. The first pretext was also used by the MDC and by ZEC. They all pointed to the fact that with over 9,000 polling stations tabulation of the results was onerous and time-consuming. All disingenuously ignored the fact that the summation of the polls into four columns of 210 figures had already been done and published at constituency level.

ZESN ought therefore, without announcing the result, to have been in a position to simply publish the 210 returns which had already been published at constituency level and let the reader do his or her own addition. Instead, and to the bewilderment of journalists and other NGOs, ZESN called a press conference at which they gave an overview of the conduct of the poll and called on ZEC to release the figures speedily (rather than debunking the given reason for the delay). To the astonishment of journalists and others, rather than releasing the figures collected by its observers ZESN then announced a 'poll projection' from which the presidential result could be deduced within defined parameters. This extrapolated projection relied on a 'random' sample of data from 435 polling stations. The 'random' sample was said to be representative and 'stratified by province and urban rural areas'. ZESN stated that a 'proven' technique known as Sample Based Observation had been used by professional statisticians to arrive at the projection. However, the projection raised more questions than it answered. Why was it necessary to rely on extrapolation in the first place? Why were polling station returns rather than constituency returns relied on? Why had only 435 polling stations (less than 5 per cent) been used for the projection? What number of polling station results was known? If many figures remained unknown, how could the sample be deemed representative? How did the extrapolation from polling stations compare with known constituency level results? How did the projection deal with the lack of homogeneity in wards and constituencies which had shown unexpected spikes in vote numbers and preference?

ZESN's projection gave Tsvangirai 49.4% of the vote with a 2.4% margin of error, meaning that his poll was estimated to lie between 47% and 51.8%. For Mugabe they projected 41.8% with a 2.6% error, making the range between 39.2% and 44.4%. A similar projection was arrived at by the Research and Advocacy Unit by comparing House of Assembly and Senate results.[6] A simple tally of votes in the parliamentary elections as

---

6 Matyszak, Derek and Anthony Reeler (2008): *Zimbabwe Elections 2008: Examining The Popular and Presidential Choice - Hiding or Run Off?* Research and Advocacy Unit, Harare. Also available on www.kubatana.net.

a means of deducing the presidential result was not possible, because the leadership of the Mutambara formation of the MDC had recommended that its members vote for Simba Makoni in the presidential election and it was thus necessary to deduce how many actually did so. This analysis obtained similar results to those of ZESN, suggesting a maximum of 50.7% and minimum of 48.5% for Tsvangirai. With a voter turnout of just over 2.5 million, 1% represents 25,000 votes, the equivalent of just under the average number of registered voters per constituency. The voter turnout was 42.7%, giving an average of about 11,000 voters per constituency. Each 1% of the vote thus represents just over the combined votes for more than two constituencies; in order to 'massage' Tsvangirai's vote from over 50% to the ZEC's declared 47.9%, over 50,000 votes would have to have been reallocated. That in turn would require allocating all votes from four constituencies to Mugabe or reducing the vote allocated to Tsvangirai in many more constituencies. The difficulty in so doing is that such fraudulently reduced tallies would need to be compatible with the parliamentary results. More than a little suspicion would arise if a parliamentary seat was won by an MDC candidate with a greater number of votes than that obtained by Tsvangirai in the same constituency for the presidential election; it would strongly suggest a fraudulent reallocation of votes from the MDC presidential candidate to one of the other contenders. This kind of analysis is conspicuously absent from the post-election reports of ZESN and other NGOs.

ZEC could have dispelled speculation of vote tampering by revealing the results of the presidential poll on a constituency basis when it finally announced the results. It failed to do so and has not, to date, released these figures. ZESN likewise ought to have been able to dispel or confirm any manipulation of the results by publishing the ZEC's announced result of the presidential poll against its own figures, or by comparing the results of the presidential poll on a constituency basis with the results of the constituency based parliamentary poll. Both the MDC and ZESN appeared unwilling or unable to do so. ZESN's explanation for this, given in its post-election report, is unconvincing:

> ZESN however could not verify the presidential results that were announced by ZEC on 2 May 2008 as the ZEC National Command Centre was closed on the 6th of April and only opened on the 1st of May for tabulation of Presidential results. The fact that ZESN was not aware of the chain of custody of the ballot materials during the aforementioned period further rendered substantiation of ZEC figures impossible.

This explanation sheds no light on the reason why ZESN was unable to obtain the presidential tally from the results published at constituency level. Although ZESN does indicate that there was no compliance with the requirement to post results at constituency centres in Zvimba North, Zvimba West and Makonde, these figures could have been deduced from the provincial tallies subsequently published by ZEC and reproduced in ZESN's report. Similarly, when the MDC finally released figures to support Biti's claim of a 51.7 per cent poll by Tsvangirai, these figures broke the poll down by province and not by constituency, as would have been required to provide a convincing and verifiable challenge to ZEC's figures.

ZESN's failure to release these figures has been dealt with at some length not only because ZESN was the key NGO during this period, but because the collation of constituency results went to the core of duties others expected it to perform and proved to be a vital omission for the events that followed. When Biti was subsequently arrested for treason and for announcing the result of 51.7 per cent for Tsvangirai in the first round, ZESN was unable to provide any convincing backing for his claim, other than that the figure fell within the range of its projection. The MDC was unable to challenge the figures presented by ZEC during the verification and collation of the presidential result by the Chief Elections Officer and, unable or unwilling to present figures of its own from posted constituency returns, weakly demanded without legal grounds for doing so that returns from the polling stations themselves be reassessed.

The MDC's subsequent claim that ZEC had massaged the figures for the presidential poll to bring Tsvangirai's tally to below 50 per cent could be neither supported nor gainsaid by ZESN. The MDC continued to claim that it had won the election outright and thus would participate in the run-off under protest. When Mbeki also urged that the run-off be cancelled in favour of a unity government, convincing evidence from ZESN that the MDC had in fact won outright might have significantly affected subsequent events and the MDC's bargaining leverage in negotiations which followed the 27 June election. Such evidence would have further discredited Mugabe's already farcical claim to be the legitimately elected president of Zimbabwe.

Tallying the presidential votes in the 210 constituencies was not an onerous logistical exercise. In fact, it should have been so easy to accomplish and was of such importance that a large question mark arises from the apparent failure of ZESN and the MDC to do it. The delay in releasing the presidential poll result could not but support the notion that the results were being manipulated in favour of Mugabe. If ZESN's and the MDC's figures agreed with ZEC, this would certainly provide a motivation for non-disclosure, as disclosure would then douse suspicions the MDC may have been anxious to fuel.

In April, 2008 ZESN's offices were raided and searched by the police and senior staff were extensively questioned. The police focus was on documentation surrounding the presidential results and ZESN's projection. The purpose of the raid could have been as much to find information corroborating ZEC's figures, as it was to determine the source of the MDC's claim of 51.7 per cent for Tsvangirai.

The pre-presidential election run-off period
– the run-up to the run-off

Following the 29 March election, ZANU(PF) embarked on a widespread and systematic campaign of violence aimed at re-establishing blanket control over all rural areas. Incidents varied in nature and extent from individual harassment, intimidation and assault, to murder, attempted murder, rape, severe assault, arson, malicious injury to property and forced displacements. ZANU(PF) adopted a strategy of seeking to have a maximum intimidatory effect locally, to cause comprehensive fear and terror, and simultaneously seeking to conceal the campaign from the international community. To accomplish this, the violence perpetrated by ZANU(PF) militia and the military assumed a particularly gruesome and sadistic form, often accompanied by a macabre theatricality which ensured that accounts of the brutality spread throughout communities. Many reported that the violence was reminiscent of that used during the notorious Gukurahundi massacres and the atrocities of the liberation war – presumably deliberately so. In an attempt to conceal this from the international community, the militia imposed curfews in rural villages and restricted freedom of movement, preventing villagers from moving from their villages without letters of authorisation from ZANU(PF)-aligned traditional leaders. Victims of violence were prevented from seeking medical treatment and filing reports with police.

Immediately after determining to embark on the campaign of violence, ZANU(PF) also sought to justify its loss in the March election and to prepare a rationale for an implausible 'vote swing' in favour of Mugabe in the run-off. ZANU(PF) heavyweight Emmerson Mnangawa issued a statement in the press that ZEC officials had falsified results due to corrupt activities by ZESN monitors and polling agents. Much of the post-March violence specifically targeted polling agents and monitors, and clerical and transposition errors in figures were used as a basis to arrest junior ZEC officials. The criticism of ZESN mentioned above should in no way detract from the remarkable courage of its staff, who carried out their duties in the prescient knowledge that they could be targets of ZANU(PF) violence. One of their members was beaten to death in April, twelve others assaulted, 71 reported intimidation and harassment, sixteen had houses burnt down, and four had property destroyed.

On 4 June 2008, the Minister responsible for social welfare issued a directive that all NGOs were to cease field operations with immediate effect. The government sought to justify this by alleging that humanitarian NGOs were distributing food on a partisan basis. In fact, numerous reports indicated that governmental food networks were controlled by

ZANU(PF), who demanded party cards from villagers before distributing food relief and used other means (particularly through food relief lists compiled by ZANU(PF)-aligned traditional leaders) to ensure that MDC supporters were excluded from food programmes. Impartial NGO food relief undermined this control by ZANU(PF) and was a partial motivation for the ban. But also, and importantly, in line with that party's attempts to conceal information about its campaign of terror from the international community, the fact that humanitarian NGOs were well placed to observe the events in the countryside and to feed this information through to human rights NGOs and the international community was important. Action Aid, for example, mapped out all parts of Zimbabwe according to whether they were no-go areas for its operations, restricted areas, or areas where operations could continue. The ban on NGOs was intended to remove humanitarian workers' eyes and ears from areas of terror. The directive given by the Minister had no legal basis and no legislation gave the Minister any authority to issue a directive of this nature. Furthermore, although the directive had been for NGOs to halt field operations, the police directed all NGO offices to close their doors as well. As a result, most NGOs had to find other ways to continue their operations where possible.

The ZPP was able to continue monitoring violence to some degree, but it did report that levels of violence, already large and indicative of a widespread and systemic campaign, were in fact under-reported due to the difficulties of monitoring and restrictions on the movement of victims. The situation had become particularly severe by June, which partly explains the drop in incidents of violence over this period. ZPP produced several post-March election reports. They showed 4,375 incidents of violence in April, 6,288 in May and 3,653 in June. By July the cumulative total had risen to 17,605 which included verified cases of 171 murders, 9,148 assaults and sixteen rapes.

These reports were of crucial importance, particularly in view of the fact that the government made no attempt over this period to comply with electoral regulations allowing airtime to the MDC. Broadcasting officials who had complied with the regulations for 29 March were summarily dismissed and replaced. As MMPZ revealed in detail, there was a complete ban on MDC advertising materials or any positive reporting on the MDC. The state-controlled *Herald* cynically ignored the levels of violence in the country, reporting instead a few limited instances of political violence which it invariably attributed to the MDC. Violence reports such as those produced by ZPP provided an important source of information and corroboration for international journalists who were thus able to undermine ZANU(PF)'s strategy of denial to the international community, and to South Africa in particular. The Director of ZPP, Jestina Mukoko, was abducted by state agents in December, and, after several weeks of being held in an undisclosed location, was handed into the custody of the police.

At the time of writing, she was being held in prison with several others on obviously spurious charges of recruiting persons to be trained in 'banditry'. It has been suggested that her arrest be more accurately viewed as state revenge for ZPP's exposure of the violence.

The level of violence, and the closure of democratic space and access to rural areas, compelled Tsvangirai to withdraw from an election in which his supporters would either have been unable to vote, or unable to vote for a candidate of their choice. Those who have criticized this withdrawal cannot have read the violence reports produced by ZPP, the Forum, ZESN itself, and others.

Conclusion

The closure of the rural areas meant that there could little monitoring of the 27 June presidential run-off. The importance of this work by civil society was highlighted when ZEC announced the implausible result of an electoral charade in which Mugabe claimed an additional one million votes to his tally in March, despite the fact that those MDC members who were not coerced to vote boycotted the election from which their candidate had withdrawn. Mbeki sought to reward Mugabe for his bloody electoral farce. He pressurized the MDC, the winner of the elections, into a power-sharing arrangement with the loser, an agreement in which the MDC was to be the vastly inferior partner.[7] Civil society maintained a healthy distance from the MDC during the negotiation process and demanded to be included in the negotiations. In a July 2008 statement, the National Association of NGOs (NANGO) rejected the notion of a power-sharing agreement and demanded a transitional government leading to the adoption of a new constitution to govern fresh elections. To the annoyance of the MDC, but again showing independence, civil society further demanded that the transitional government be led by a neutral person unaligned to any of the political antagonists.

Throughout the long election process, civil society played a crucial role in exposing democratic malpractice in the face of state oppression and at great personal risk to its staff members. As a result of its actions, including the dissemination of information about human rights abuses, claims by Mugabe to be the legitimately elected president of Zimbabwe are endorsed by few other than the most deliberately obtuse of his supporters.

[7] Matyszak, Derek (2008) (b): *Losing Focus: Zimbabwe's 'Power-Sharing' Agreement.* Research and Advocacy Unit, Harare. Also available on www.kubatana.net.

9

Zimbabwe's 2008 Harmonized Elections
Regional & International Reaction

Simon Badza

Introduction

The unprecedented harmonized elections that Zimbabwe conducted on 29 March 2008 were generally accepted as relatively free though not necessarily fair. They thinly complied with the SADC Principles and Guidelines Governing Democratic Elections. However, the subsequent, controversial presidential election run-off of 27 June 2008 was inexcusably flawed and therefore discredited, particularly by the West. It was also condemned at regional level. Yet, despite that condemnation, and the growing crisis of legitimacy, Robert Mugabe began his fourth presidential term of office on 29 June 2008. Inevitably, under the circumstances, this triggered a political impasse among ZANU(PF), MDC-T and MDC-M which was eventually solved, albeit temporarily, by an illusive Power Sharing Agreement (PSA)[1] that was signed formally on 15 September 2008 by these three political parties. The PSA was a result of a long SADC-facilitated mediation process led by South Africa's former president, Thabo Mbeki. In the interim, for over ten months, until the power-sharing government was finally formed in February 2009, Zimbabwe was under an illegitimate *de facto* government.

Using selected organizations and countries as examples this chapter assesses the regional and international reaction to Zimbabwe's 2008 harmonized elections, including the subsequent controversial presidential election run-off and, in passing, the PSA. Its central position is that regional and international reaction has been marked by continuities rather than discontinuities of the policies governing the world's diplomatic interactions

---

1   It is otherwise referred to as the 'Global Political Agreement' (GPA) and it has been regarded, at least by SADC and the AU, as the inevitable short-term solution to the post-election political impasse.

149

with the government of Zimbabwe. As such, the reaction, by and large, has been a function of old perceptions about the near-decade-long Zimbabwe crisis. The chapter also argues that although the government of Zimbabwe has struggled for nearly a decade under various forms of pressure, mainly applied by the West, its reputation and international standing were considerably worsened by the appalling manner in which the 2008 harmonized elections – particularly the subsequent presidential election run-off – were conducted. As a necessary first step, therefore, the chapter begins by considering the broad dynamics of Zimbabwe's international relations for they facilitate a better understanding of the context within which the elections were conducted.

Contextualising Zimbabwe's international relations before the harmonized elections

Since the violent farm occupations that began early in 2000, otherwise known as the Fast Track Land Reform, or in revolutionary parlance, the 'Third Chimurenga', Zimbabwe's international relations were characterized by increased international proscription particularly by the West and the influential international institutions that it also dominates such as the World Bank and the International Monetary Fund (IMF). For example, all development aid and balance of payments support was indefinitely suspended. Zimbabwe's voting right in the IMF and its eligibility for financial assistance were also suspended due to its overdue financial obligations that by the end of August 2001 had totalled US$53 million.[2] Its ruling elite were also under targeted sanctions[3] that include travel bans and asset freezes. However, the same Western powers continued to provide humanitarian assistance to Zimbabwe albeit through United Nations (UN) specialised agencies such as the World Food Programme, World Health Organization, United Nations Children's Fund and other humanitarian aid organizations. In December 2003, Zimbabwe also withdrew its membership of the Commonwealth. Last, but not least, most Western investors pulled out of Zimbabwe because they considered that the country not only lacked political and economic stability, but also dishonoured Bilateral Investment Protection Agreements.

Zimbabwe pragmatically used the diplomatic stand-off with the West as a pretext to proclaim its 'Look East' foreign policy under which it sought to strengthen its diplomatic, trade and economic ties with Asian and Middle Eastern countries from where most foreign investors and tourists have since been drawn. The policy has also encompassed the strengthening of

---

2   See Press Release: IMF Declares Zimbabwe ineligible to use IMF Resources,http://www. imf.org/external/np/sec/pr/2001/pr0140.htm (Accessed 27/5/09).

3   The government of Zimbabwe claims that sanctions are illegal and not targeted at all.

ties with Latin America and, essentially, the rest of the Third World, which commands a numerical majority at the UN. It was strategically rooted in regime security and survival concerns camouflaged as 'national interests'.[4]

Most Third World countries in Africa, Asia and Latin America had, however, continued to support the government of Zimbabwe within the general broad framework of the Non-Aligned Movement (NAM) and the G-77. Russia and China as well as some countries in the Middle East, particularly Iran, also continued their support for the Mugabe administration. Perhaps most importantly, SADC countries, with the exception of Botswana and Zambia, also remained supportive. Thus the international community was tensely polarised. Critics of Mugabe had hoped that the harmonized elections would peacefully conclude the fomer's era and usher in a Tsvangirai regime while Tsvangirai's opponents regarded the 2008 elections as a timely opportunity to prevent, once and for all, 'foreign sponsored regime change'.[5] Such were the dynamics of Zimbabwe's international relations within which the 2008 harmonized elections and the subsequent controversial presidential election run-off were conducted.

The 2008 harmonized elections & the subsequent presidential election run-off

Zimbabwe's harmonized elections of 29 March 2008 were conducted within a political context that had been created through the facilitation of SADC. The regional body became more actively involved in the Zimbabwe crisis following the political violence of 11 March 2007 that saw the brutal assault of opposition MDC-T leaders and supporters by the police in Harare, and subsequent acts of politically motivated arson across the country.

The Communiqué released by the subsequent Extra-ordinary Summit of SADC Heads of State and Government that met in Dar es Salaam, Tanzania on 29 March 2007 to discuss the political situation in Zimbabwe (among other important regional matters) mandated Mbeki to continue facilitating dialogue among Zimbabwe's three main political parties and report back to SADC's Organ on Politics Defence and Security (OPDS) Troika. It also mandated the SADC Executive Secretary to undertake a study of the economic situation in Zimbabwe and to propose measures about how best SADC could assist Zimbabwe's economic recovery. Furthermore, it reiterated its appeal to Britain to honour what it referred to as 'its compensation obligations' with regard to the land reform, in line with the Lancaster House Agreement of 1979. Finally, it also appealed for the lifting of what

4   This is a hotly contested concept in the Third World, especially in party-states such as Zimbabwe.
5   The MDC has always been considered by ZANU(PF) as the puppet of the West without domestic roots and a legitimate cause.

it referred to as 'all forms of sanctions against Zimbabwe'.[6]

Eventually, the SADC-facilitated dialogue resulted in the enactment of Constitutional Amendment Number 18 that provided for the harmonization of the presidential, house of assembly, senatorial and local government elections. The amendment to the Electoral Act also provided for the posting of election results at the polling stations. Generally, SADC facilitated the creation of a relatively level election playing field that, comparatively speaking, enabled the opposition to freely access and campaign in what had traditionally become 'opposition-no-go-areas'. The elections were legitimately expected to be relatively free and fair, and thus democratically credible. Unfortunately, they defied expectations as they turned out not to be.

While the harmonized elections of 29 March 2008 were almost in line the SADC guidelines, the subsequent presidential election run-off of 27 June 2008 was marked by inexcusable acts of violence, intimidation, loss of life and property, displacement and the repression, in particular, of opposition supporters. The main opposition MDC-T leader, Morgan Tsvangirai, was arrested several times; many people were detained after April 2008 athough most of them were later released. Many were treated for injuries. some of whom died, and thousands were displaced particularly in the rural areas.[7] Humanitarian aid organizations were banned on 5 June 2008.[8] MDC-T's access to state media was also barred and most of its campaign rallies were disrupted, at times even in full view of foreign election observers. It was under these circumstances that Tsvangirai withdrew from the presidential run-off election, effectively rendering it a controversial 'one-man race'.

Unprecedented and explicit condemnation came from the southern African region, Africa, and the UN; that it came from the West was no surprise. Even former liberation movements and ruling parties such as the African National Congress (ANC) in South Africa,[9] the Tanzania African National Union[10], the Botswana Democratic Party, and the Movement for

---

6   See: Communiqué, Extra-ordinary SADC Summit of Heads of State and Government, 28-29 March 2007, Dar es Salaam, Tanzania. See also http://www.dfa.gov.za/docs/2007/ sadc0330htm (Accessed 23/10/08).

7   See, for instance, the Electoral Institute for Southern Africa's report, Zimbabwe: 2008 Post-harmonized election violence (continued) at: http://www.eisa.org.za/WEP/ zim2008postd2.htm (Accessed on 28/5/08).

8   They were suspected of campaigning for the MDC-T.

9   Baleka Mbete, Chairman of ANC and Speaker of Parliament said on 15 April 2008 that Zimbabwe's failure to release results was an example of a democratic process gone wrong. See: *ANC hits out at dire Zimbabwe situation*, http://www.guardian.co.uk/ world/2008/apr/15/anc.Zimbabwe (Accessed 20/10/08)

10   On 19 June 2008, Tanzania's Foreign Affairs Minister, Bernard Membe said: 'Zimbabwe has been our great friend. We have stood by them since the Lancaster House agreement on land issues in 1980, but on governance issues, we have started to differ with the incumbent president.' See: *Tanzania Parliament Endorses Government's Tough Stance on Zimbabwe*, http://www.danielmolokele.blogspot.com/2008/06/tanzania-parliament-endorses-government.html (Accessed 22/10/08).

Multiparty Democracy in Zambia all condemned the violent presidential run-off election campaign. Election observer teams from the AU, the Pan-African Parliament (PAP) and SADC recommended the postponement of the presidential election because the situation on the ground was undisputedly not conducive to a free, fair and credible election.[11] The UN Secretary General, Ban Ki-moon, also recommended postponement, citing 'too much violence and too much intimidation'. Yet, in an assertive display of absolute sovereignty and self-determination, the presidential election run-off was conducted as scheduled and Robert Mugabe 'won' a fourth presidential term of office with an unprecedented 85 per cent of the votes cast. There were mixed reactions.

Understanding the regional and international reaction

Perceptions are very important in international relations. They significantly influence the reaction of actors to multi-dimensional developments taking place in other parts of the world. The first perception is that the Zimbabwe crisis is simply an ordinary democratic contest between two major competing political parties namely, ZANU(PF) and MDC-T. Both domestic and foreign supporters and sympathisers of the opposition MDC-T and Morgan Tsvangirai are influenced by this perception. The second perception is that the crisis in Zimbabwe is a serious conflict between African revolutionaries and imperialist-backed reactionaries disguised within democratic movements that are being used to reverse the 'gains of independence', particularly land acquisition. As such, domestic and foreign supporters and sympathisers of the ZANU(PF) government are influenced by this perception. They regard Mugabe as a true African hero, fighting an African cause, and regard Tsvangirai as a puppet of the West. To them the Zimbabwe crisis is part of a grand imperialist conspiracy to forcibly reform or, if this fails, dislodge, all African 'revolutionary' liberation movements, leaders and rulers, with Zimbabwe just being the pilot project. Governments influenced by this perception therefore insist on unconditional solidarity with the ZANU(PF) government as the most appropriate strategy to guarantee the security and longevity of incumbent revolutionary parties and their leaders. They also emphatically insist on African solutions to African problems.

From another perspective, the Zimbabwe crisis is just a microcosm of a larger political contest between, at least, two emerging categories of African leadership. The first category comprises the heroic but old-style conservative leadership, the vanguard of the liberation struggle, which brought independence from colonial rule. It inflexibly believes in absolute sovereignty

---

11 See also Communique, Extra-ordinary Summit of OPDS Troika, 25 June 2008, Manzini, Swaziland.

regardless of the changing times and, occasionally, it is also radical. It publicly claims to be correcting the injustices of the past even as it creates its own share of injustices. It has less enthusiasm for substantive political and economic liberalization. It pays lip service to democratically acquired popular legitimacy. It does not trust the Western world that it blames for most, if not all, past (colonial) and current injustices. Moreover, it suspects the West of harbouring sinister motives in Africa. It regards neo-liberalism as a western-propelled strategy to re-conquer and exploit the natural resources of the Third World in general, but Africa in particular. Last, but not least, it refrains from supporting democratic trends in other countries hiding behind the façade of the 'non-interference' clause in Article 2 of the United Nations Charter. Thus, the international relations of this category of African leadership are primarily motivated by its regime security and survival concerns. In the circumstances, national interests become consequential.

The second category consists mostly of a new and young generation of modern, pragmatic and forward-looking African leaders who appear to be politically and economically reform-oriented. This group, currently predominant in the opposition, promises to depend on democratically acquired popular legitimacy to govern successfully. Whilst it remembers the past and attaches great importance to acquired inalienable values such as independence and sovereignty, it believes that these are, practically, relative rather than absolute. Equally, it believes that contemporary international relations produce relative rather than absolute gains since actors 'take' in return for 'giving', a basis which forms the essence of diplomacy. It is seemingly determined to move African countries forward, in tandem with the demands of a globalizing world so as to maximize its relative benefits, and also believes in the inevitability of legitimate expectations of internal peaceful democratic political change. Furthermore, it exhibits a stronger preference for constructive engagement and integration with the Western world rather than confrontation and de-linking. Its international relations are motivated not by suspicions and fear but by a combination of aspirations and hopes. It openly supports democratic trends in other countries. Thus, African countries in this category insist that pan-African solidarity should be strictly qualified rather than distorting it for the sake of unconditionally preserving discredited incumbent parties and leaders.

At the risk of oversimplification, most of the leadership in SADC and AU member states fit smartly into the first category. To some extent, the leadership in countries such as Botswana may fit into the second category. South Africa may exhibit a mixture of the positive attributes of both categories, thus suggesting a possible third category; and there may be countries in north Africa that defy this categorization altogether.

Therefore, even though election observer teams had strong reservations regarding the widely condemned and discredited presidential run-off, predictably both SADC and the AU refrained from disparaging it, or from preventing Mugabe's attendance at the subsequent summit meetings as Zimbabwe's Head of State and Government, first in Sharm El Sheikh, Egypt from 30 June 2008 to 1 July 2008 and second, in Johannesburg, South Africa on 17 August 2008. Thus at the institutional level, both the AU and SADC tacitly endorsed the presidential election run-off and its outcome as credible and legitimate.

Possible explanations for the unpopular AU and SADC reactions to the harmonized elections are not difficult to find. In part, the two organizations are traditionally opposed to what appear to be double standards, i.e. the West deliberately ignoring or seriously supporting, for strategic reasons, political systems worse than Zimbabwe's. The sustained use of political rhetoric and propaganda by the Mugabe administration also successfully contributed to shaping such reactions. Essentially, it reduced the political crisis to the level of a bilateral dispute between Britain and Zimbabwe, specifically over the generally sensitive land question, but one that the British Labour government is accused of having unnecessarily internationalized. Accordingly, the Mugabe administration has continuously blamed the British and the American governments, together with their friends and allies, of causing most of the problems bedevilling Zimbabwe. This is supported by the notion that that runs deep and wide in the Third World: that both the government of Zimbabwe and Mugabe are being punished not for bad governance or for violating human rights, but for daring to take land from the white commercial farmers and directly confronting the West.[12]

Dissecting the SADC reaction

SADC is now a regional security complex, a group of countries sufficiently linked that their national security concerns cannot be realistically considered separately.[13] A security threat anywhere in SADC is regarded as a potential threat to the security of all.

Historically, Zimbabwe has been a key player in southern Africa partly because of the size of its economy and its geographically strategic location. It has had a significant impact on the regional economy as it links most of the regional transport and energy systems. It was once the breadbasket of the region. It also once set positive political standards for some, if not all, of its neighbours. Furthermore, it has in the past actively contributed to promoting regional and international peace and security. Refugees from all directions used to find a second home in Zimbabwe. Sadly, it is no longer able to play such critical, positive roles. Naturally, therefore, a politically

---

12 In fact, Robert Mugabe is a hero to many people in and outside Zimbabwe for standing firm against the West and what he believes is right.

13 See Buzan, B. (1991) *People, States and Fear: An Agenda for International Security Studies in the Post-Cold War Era.* Harvester/Wheatsheaf, London and New York, p. 190.

unstable Zimbabwe with the fastest declining economy in the region, which now sends out refugees in all directions, unsettles its neighbours.

There have been numerous SADC Summit and OPDS Troika meetings to solve the Zimbabwe crisis, but it appeared to defy all such attempts until the historic 15 September 2008 PSA. Since 11 March 2007, SADC had been closely monitoring and reacting to developments in Zimbabwe. Indeed, as noted above, SADC is credited for the relatively peaceful and free harmonized elections of 29 March 2008 and for the PSA itself. The SADC Election Observer Mission (SEOM), which comprised 163 members drawn from eleven member states, prematurely endorsed the 29 March 2008 harmonized elections as being a peaceful and credible expression of the will of the people. However, in what may have sounded like a threat, the team leader, Angola's Minister of Youth and Sport, Marcos Barrica, urged Zimbabweans to consider the peace in their country stressing that, 'You have to avoid conflict. I have seen war, and you should avoid it.'[14] It is fair to argue, however, that SADC was significantly discredited by allowing, or at least failing to prevent, the atrocities surrounding the controversial presidential run-off election.

The OPDS Troika met in Sandton, South Africa on the margins of the 28th Ordinary SADC Summit meeting on 16-17 August 2008. The Troika appealed to the political parties in Zimbabwe to sign any outstanding agreements and conclude the negotiations as a matter of urgency in order to restore political stability in Zimbabwe.[15] On 20 October, the OPDS Troika met again in Mbabane to review the political situation in the region, focusing specifically on Zimbabwe, the DRC and Lesotho. The MDC-T leader did not attend the meeting, allegedly because he did not have a proper travel document. Authorities in Harare cited shortages of the necessary passport paper and ink arising from what they referred to as 'sanctions'. Ironically, the Troika remained silent, at least publicly, on the 'technicalities' that had prevented Tsvangirai from attending the supposedly crucial meeting and, instead, decided to postpone and relocate the meeting.

The Extra-ordinary OPDS Troika meeting held in Harare on 27-28 October failed to resolve the deadlock, and recommended a full SADC Summit meeting[16]; this was held on 9 November in Sandton, Johannesburg, and also failed. Instead, it 'ruled' that a unity government be formed forthwith and that the contested Ministry of Home Affairs be co-shared between ZANU(PF) and MDC-T. The MDC-T rejected the 'ruling' and appealed for both the AU and the UN to intervene to salvage the threatened PSA, which many regarded as the only viable solution to the crisis. It is important to stress that, contrary to what many believe, SADC is not a

---

14 See *The Herald*, 31 March 2008.
15 See Communique, Extra-ordinary Summit of OPDS Troika, 17 August 2008, Sandton, South Africa.
16 See Communique, Extra-ordinary Summit of OPDS Troika, 27-28 October, Harare, Zimbabwe.

sovereign authority above the government of Zimbabwe with the mandate to 'rule' or impose solutions. It can only recommend.

SADC has clearly been very cautious about openly criticizing Mugabe and the ZANU(PF) government. Instead, it has pursued 'quiet diplomacy', which essentially avoids applying open, direct criticism or pressure on Mugabe. In adopting this approach, SADC may have hoped to achieve some limited changes that fell short of 'regime change'. Such an approach is strategically aimed at a situation that Fisher and Ury aptly describe as 'getting to yes: negotiating an agreement without giving in'.[17] Thus SADC assisted ZANU(PF) to negotiate the PSA 'without substantively giving in'.

However, there were emerging signs of difference that threatened to tear the regional bloc apart. As noted earlier, Botswana, Zambia and Tanzania openly expressed concern over the delays in releasing the first presidential poll results and the implausible manner in which the run-off election campaign was conducted. Yet, only Botswana and Zambia refused to formally recognize Mugabe as the democratically elected president of Zimbabwe until after the PSA was signed. Each SADC country had its own foreign policy principles to adhere to and national interests to safeguard in relation to the crisis. It is, for example, common knowledge that the influx of refugees and the associated societal challenges of crime, health[18] and prostitution as well as pressure over scarce resources, are potential causes of xeno-phobic violence similar to that which occurred in South Africa in 2008.

In some measure, the SADC reaction to the election crisis in Zimbabwe was also caused by a fear of internal political instability, a threat constantly insinuated by ex-freedom fighters as likely to occur in the event of Mugabe losing the elections. It was also due to distorted pan-African solidarity that, as many would now believe, seemingly seeks to ensure the unconditional security of the incumbent party and leader. Furthermore, it is an indication of the growing resentment among some Africans leaders against perceived Western attempts to effect what they, rhetorically or otherwise, refer to as 'unconstitutional regime change'. Most African leaders have a political culture of acquiring and retaining power through undemocratic methods. Generally, the patriarchal African political culture also considers it un-African to criticize elders, especially those with Mugabe's revolutionary credentials. Moreover, SADC does not want to be perceived as paving the entrance for the opposition lest it sets what most incumbents throughout the continent generally regard as a 'negative' precedent.

SADC's reaction was also partly influenced by its elitist concept of security, which it defines in almost exclusively military terms and in direct reference to the incumbent. Seemingly, the state enjoys the singular prerogative of defining – and making itself the single most important referent

---

17   Fisher, R. and W. Ury (1999), *Getting to Yes: Negotiating an agreement without giving in*. Random House, London.

18   At the time of writing, South Africa and Botswana had begun to grapple with the cholera epidemic that was allegedly traceable to Zimbabwe.

object of – security. Such notions of security are too deficient to guarantee human security in a situation in which the state, quasi-state and quasi-military institutions may be the major causes of human insecurity. As Francis Makoa lamented, SADC has not yet shown its readiness to acknowledge that insecurity and instability in southern Africa also have systemic and structural causes.[19] SADC's lack of legitimately expected political will to react appropriately to the election crisis in Zimbabwe testifies to its institutional weaknesses.

The language used in the various treaties, protocols and defence and security co-operation pacts illustrates SADC's guiding approach to regional peace and security. For example, Article 7 of the SADC Mutual Defence Pact stresses the strict adherence by member states to the fundamental principle of sovereignty and non-interference in the internal affairs of other states. Article 8 also deals with what are vaguely referred to as 'Destabilizing Factors'. It reads:

> State parties undertake not to nurture, harbor or support any person, or group of persons or institutions whose aim is to destabilize the political, military, territorial and economic or social security of a State Party.

With the exception of Botswana, and Zambia under the late President Levy Mwanawasa, most SADC countries have religiously adhered to such vague provisions that may lack objective and universally applicable definitions. Thus, SADC's reaction to the election crisis in Zimbabwe effectively guaranteed the security and longevity of the incumbent. As Maxi Schoeman observed:

> The protracted implosion of Zimbabwe continues unabated and it is clear that SADC member states cannot ... intervene in the name of SADC principles to stop the degradation of the rule of law and human rights or stop the blatant and violent attacks on ordinary people who seem to be punished for their opposition to the regime in the country. On paper everything is in place to address the situation in Zimbabwe. In practice, there is a rift in the organization and the 'old guard' under the leadership of Mugabe is clearly in charge, at times making a mockery of the organization's principles and objectives.[20]

SADC seemingly disregarded the first round presidential election results as both politically and practically insignificant and, instead, made its critical decisions, with far-reaching consequences, primarily on the basis of the results of the presidential election run-off in June. Thus, to Africa and in the rest of the Third World, SADC effectively legitimized Robert Mugabe as the democratically elected President of Zimbabwe. Critics accuse SADC of complicity in subverting the freely expressed democratic will of the people

19 F. K. Makoa (2005) 'Managing Conflict in an Integrated Southern Africa: Peace, Security and Stability in Lieu of Democracy?' in *Monitoring Regional Integration in Southern Africa Year Book* Vol. 5, p. 113.
20 See Schoeman, M. (2006) 'Towards a Collective Security Identity?', in *Monitoring Regional Integration in Southern Africa Year Book* Vol. 6, p. 255.

of Zimbabwe as expressed in the 29 March elections. Equally, they accuse SADC of contributing to the Zimbabwe crisis all the necessary ingredients for its potential escalation in future. Therefore, there is growing pessimism regarding SADC's future credibility in handling crises similar to that of the Zimbabwe election.

SADC's approach of seeking to ensure only 'change without regime change' has been echoed by Eldred Masunungure who describes it as a 'pro-regime policy change approach'.[21] However, the highly mysterious nature of politics in general, and Zimbabwean politics in particular, suggests that the potential of 'regime policy changes' to inevitably result in regime change should not be underestimated. In fact, the amendments to the Electoral Act contributed to the creation of an enabling environment for the March harmonized elections that nearly resulted in a 'constitutional regime change', thanks to the ZEC's 'meticulous' verification of results.

Lastly, SADC is still captivated by the, arguably, indelible historical fact that Mugabe is one of the key regional statesmen who initiated the processes of regional co-operation in southern Africa under the aegis of the Frontline States. Indeed, it was Mugabe rather than Tsvangirai who signed the SADC Treaty that enlisted Zimbabwe as one of its core member states. To this extent, SADC's reaction to the Zimbabwe election crisis would suggest that its continued support for Mugabe, and for ZANU(PF), remains likely as long as the solidarity among liberation movements and leaders, as well as incumbent political parties, remains strong. Quiet diplomacy will remain the cornerstone of SADC's approach towards any negative political developments in Zimbabwe until Mugabe's voluntary, peaceful and dignified exit takes place at a time of his own choosing. SADC is very unlikely to adopt Botswana's preference for 'megaphone diplomacy'.

The African Union reaction

The AU has a Charter on Democracy, Elections and Governance. Chapter 7, Articles 19 to 24 deal with democratic elections while Chapter 8, Articles 25 to 28 specifically provide for 'Arrangements and Sanctions' in cases of unconstitutional changes of government. The AU election observer team was made up of 21 observers drawn from across the continent. It was led by former Sierra Leone President Ahmed Tejan Kabbah who described the pre-election environment as peaceful.[22] The co-ordinator of the mission, Professor Raphael Omotayo Olaniya, said that the presence of the AU observer team constituted proof of the AU's commitment to the promotion of democracy and the rule of law on the continent. He stressed that

21 In an unpublished paper presented at workshop that was organized by OSSREA on the theme: 'Zimbabwe Political Situation'. Holiday Inn, Harare, 8 September 2007.
22 See *The Herald*, 28 March 2008.

the mission's main objective was to provide an honest, independent and impartial observation and assessment of the organization and conduct of the harmonized elections.[23] Their recommendation for the postponement of the presidential run-off election, like that of SEOM, was also ignored by the Zimbabwe Electoral Commission (ZEC).

While the AU mission expressed concern over the delays in the announcement of results, the Pan-African Parliament (PAP) election observer mission concluded that on the whole, the basic conditions for credible, free and fair elections as contained in the OAU/AU Principles of Governing Democratic Elections in Africa (2002) existed.[24] But, as it turned out, such verdicts were only relatively accurate with reference to the period immediately prior to and during the actual voting days. The observer mission also naively recommended the postponement of the presidential run-off election. Another reaction to the election crisis came from 40 eminent African personalities, including former UN Secretary-General Kofi Anan and some retired presidents, who in the run-up to the presidential election run-off wrote to Mugabe asking him for an assurance that it would be free and fair.[25] They were naive because, as it turned out, they were ignored.

Although it naturally expressed what it referred to as 'deep concern with the prevailing situation in Zimbabwe based on the negative reports of SADC, AU and PAP election observers about the presidential election run-off held on 27 June 2008 and the loss of life that occurred in Zimbabwe,'[26] the 11th Ordinary Session of the AU Assembly of Heads of State and Government in Sharm El Sheikh failed to prevent Mugabe from attending the meeting and made no attempt to chastise him. The AU Peace and Security Council held its talks at the same time but, reportedly, no mention was made of Zimbabwe as a serious case for consideration. Instead, the Assembly welcomed Mugabe as the Head of State and Government of Zimbabwe. It encouraged he and Tsvangirai to honour their commitment to initiate dialogue with a view to promoting peace, stability, democracy, and the reconciliation of the Zimbabwean people. Furthermore, it pledged support for both the creation of a Government of National Unity (GNU) and the SADC facilitation.[27]

The AU also welcomed the PSA of 15 September 2008 and pledged to be one of its guarantors. Therefore, in future, the AU is most likely to follow SADC's preferred approach of 'quiet diplomacy' towards Mugabe. The preference will only last until the Zimbabwe crisis has escalated to an unacceptable humanitarian catastrophe constituting a threat to international peace and security. But, using African standards, such a stage may never be reached in the lifetime of many.

23 Ibid.
24 *The Herald*, 1 April 2008.
25 *The Standard*, 15-21 June 2008.
26 AU Summit Resolution on Zimbabwe, 2 July 2008, Sharm El Sheikh, Egypt.
27 Ibid.

The reaction of the United Nations

On 21 April 2008, opposition MDC-T leader Morgan Tsvangirai met the UN Secretary-General on the sidelines of the UN Conference on Trade and Development in Accra and urged UN and AU intervention. In response to the delays in releasing results of the presidential election, the UN Security Council held a special session on Zimbabwe on 29 April 2008. The Secretary-General also expressed concern over the unprecedented delay, and warned that the situation in Zimbabwe could deteriorate. He further expressed frustration with regional (SADC) leaders' continued suggestion that the rest of the world had no role to play in the Zimbabwe situation, and said that the credibility of the democratic process in Africa was at stake.[28]

The Secretary-General had vainly insisted that international election observers be present to monitor the presidential run-off election. While Latin American and EU members wanted to send a special envoy to Zimbabwe, this was prevented by South Africa which chaired the meeting. However, the Security Council issued a statement on 23 June 2008 condemning the violent run-off election campaign by ZANU(PF) and expressed regret that the violence had made a free and fair election impossible. The UN remained concerned about the situation in Zimbabwe. A Seurity Council resolution to impose a multilateral arms embargo, travel bans and financial sanctions on Zimbabwe was vetoed by Russia and China on 11 July 2008. The Secretary-General welcomed what soon became a not so historic 15 September 2008 PSA that defied implementation. He hoped that the PSA would pave the way for durable peace in Zimbabwe. He acknowledged Thabo Mbeki for his tireless efforts to facilitate the agreement.

In a related development, Zimbabwe appeared to have become allergic to any visit by UN envoys, especially after two of them, Anna Kajimulo Tibaijuka and John Eageland, had produced allegedly 'biased' reports on the situation in Zimbabwe in 2005. This had happened during Kofi Annan's term as Secretary-General. Since then, Zimbabwe has not unconditionally facilitated any such 'fact-finding' missions. For example, on 21 November 2008 a team of 'Elders' led by the same Kofi Annan was refused entry into Zimbabwe largely because of ZANU(PF)'s suspicions that they were coming to bolster MDC-T.[29] But on 22 November 2008, Zimbabwe's Foreign Affairs Minister, Simbarashe Mumbengegwi, argued that Zimbabwe

28 See also 'Strong Talk About Zimbabwe at the UN', (The *New York Times*, 17 April 2008), http://www.nytimes.com/2008/04/17/worldafrica/17zimbabwe.html?r=&oref=slogin (Accessed 1/4/08)

29 A ZANU(PF) Spokesperson, Christopher Mutswangwa, openly accused Kofi Annan of shedding 'crocodile tears' while he had allegedly legitimized USA sanctions against Zimbabwe by remaining silent. See: 'Kofi Annan Not Welcome in Zimbabwe', SABCNews.com (Accessed 21/11/08).

had not barred the 'Elders' but had, instead, postponed their visit because Mr Annan had not made prior consultations with the government of Zimbabwe on the 'timing and programme'.[30] The 'Elders' resorted to meetings in South Africa with civic society groups operating in Zimbabwe. They also met Morgan Tsvangirai. From these meetings the 'Elders' obtained critical information about the post-election crisis in Zimbabwe. However, the UN decided to support the AU position of backing the SADC 'quiet diplomacy' initiatives. As long as the Zimbabwe post-election crisis does not threaten international peace and security, the UN will likely maintain this approach of backing the regional organizations in line with Chapter VIII of its Charter.

The European Union (EU)

The European Union and Zimbabwe have enjoyed fruitful co-operation since 1981, but since 2002 the relationship has deteriorated due to major disagreements over essential elements of the Cotonou Partnership Agreement resulting in restrictions on the co-operation.[31] In February 2002, the EU partially suspended co-operation and assistance under the European Development Fund. It also adopted restrictive measures such as an arms embargo, visa bans, and the freezing of assets against some 168 senior officials.[32]

The EU considered the results of the harmonized elections as relatively credible but declared the June presidential run-off election results illegitimate and unacceptable. On 22 July 2008, it extended its list of sanctions that for the first time included companies linked to ZANU(PF). On 15 September 2008, the EU General Affairs and External Relations Council, which comprises 27 EU Foreign ministers and the EU commission, issued a statement welcoming the conclusion of the PSA. It thanked Mbeki for his mediation. However, the Council stressed that it would study the details of the agreement and would be attentive to its implementation. It further stressed that the agreement should provide the Zimbabwean people with the reforms they awaited, which included democracy and the rule of law, respect for human rights and the restoration of the country's economic and social situation. The EU promised that it stands ready to adopt a new set of economic measures to support a transitional government observably taking steps to restore democracy and the rule of law in Zimbabwe particularly

---

30 See *The Sunday Mail Online*, 23 November 2008 at: http://www.sundaymail.co.zw/ inside aspx?sectid=926&cat=12. (Accessed 23/11/08). Given Kofi Anan's long experience in high-level diplomatic service, the reasons given by the government of Zimbabwe sound weak.

31 These mainly centre on good governance, rule of law, and promotion of human rights, among other conditionalities for development co-operation.

32 The arms embargo was imposed in reaction to Zimbabwe's intervention in the DRC in 1998.

by organizing transparent multi-party elections and promoting economic rehabilitation of the country. It however decided to postpone any decisions on sanctions until its October 2008 meeting.[33]

On 13 October 2008, the EU Foreign Ministers meeting in Luxemburg condemned what they described as Mugabe's 'unilateral decision to form a new government which had not been agreed by all parties' and it threatened a fresh wave of sanctions if the PSA continued to be blocked.[34] Nonetheless, the EU said it remained ready to undertake a political dialogue with Zimbabwe as defined in the provisions of Article 8 of the Cotonou Partnership Agreement and it attached importance to future EU-Zimbabwe co-operation. Clearly, the EU approach towards the government of Zimbabwe will, predictably, remain a function of the confidence-building measures to be adopted by the envisaged inclusive government of Zimbabwe. Essentially, it will be performance-based.

South Africa

Hennie Strydom[35] has correctly observed that post-apartheid South Africa's ideological choice to join the developing world in transforming international relations and to bring about a more just world order based on multilateralism and respect for the purposes and principles of the UN is a function of the country's history, its position in Africa and its membership of NAM. South Africa is a formidable economic and military power house in the sub-region and the continent as a whole. Until the momentous end of apartheid rule in April 1994, southern African countries, including Zimbabwe, had experienced adversarial relations with their neighbour, essentially as its victims. Since 1994, South Africa has therefore been cultivating a confidence- and trust-building foreign policy strategy towards its immediate neighbours, Africa and the rest of the world. It has not been keen on being perceived as a relic of the former apartheid regime. Thus, since joining the United Nations, South Africa has championed the cause of the Third World, particularly Africa. It has sought to contribute towards reforming the Security Council on the basis of proposals put forward by such organizations as the AU and NAM. Its approach towards the crisis in Zimbabwe should be understood within this broad context of post-apartheid foreign policy.

33 See 'EU Council Conclusion on Zimbabwe', The *Zimbabwean* 17 September 2008, http://www.thezimbabwean.co.uk/index.php?option=com_content&view=article&id=15/eu-council-conclusion-on-zimbabwe&catid=31:top%20zimbabwe%20stories&itemid=66 (Accessed 17/09/08)
34 See 'EU Slams Mugabe, Threatens new Sanctions against Zimbabwe'. AFP report in *Eubusiness*: http://www.eubusiness.com/news-eu/1223902928.18 (Accessed 13/10/08)
35 Strydom, H. (2007) 'The Context and Determinants of South Africa's New Role in the United Nations', p. 28, in *Strategic Review for Southern Africa*, Vol. XXIX No. 1, May 2007, (pp. 1-37). Institute for Strategic Studies, University of Pretoria, Pretoria.

Since its tenure as a non-permanent member of the Security Council in January 2008, South Africa has come under increasing criticism, particularly from Britain and the United States, for preventing grave human rights abuses in Burma, Sudan and Zimbabwe from being included in the Security Council's agenda. South Africa has defended its position by arguing that not all human rights abuses are a threat to international peace and security and therefore need not be discussed in the Security Council. Its reaction to the election crisis in Zimbabwe was, at least in part, a function of its foreign policy principles.

On 29 April 2008 ,when the Scurity Council held a special session on the situation in Zimbabwe, some EU and Latin American members wanted to send out a special envoy but this was successfully prevented by South Africa which chaired the session. They further vetoed any draft resolution on Zimbabwe in the period before the 27 June 2008 run-off election and subsequently, arguing that the UN risked complicating the situation in Zimbabwe that at the time had not reached the levels of Kenya's December 2007 post-election violence. Furthermore, when the Security Council met on 12 July 2008 to agree on a US- and UK-sponsored draft resolution that sought to impose sanctions on Zimbabwe, South Africa together with Russia, China and Vietnam voted against it. Partly as a result of South Africa's actions and inactions (alongside those of China and Russia) the Security Council has not been able to pass a resolution on Zimbabwe. Thus, South Africa has consistently shielded Mugabe from potentially devastating US- and UK-sponsored international action.

However, support for Robert Mugabe within the ANC has not always been consistent. For one thing, Nelson Mandela regards Mugabe as a despot.[36] Regarding the harmonized elections, there were conflicting views between the ANC position as articulated by its president Jacob Zuma and that of the South African government as articulated by President Thabo Mbeki. Mbeki has always been reluctant to explicitly criticize Mugabe even when it was prudent and necessary to do so thereby undermining his credibility as an impartial mediator. Yet, during a visit to Zimbabwe shortly before the run-off election, former ANC Deputy President – who soon afterwards succeeded Mbeki – President Kgalema Motlanthe, together with the ANC Secretary General, echoed support for ZANU(PF) citing strong historical ties between the two liberation movements; and in November 2008, ANC Youth League representatives visited Harare as a sign of solidarity. At the occasion of the official signing ceremony of the PSA on 15 September 2008 in Harare, former South African Deputy Foreign Affairs Minister Aziz Pahad told the SABC News Zimbabwe correspondent Thulasizwe Simelane that the PSA was a vindication of South Africa's approach and that he hoped the historic agreement had put to rest

36 Robert Guest (2004) *The Shackled Continent: Africa's Past, Present and Future.* Pan Books, London, p. 229.

'the fallacious notion of "quiet diplomacy" because it had always been our view that diplomacy by its very nature is quiet.'[37]

In October 2008, the South African government approved a R300 million (US$28 million) package to help Zimbabwe procure agricultural inputs ahead of the 2008/09 summer cropping season. It also called for an international united approach to help in the reconstruction and reconciliation of Zimbabwe.[38] However, in an unusual manifestation of rare impatience, on 20 November 2008 the South African Cabinet issued a statement indicating that it had decided to withhold this support until a representative government had been established.[39]

In the final analysis, Mbeki's seemingly endless mediation may have been intended simply to create an impression of commitment to crisis management. In any case, he has always stressed that it is ultimately the singular right and duty of Zimbabweans to solve their own problems. Clearly, South Africa does not want to share the responsibility or blame for contributing to the fall of the Mugabe administration. Unfortunately, retrospectively, both South Africa and Mbeki will be remembered less for any good they might have done and more for the good they did not do and the bad they did.

Nonetheless, in the foreseeable future and assuming South Africa's internal political dynamics, foreign policy principles and, indeed, its strategic self-interest considerations, remain the same, 'quiet diplomacy' is likely to remain the cornerstone of its approach towards the Zimbabwe crisis.

Botswana

President Ian Khama was the first SADC leader to openly criticize Robert Mugabe after the latter lost the first round of the presidential election on 29 March 2008. However, Botswana-Zimbabwe relations had waned since the SADC Parliamentary Forum dismissed the controversial 2002 presidential election, which gave Robert Mugabe a third presidential term, as having been neither free nor fair. While Botswana recognized the results of the harmonized elections of 29 March 2008, it closely followed events leading up to the presidential election run-off. It expressed serious concern about the deteriorating political situation and made repeated calls on the authorities in Zimbabwe to take the necessary steps to ensure a climate conducive to the holding of a free and fair presidential election run-off. It argued that the process that led to the run-off election did not conform to the SADC guidelines governing the conduct of democratic elections. It advised that in line with the AU Declaration on the Principles Governing

---

37 SABC International, Live Interview, Harare, 15 September 2008.
38 See *The Herald*, 14 October 2008.
39 See South Africa Cabinet Statement on Zimbabwe: http://www.newzimbabwe.com/pages/mbeki235.19047.html (Accessed 22/11/08)

Democratic Elections, conditions should be established as soon as possible for the holding of free, fair and credible elections.

On 12 June 2008, Botswana's Ministry of Foreign Affairs and International Co-operation summoned the Ambassador of Zimbabwe, Thomas Mandigora, to express strong concern over the 'arrest and detention of opposition leaders' that, Botswana argued, undermined the process of holding a free and fair election.[40] According to a press statement released by its Ministry of Foreign Affairs and International Co-operation on 4 July 2008, entitled *'Botswana's Position on Zimbabwe'*, Botswana argued that as a country which practices democracy and the rule of law, it could not recognize the outcome of the 27 June presidential election run-off because it violated the core principles of the SADC, the AU and the UN. It called on other SADC member states to adopt the same position. On 1 July 2008, it called on both the AU and SADC to exclude Zimbabwe from their meetings because 'a disputed election did not give the government of President Robert Mugabe legitimacy'.[41] It vainly recommended the suspension of Zimbabwe from SADC Summit meetings until it demonstrated its commitment to strictly adhering to the SADC principles. It argued that such steps would enhance the credibility of SADC and provide an enabling environment for the people of Zimbabwe to find lasting solutions to their problems. It agreed with the AU position that mediation efforts should continue, but insisted that such mediation had to be expeditious, given a definite time frame, and conducted in an atmosphere of mutual trust and good faith where both parties are treated as equal partners.[42]

In his State of the Nation Address on 3 November 2008 on the occasion of the opening of the Fifth Session of the Ninth Parliament of Botswana, President Khama stressed that while Botswana respected the principle of non-interference in the internal affairs of sovereign states, it discharges its international responsibilities in line with its own values, regional protocols, and global consensus, voicing its own opinion as and when it feels that it is justified to do so. He added that this is exactly what Botswana had been doing in the context of developments in Zimbabwe about which it remained seriously concerned regarding the failure to form a legitimate government. Botswana reiterated the importance of SADC member states upholding the regional standards that they have collectively and voluntarily adopted. Above all, he strongly believed that one viable way forward for Zimbabwe was to have a re-run of the run-off presidential election but

---

40   See New Zimbabwe.com, 13 June 2008: http://www.newzimbabwe.com/pages/botswana20.18333.html (Accessed 5/10/08)

41   Botswana's Vice President Mompati Merafhe made these remarks during his speech at the AU Heads of State and Government Summit on 1 July 2008 in Sharm El Sheikh. See the full speech on Mmegi Online, http://www.mmegi.bw/index.php?sid=1&aid=1&dir=2008/july/Thursaday3 (Accessed 22/10/08)

42   See   http://www.mofaic.gov.bw/index.php?option=com_content&task=view&id=301 (Accessed 23/10/08)

under full international sponsorship and supervision.[43] In response, Zimbabwe's de facto Minister of Justice, Legal and Parliamentary Affairs, who had also been one of the ZANU(PF) chief negotiators in the long SADC facilitated talks, said Khama's statement was unstatesman-like, unwarranted and unjustified interference in Zimbabwe's internal affairs as well as an act of extreme provocation.[44]

Relations worsened when Zimbabwe accused Botswana of interfering in its internal affairs by allegedly, and since 2002, facilitating the training of MDC-T militia to destabilize Zimbabwe with the assistance of both Britain and the United States. According to the *Standard Online*, Botswana said it was invited to an extra-ordinary meeting of the SADC OPDS Inter-State Defence and Security Committee (ISDC) in Maputo, Mozambique, on 5 November 2008. The ISDC requested that Zimbabwe provide documentary evidence to support its allegations. The paper further stated that Botswana re-affirmed its continued adherence to the principles and policies of good neighbourliness, non-interference in the internal affairs of other states and the peaceful resolution of disputes. Botswana also said that it reminded Zimbabwe of the existence of mechanisms for the management of bilateral relations such as the Botswana-Zimbabwe Joint Permanent Commission on Defence and Security that has held over 25 annual meetings since its establishment.[45]

On 14 November 2008 Botswana's Foreign Affairs Minister, Mpandu Skelemani, said that his country did not share the SADC consensus on Zimbabwe, especially regarding the co-management of the Ministry of Home Affairs. He reiterated that if the PSA could not be quickly implemented, then the international community should demand a re-run of the presidential election under international supervision.[46]

To show its concern about the Zimbabwe crisis, Botswana began a half-hour television programme, *Zimbabwe: The Voice from Within*, which was aired live every Wednesday evening. It focused specifically on the unfolding crisis in Zimbabwe. Botswana has thus unreservedly become Zimbabwe's leading regional critic. It has openly stated that it shares with the UK a common approach towards the Zimbabwe crisis, and argued that SADC's 'quiet diplomacy' had expired.[47] As a matter of principle and to

43 See http://www.prgovbw.blogspot.com/2008/11/state-of-nation-address-by-his.html (Accessed 04/11/08)
44 *The Herald*, 5 November 2008.
45 The *Standard Online*, 9 November 2008.
46 He made these remarks while briefing the Botswana Parliament on the Extra-ordinary SADC Summit of Heads of State and Government held on 9 November 2008 in Sandton, South Africa. See 'Botswana Doesn't Support SADC on Zimbabwe ministries', ZWNEWS. com, 14 November 2008: http://www.zwnews.com/issuefull.cfm?ArticleID=19683 (Accessed 16/11/08)
47 Captured on Botswana Television on 3 December 2008, 7.30 p.m., when President Khama made these remarks in an exclusive interview with Christopher Nyanga during his official visit to the UK.

prevent setting what it considers a negative precedent, one which would have seriously negative ramifications for the entire sub-region, Botswana seemingly preferred to 'stand only with a legitimate government of Zimbabwe that stands right'. While Botswana is likely to remain a lonely voice in the SADC wilderness, it is most likely that it will eventually respect and adopt SADC's approach rather than risk isolating itself from the sub-regional body.

Zambia

Zambia may have begun losing patience with the Zimbabwe crisis following the political violence in Harare on 11 March 2007. It is also important to remember that in August 2007, when SADC met in Lusaka to consider an economic rescue plan for Zimbabwe, President Levy Mwanawasa is reported to have clashed with Robert Mugabe. In reaction to the unprecedented delays in the announcement of the results of the 2008 harmonized elections, the escalating politically motivated violence and arrest of opposition supporters, Mwanawasa (as SADC Chairman) convened an extra-ordinary SADC Summit meeting on 12 April 2008, which Mugabe did not attend. Mbeki grudgingly participated for his position had remained consistent: 'there was no crisis in Zimbabwe'. Rather, he argued, events in Zimbabwe were 'politically normal' in the circumstances.[48]

Between the harmonized elections and the 15 September 2008 PSA, Zambia under Mwanawasa did not recognize Mugabe as Zimbabwe's democratically elected president. Mwanawasa's death came as a blow to what appeared to be a gathering momentum towards the possible end of SADC's quiet diplomacy, and indifference to the plight of ordinary Zimbabweans.[49] However, it also marked the beginning of the end of Zambia's open criticism of the government of Zimbabwe. The newly elected Zambian President, Rupiya Banda, who was born in Zimbabwe,[50] has never been, and is unlikely to be, openly critical of Mugabe. Indeed, he attended the PSA signing ceremony. Mugabe reciprocated by attending Banda's inauguration as Zambia's elected President.

However, the absence of Banda at the Extra-ordinary SADC Summit meeting in South Africa on 9 November 2008 was arguably a strategic tactic, to avoid 'looking Robert Mugabe straight in the eyes' and making an honest contribution to the post-election Zimbabwe crisis. Nevertheless, post-Mwanawasa Zambia has tacitly endorsed Mugabe's presidency,

---

48   Citing the example of negotiations that eventually ended apartheid, Mbeki believed that successful negotiations only took place when people were killing each other daily.
49   Dr Levy Mwanawasa suffered a stroke during the AU Summit at Sharm El Sheikh and died in Paris on 18 August 2008 at the age of 59.
50   13 February 1937 in Gwanda, Matabeleland South Province.

thus effectively distancing itself from Botswana's approach. Zambia is also likely to adopt a distorted version of positive neutrality under which it will either support the government of Zimbabwe or abstain from voting at SADC level for any decision that might be against Mugabe's desires.

Kenya

Zimbabwe's harmonized elections were held against the background of Kenya's post-election violence that had ultimately resulted in a negotiated power-sharing agreement. Indeed, even the concept of Zimbabwe's PSA was, in large measure, informed by that of Kenya. Kenya's Prime Minister, Raila Odinga, became the fiercest critic of Mugabe in east Africa over the deplorable manner in which the harmonized elections had been conducted and the controversial presidential election run-off.[51] He even referred to Mugabe as a 'disgrace' and lamented that the solidarity which some African leaders had shown towards him, was a distortion of pan-Africanism. On 23 November 2008, he recommended the deployment of AU Peacekeepers in Zimbabwe and, like President Khama of Botswana, said that the PSA was dead. Odinga suggested that fresh elections under international supervision were the only lasting solution to the Zimbabwe crisis. The government of Kenya is most likely to endorse Mugabe despite Odinga's views. The latter is, however, most likely to use every opportunity to openly criticize Mugabe.

The United Kingdom

Relations between Zimbabwe and Britain started to deteriorate soon after the British Labour Party, under Prime Minister Tony Blair, came to power in 1997. This coincided with increasing differences between the two governments over the modalities surrounding the funding of the land reform programme. Following the disputed 2000 and 2002 general and presidential elections, Britain imposed sanctions against selected members of the government of Zimbabwe and refused to unconditionally fund the controversial Fast Track Land Reform Programme. Since then, Robert Mugabe has primarily blamed Britain and its allies for all the problems facing Zimbabwe and has successively used it as an election campaign and propaganda tool in extremely vitriolic language. The British Prime Minis-

---

51 Raila Odinga compares himself with Morgan Tsvangirai. Both consider themselves as the undeclared winners of the presidential elections in their two respective countries. Equally, he compares Robert Mugabe with Mwai Kibaki as the illegitimate winners of those elections. Odinga preceded Tsvangirai as the victim of a power sharing arrangement, a concept that is increasingly becoming institutionalized as Africa's solution to its election crises.

ter boycotted the December 2007 EU-Africa Summit in Lisbon, Portugal, to avoid a potentially difficult encounter with Mugabe.

Britain's reaction to Zimbabwe's election crisis was predictably forthright. On 11 April 2008 Mugabe described British Prime Minister Gordon Brown as 'a little tiny dot in this world', accusing him of trying to be the 'international community'.[52] Apparently reacting to the delayed announcement of the presidential election results on 21 April 2008, Foreign Secretary David Miliband described the situation in Zimbabwe as a 'constitutional crisis', adding that Mugabe was trying 'to steal the election'.[53] Also on 23 April 2008, Gordon Brown, together with Jacob Zuma, then President of South Africa's ruling ANC, issued a joint statement in which they described the situation in Zimbabwe as a crisis and called for an end to violence and intimidation. Both stressed the importance of respect for the sovereign people of Zimbabwe and the choice they had made at the ballot box. Along with Amnesty International, Brown also called for the imposition of an arms embargo on Zimbabwe.

Britain promised to ensure that the EU maintained the sanctions against some 131 individuals in the ruling elite, including President Mugabe, on the grounds of human rights abuses.[54] It threatened to extend the sanctions to other individuals when necessary. However, it supported the mediation efforts of Presidents Jakaya Kikwete of Tanzania in his capacity as the Chairman of AU and Thabo Mbeki, the official SADC mediator.

Reacting to the PSA, Miliband said that his government welcomed the prospect of a turn in the tide of suffering in Zimbabwe. He hoped that the agreement would allow Zimbabwe to chart a new course towards economic recovery and political stability. He stressed that his government would study the details of the agreement, adding that what mattered was not just the words of the agreement but the way in which it would function and the actions and policies that the new government would pursue, and hoped that it would reverse what he referred to as 'the tragic policies and decline of recent years'. In his view, the new government needed to start re-building the country and, if it did so, he promised, Britain and the international community would be quick to support it.[55]

However, while in Luxemburg on 13 October 2008, Miliband condemned what he believed was 'Mugabe's attempted power grab' saying:

> I think it is very important that a European signal goes out that we will have no part, and play no part, in supporting a power grab by the Mugabe regime...

52 He made these remarks after briefly meeting Mbeki at State House. The latter had stopped on his way to the Extra-ordinary SADC Summit meeting that had been called for by the late Zambian President Mwanawasa on 12 April 2008.
53 See Wikipedia, the free encyclopedia: Zimbabwe Presidential Election 2008.
54 The full list has since grown to include journalists and companies that are accused of having strong allegiances to or links with ZANU(PF).
55 See: *In Quotes: World reaction to power sharing deal signing*:http://www.newzimbabwe. com/pages/mbeki165.18764html. (Accessed 15/09/08).

It is important that there be an international united response that says that the results of the Zimbabwean (March 29) elections need to be respected and that a power grab will not be respected.[56]

Britain is expected to continue working with or through Zimbabwe's neighbours to achieve its preferred foreign policy goals in Zimbabwe. Equally, it is likely to continue to provide Zimbabwe with humanitarian assistance, but channelled through NGOs and UN agencies.[57] Its approach towards Zimbabwe will, therefore, remain performance-based and essentially punctuated by deserved rewards and necessary punishments.

The United States of America

Together with Britain, the USA has been at the forefront of putting pressure on the government of Zimbabwe to reform. On 4 December 2001, the US Congress passed into law the Zimbabwe Democracy and Economic Recovery Act (ZDERA) that became the cornerstone of US foreign policy towards Zimbabwe. Under this Act, the US preconditions for aid and financing are the restoration of the rule of law, free and fair elections, civilian controlled military and police force, and a commitment to a transparent, equitable and legal land reform programme. The financial sanctions under ZDERA prohibit any US person from engaging in any financial transactions with any person or entity found to be undermining democratic institutions and processes in Zimbabwe. Under ZDERA, Zimbabwe has not benefited from the Africa Growth Opportunity Act, which offers tangible incentives for African countries that open their economies, build free markets and embrace political pluralism.

The USA openly opposed China's shipment of arms to Zimbabwe during the election crisis.[58] As Assistant Secretary of State for African Affairs Jendayi Frazer argued, the US did not think it appropriate at the time, given the political upheaval that was occurring in Zimbabwe, for any country to supply weapons to Zimbabwe's security forces. The US Foreign Affairs Chairman Howard Berman also praised the African nations for blocking the shipment of small and light weapons to Zimbabwe.[59] The list of individuals and companies under US targeted sanctions has been regularly

---

56 See www.eubusiness.com, ibid.
57 According to 'Britain and Zimbabwe' (British Embassy, Harare, 2007) Britain annually provides an estimated £40m of humanitarian aid to Zimbabwe. In 2007, it donated a further £8m through the World Food Aid programme.
58 The Chinese ship *An-Yue Jiang* carried a consignment of weapons destined for Zimbabwe. It was prevented from docking at any South African port by labour unions and pressure groups. Reports that it returned the consignment to China remain unconfirmed.
59 See Kellerhals, M.D. (Jr), 'US Supports African Stance Against Arms Shipment to Zimbabwe': http://www.america.gov/st/peacesec-english/2008/april/20080422162313d mslahrellek0.3094904.htm (Accessed 23/04/08)

updated, most recently in November 2008 when four individuals linked to the Mugabe administration were added to the list in reaction to the stalled PSA. Nonetheless, the USA has remained cautiously optimistic about the power sharing agreemeent. In an interview with Blessing Zulu of VOA News on 17 September 2008, the US Ambassador to Zimbabwe, James McGee, clearly articulated the criteria under which the US would measure the success of the agreement. He called for 'ratcheting up' towards adherence of key principles that include: the restoration of the rule of law, respect for human rights, a crackdown on corruption, and the restoration of a market economy, adding that if the envisaged unity government could show that it is moving to meet the principles set out by the US, 'we will be very pleased with this arrangement'. He added that America's re-engagement with Zimbabwe would be based on performance: 'If this government is moving in a positive direction then our response will be a very positive one. But if the government continues along the same path as previously, our response will be... likewise in that same direction.'[60]

Regardless of the congratulatory message that Mugabe sent to the US President-elect Barack Obama, and given the permanency of American self-interest as well as Obama's determination to succeed where his predecessor failed, ZDERA will remain the cornerstone of US policy towards Zimbabwe. Like the British government, the Obama administration will continue to insist on performance as a necessary precondition for re-engagement with the government of Zimbabwe.

The People's Republic of China

China has supported ZANU(PF) and, by extension, the government of Zimbabwe, since the onset of the liberation struggle. Its current policy is best understood within the framework of a 'Look East' policy that is largely premised on party-to-party solidarity. China has taken the opportunity provided by Western disengagement to offer itself as an alternative source of no-strings assistance and investment. It claims to adhere to the non-interference norm in its international relations but only to the extent that its strategic self-interests are not significantly compromised. As such, it did not criticize Mugabe or ZANU(PF) or indeed anybody, for the manner in which the harmonized elections and the presidential run-off elections were conducted. However, China was widely criticized for sending the *An-Yue Jiang* to deliver a consignment of ammunition and weapons during the election crisis. The timing of the delivery naturally raised suspicions about China's interests in Zimbabwe.

China has repeatedly vetoed any proposed UN Security Council res-

60 For a full interview, see http://www.voanews.com/english/archive/2008-09/2008-09-17-voa64.cfm?CFID=5908777&CFTOKEN=73016293 (Accessed 17/09/08)

olution to put pressure on Zimbabwe. The latest instance was after the harmonized elections, when alongside Russia, Vietnam and South Africa, China vetoed a proposed resolution on Zimbabwe that had been co-sponsored by the USA and Britain. Zimbabwe is likely to maintain its heavy reliance on China which, in turn, is also likely to maintain fraternal relations in line with its Africa policy.[61]

The Russian Federation

Russia's ties with Zimbabwe have grown stronger following the unilateral invasion of Iraq by the US-led 'Coalition-of-the-Willing' in March 2003, which coincided with the unprecedented US pressure on Zimbabwe following the 2002 elections. Like China, Russia is strongly opposed to the occasional unilateral tendencies of the US, increasingly favouring multilateralism, which in its weaker position since the end of the Cold War, gives it an assumption of power. Russia has always vetoed any Security Council proposals aimed at putting pressure on Zimbabwe. Indeed, it vetoed one resolution in spite of President Dimitri Medvedev's previous assurances at the 2008 G-8 Summit in Japan that it would not do so. Russia's approach to Zimbabwe at the UN can be read as a reaction to the tendency of the USA (under the presidency of George Bush) to disrespect bilateral arms control and disarmament agreements and show contempt for multilateralism. This approach, coupled with what are interpreted as provocative policies towards countries which once had strong ties with the Soviet Union, such as the Ukraine, Poland, Lithuania, Czech Republic and Georgia, Russia is likely to continue to veto any US and UK attempts to put Zimbabwe on the Security Council agenda, but only to the extent that the US maintains its provocative policies towards Russia. However, Russia will at most condemn but not prevent any US and UK unilateral actions against Zimbabwe.

The Islamic Republic of Iran

As with China, Zimbabwe's relations with Iran are part of its 'Look East' policy. Both countries have a common adversary in the West in general but the UK and the US in particular.[62] (Indeed, in 2008, the US Secretary of State, Condoleezza Rice named both Zimbabwe and Iran in a list of so-called 'outlaw states' as 'remaining outposts of tyranny'.) The bilateral

---

61 China has been quietly pursuing an aggressive Africa policy as it seeks to acquire minerals and other natural resources.

62 The US government under president George W. Bush named Zimbabwe, Iran, Iraq and North Korea 'remaining outposts of tyranny'. http://www.newzimbabwe.com/pages/powell18.12161.html

relations between the two countries have been growing stronger since Zimbabwe opened its embassy in Teheran in 2003. Iran has assisted in the modernization of Zimbabwe's state television and radio services. It has also invested in various sectors including agriculture, industry, power and energy, and has extended lines of credit at a time of dire need. It endorsed the results of both the 29 March 2008 harmonized election and the presidential run-off election. Predictably, it also hailed the PSA saying it would provide a solution to the challenges facing the country. It has solidly supported Zimbabwe at various international forums including the United Nations where it has called for the immediate lifting of what it considers as 'sanctions against Zimbabwe' so as to expedite the country's economic recovery. With common western adversaries, shared perceptions regarding the contemporary global order, common principles regarding the inviolability of state sovereignty and non-interference, shared values and aspirations, Iran will most likely maintain its friendly stance towards Zimbabwe but only to the extent that its national self-interests are safeguarded.

Conclusion

This chapter has attempted to show that Zimbabwe's 29 March 2008 harmonized election and the subsequent presidential run-off election of 27 June received varied regional and international reaction. Most foreign election observer teams, including the PAN, SEOM, AU, COMESA and the East African Community, endorsed the harmonized elections but not the presidential run-off election. Most Western governments reacted similarly. Only Russia, China, Iran and most African and Third World governments endorsed both. Similarly, the PSA received mixed regional and international reaction. While some saw it as a necessary compromise and significant first step towards taking the country forward, others were cautiously optimistic, avoiding premature celebration. Still, there were those who regarded the PSA as both potentially fragile and unrealistically ambitious given the traditional levels of enmity between ZANU(PF) and MDC-T. The implementation of the PSA was initially stalled, although a power-sharing government was eventually instituted in February 2009. Thus, the potent winds of Zimbabwe's peaceful democratic transition that came with the harmonized elections were effectively blocked by the presidential run-off election and the subsequent SADC-facilitated settlement, the PSA.[63]

Zimbabwe conducted its harmonized elections using its own preferred 'principles and guidelines' partly because the SADC Principles and Guide-

---

63 Increasingly becoming the preferred African solution to African political crises such as post-election disputes, power-sharing governments usually disadvantage the winners, substantively reward the losers, and tend to be imposed on the people, regardless of their otherwise democratically expressed will.

lines Governing Democratic Elections are not mandatory. Whilst it may have lost its historically positive reputation as a regional political pace-setter, Zimbabwe has shown that in *realpolitik* the independent sovereign state is the ultimate arbiter in matters of political life and death. In future, other African governments, with assertive sovereignty and determination similar to that of Zimbabwe, are also likely to conduct their own elections in their own preferred style. Both SADC and the AU exhibited an inexcusable lack of commitment to enforcing their own institutional principles on member states. SADC created a false impression that the Zimbabwe election crisis was unique. In doing so, it lost its credibility. It took longer than necessary to solve the post-election Zimbabwe crisis in part because its 'quiet diplomacy' had no benchmarks, deadlines and viable alternatives; the mediator was also visibly biased in favour of one party and against the others. To successfully solve similar future election crises, it is critical that mediators should remain neutral, impartial, honest and trustworthy as well as enjoying public confidence. Equally, there should be alternative approaches to election crisis management. Perhaps, most importantly, future mediators should not be picked from the list of incumbent leaders. Ultimately, the only lasting solution to any election crisis can be one that affords primacy to the freely expressed democratic will of the people rather than the preferences of political gladiators; otherwise, the lives of many citizens will be 'short, nasty and brutish'.

Contributors

Simon Badza is a lecturer in the Department of Political and Administrative Studies at the University of Zimbabwe, where he received a B.Sc. in Political Science and Administration and an M.Phil. in International Relations. He teaches International Relations, Political Theory and International Peace and Security Studies. His research areas include: Zimbabwe's foreign relations and political transition, security sector governance and reform in transition societies, conflict transformation, and the evolution of SADC sub-regional and AU regional security architectures. He co-authored *Zimbabwe: The Next 25* Years (2005), *Transparency International Zimbabwe Country Report 2007* and 'Zimbabwe's 2008 Elections and their Implications for Africa' in the *African Security Review.*

Greg Linington is lecturer in Constitutional Law in the Department of Political and Administrative Studies at the University of Zimbabwe. A graduate of the University of Zimbabwe Law faculty, he holds an M.A. in International Relations from the same university and an M.A. in Constitutional Law from the University of South Africa. He is the author of *Constitutional Law of Zimbabwe* (2001).

John Makumbe is an Associate Professor of Political Science at the University of Zimbabwe, and author (with Daniel Compagnon) of *Behind the Smokescreen: The Politics of Zimbabwe's 1995 General Elections,* (2000), and several other books. He is the founder Chairman of the Zimbabwe Chapter of Transparency International and the Zimbabwe Albino Association, and a board member of the Mass Public Opinion Institute. He has carried out consultancy assignments in the areas of management training, institutional evaluation, programme evaluation, democracy and good governance, and in the management of the information sector for democratic development and public participation.

Eldred V. Masunungure studied at the Universities of Zimbabwe and Dalhousie (Canada) and teaches in the Department of Political and Administrative Studies at the University of Zimbabwe. His current research interests include the political economy of transitions, elections, governance, and policy making. He is the Executive Director of the Mass Public Opinion Institute, and is widely published in local and international publications, including *African Affairs* and the *Journal of Democracy.*

176

Derek Matyszak graduated from Cape Town University, and left private legal practice to lecture at the Law Faculty at the University of Zimbabwe in 1991. In 2007, he joined the Research and Advocacy Unit in Zimbabwe as a senior researcher, focusing on issues of governance, human rights and transitional justice, and has written widely about the impact of Zimbabwean legislation on these issues.

Andrew Moyse trained as a journalist in Britain, and worked in Fleet Street and at the BBC World Service before coming to Zimbabwe in 1980. After four years with Zimpapers he became Editor of *Parade* magazine, raising its circulation from 18,000 to 100,000 in six years. In 1990 he established *Horizon*, a monthly magazine featuring topical investigative news analysis; the magazine was a victim of the collapse of the Zimbabwe dollar in 1997 and closed in 1999. Moyse edited the independent Sunday paper, *The Standard*, for six months, and in April 2000 joined the Media Monitoring Project Zimbabwe as its co-ordinator.

Ethel Muchena holds a B.Sc. in Politics and Administration from the University of Zimbabwe. She joined the Mass Public Opinion Institute in 2003 where she is now a Research Officer. She has considerable experience in political research methodologies including polling, focus-group discussions and key informant interviews.

Anyway Ndapwadza holds a B.Sc. in Economics and an M.A. in Population Studies from the University of Zimbabwe. She has led a number of research projects both at Population Services International, where she worked as the Research Co-ordinator, and currently at the Mass Public Opinion Institute, where she is the Principal Researcher. She also undertakes consultancy and training on research methodology, and data analysis and reporting.

Eustinah Tarisayi earned her B.Sc. in Politics and Administration and M.A. in Public Administration from the University of Zimbabwe, where she teaches in the Department of Political and Administrative Studies.

www.ingramcontent.com/pod-product-compliance
Lightning Source LLC
Chambersburg PA
CBHW021818270326
41932CB00007B/239